Did Jesus Correct Moses?

Expanded

by

Mark Quincy Bullen

Did Jesus Correct Moses?

Expanded

Mark Quincy Bullen

Apprehending Truth Publishers

Brookfield, Missouri

Did Jesus Correct Moses?

ISBN-13: 978-0615686301
ISBN-10: 0615686303

All Scripture quotations are from the Authorized King James Version, unless otherwise noted.

Cover Design by PureLight Graphics

AT 10 9 8 7 6 5 4 3
170301

Living Faith Books is an imprint of:
Apprehending Truth Publishers
PO Box 249
Brookfield, Missouri 64628
http://www.ApprehendingTruth.net

Did Jesus Correct Moses?

Expanded

Contents:

Chapter One
Did Jesus Correct Moses?

What is the proper relationship between the **Old Covenant** and the **New Covenant**; between **Moses** and **Jesus**; and between **God's Law** and **God's Grace**? I am grieved at the vast amount of misinformation being taught concerning these sacred and vital relationships. Satan has worked hard to muddy the waters and obscure the light; and man's lack of concern and diligence has only helped further Satan's agenda. If you believe wrong, you live wrong; and in living and believing wrong you misrepresent Christ and jeopardize your soul as well as the souls of all those you influence. God is gracious; but that grace only extends so far and does not nullify the sobering truth of Jesus' words:

*Mt 15:14 ...they be blind leaders of the blind. And if the blind lead the blind, **both shall fall into the ditch.***

It does matter what you believe and whom you follow; and what we will learn in this book can be documented, verified, and thus proven from the Word of God and history. **Sincerity is not enough,** or deception would not be a problem or concern. The Bible **never** assures us that *being sincere in a deceived state* or *sincere in believing heretical doctrine* is safe! St. Paul warned numerous times in various ways that following the *wrong Jesus*, *wrong gospel*, or *wrong spirit* could lead to damnation rather than salvation.

1

2Co 11:2 For I am jealous over you with godly jealousy: for I have espoused you to **one husband,** that I may present you as a chaste virgin to Christ. 3 But I fear, lest by **any** means, **as the serpent beguiled Eve** through his subtilty, so your **minds should be corrupted** from *[singlehearted devotion to]* Christ. 4 For if he that cometh preacheth **another** Jesus, whom we have not preached, or if ye receive **another** spirit, which ye have not received, or **another** gospel, which ye have not accepted, ye might well bear with him...13 For such are false apostles, deceitful workers, transforming themselves into the apostles of Christ. 14 And no marvel; for Satan himself is transformed into an angel of light. 15 Therefore **it is no great thing** if his ministers also be transformed as the **ministers of righteousness**; whose end shall be according to their works.

So, it definitely matters what you believe about Jesus and His mission.   The New Covenant that Jesus established was meant to be a step up to something more glorious than the Old Covenant; primarily because the New Covenant Scriptures reveal the true spiritual meaning and significance of the Old Covenant. The New Covenant is God's Holy Law written by the Holy Ghost in the minds and hearts of born again believers, as opposed to just being written on stone (2Co 3:3), and it is the spiritual fulfillment of all the types and shadows of the ceremonial laws. The Jews, according to the rabbinical writings, understood that when Messiah came He would usher in a new era. The prophets spoke of it, and the Apostles confirmed it.

De 18:17 And the LORD said unto me, They have well spoken that which they have spoken. 18 I will raise them up a Prophet from among their brethren, like unto thee, and will put my words in his mouth; and he shall speak unto them all that I shall command him. 19 And it shall come to pass, that whosoever will not hearken unto my words which he shall speak in my name, I will require it of him.

Ac 2:16 But this is that which was spoken by the prophet Joel; 17 And it shall come to pass **in the last days**, saith God, I will pour out of my Spirit upon all flesh: and your sons and your daughters shall prophesy, and your young men shall see visions, and your old men shall dream dreams:18 And on my servants and on my handmaidens I will pour out **in those days** of my Spirit; and they shall prophesy:

Ac 3:22 For Moses truly said unto the fathers, A prophet shall the Lord your God raise up unto you of your brethren, like unto me; **him shall ye hear in all things whatsoever he shall say unto you.** 23 And it shall come to pass, that every soul, which will not hear that prophet, shall be destroyed from among the people. 24 Yea, and all the prophets from Samuel and those that follow after, as many as have spoken, have likewise foretold of **these days.**

Ac 7:37 This is that Moses, which said unto the children of Israel, A prophet shall the Lord your God raise up unto you of your brethren, like unto me; **him shall ye hear.**

Many church groups build their doctrine on the belief that Jesus corrected the Law of Moses or did away with it altogether. What people say about Jesus' *preaching* and *purpose* DEFINES which Jesus they are following. If one wishes to present the **Biblical Jesus**, then they **must** present Him in the context of His **Biblical purpose** and

3

teaching. Jesus warned of "false Christ's" that would be very subtle and deceive many people. Obviously those deceived people thought they had the real Jesus; when actually they did not! According to Paul, **a *false Christ* can just be a *false concept of Christ*** due to a misrepresentation of Jesus and His message. If you don't have the time or concern to make sure you have the ***right*** Jesus; then surely you are doomed to have the wrong one.

*Mt 7:13 Enter ye in at the strait gate: for wide is the gate, and broad is the way, that leadeth to destruction, and **many** there be which go in thereat: 14 Because strait is the gate, and narrow is the way, which leadeth unto life, and **few** there be that find it.*

What is the proper relationship of the New Covenant to the Old Covenant? Was anything preserved from the Old Covenant? Why do some still keep the Old Covenant feasts and dietary laws? Are Gentiles saved *one way*, while Jews are saved *another*? Are the Old Testament Scriptures even relevant? Should we even study them?

Some believe that people were justified by God different in the Old Covenant than they are in the New Covenant. You will hear them say, *"We are not under the Law, but under Grace"* – what does that mean? If a preacher sets up rules and standards of conduct for his church, they say, *"He is preaching law and not grace"*. Were the people in the Old Covenant saved by works without grace? Are we saved by grace without works?

Should the "Sermon On The Mount" be interpreted as "Jesus correcting Moses' Law" or should it be interpreted as "Jesus correcting misconceptions about Moses' Law?" Was divorce and remarriage allowed by Moses, but forbidden by Jesus? Were the people in the Old Covenant allowed to defend themselves and participate in government, but New Covenant saints are not? Do we have any obligation to God's commandments in the Old Covenant? Is our meditation and memorization in Psalm 119 still relevant?

Ps 119:9 Wherewithal shall a young man cleanse his way? by taking heed thereto according to thy word. 10 With my whole heart have I sought thee: O let me not wander from thy commandments. 11 Thy word have I hid in mine heart, that I might not sin against thee. 12 Blessed art thou, O LORD: teach me thy statutes. 13 With my lips have I declared all the judgments of thy mouth. 14 I have rejoiced in the way of thy testimonies, as much as in all riches. 15 I will meditate in thy precepts, and have respect unto thy ways. 16 I will delight myself in thy statutes: I will not forget thy word.

Can we still whole heartedly sing Psalm 1:1-3?

*Ps 1:1 Blessed is the man that walketh not in the counsel of the ungodly, nor standeth in the way of sinners, nor sitteth in the seat of the scornful. 2 **But his delight is in the law of the LORD; and in his law doth he meditate day and night.** 3 And he shall be like a tree planted by the rivers of water, that bringeth forth his fruit in his season; his leaf also shall not wither; and whatsoever he doeth shall prosper.*

Should we still be singing Psalm 19: 7-11?

*Ps 19:7 The law of the LORD is **perfect**, converting the soul: the testimony of the LORD is **sure**, making wise the simple. 8 The statutes of the LORD are **right**, rejoicing the heart: the commandment of the LORD is **pure**, enlightening the eyes. 9 The fear of the LORD is clean,* *enduring for ever: the judgments of the LORD are **true** and **righteous altogether**. 10 **More to be desired are they than gold**, yea, than much fine gold: sweeter also than honey and the honeycomb. 11 Moreover by them is thy servant warned: and in keeping of them there is great reward.*

These are important and relevant questions that determine who Jesus really was and is today! In all my years of studying the Bible and Church History, I have discovered an extemely critical truth. **The Bible can only be properly interpreted when understood in its historic context**; for it is composed of historic documents written at specific points in time to people raised in a specific environment of doctrine and practice. Almost every heresy I have encountered is a result of interpreting the Bible outside its God ordained historical context: **Historic Judaism**. When the Bible is ripped out of its Hebrew context, all hope of proper understanding is gone. Jesus came as a Jewish man under Judaism, and He fully obeyed and taught the Law of God through Moses.

Jesus taught the Jewish people, as well as His own Jewish disciples, to obey those who sat in Moses' Seat, but not to practice their hypocrisy. Jesus taught the proper exercise of Biblical Judaism. He upheld the right and responsibility of the present religious leaders to make rules and applications of God's Word for present needs. Jesus was more stict than any Pharisee; but His strictness was in line with God's Word, not in being partial with the Word for personal gain.

*Mt 23:1 Then spake Jesus to the multitude, and to his disciples, 2 Saying, The scribes and the Pharisees sit in **Moses' seat**: 3 **All therefore whatsoever they bid you***

6

observe, that observe and do; *but do not ye after their works:* ***for they say, and do not.***

Mk 7:8 For **laying aside the commandment of God**, *ye hold the tradition of men...And he said unto them,* **Full well ye reject the commandment of God, that ye may keep your own tradition.**

Jesus didn't come as a rebel to God's religious program; but as the purifier of it just as Malachi prophesied. The Apostles continued to live as Law abiding Jews for their entire lives; and did not teach Jews to forsake Moses' Law (Acts 21). The churches that the Apostles established were established first with Jews from the local synagogues, and were all patterned after the Jewish Christian congrerations in Judaea.

1Th 2:14 For ye, brethren, became **followers of the churches of God which in Judaea are in Christ Jesus:**

The Christian assemblies were patterned and governed after the order of the Jewish Synagogue, which was the God ordained order of His "church" for approximately 500 years before Christ came. James, the bishop of Jerusalem, when writing to the churches, refers to their meeting with the word *Synagogue*; but our English Bible translates it as *assembly* (Ja 2:2). The word *synagogue* and the word *church* both refer to an *assembly*. The congregation in Jerusalem, where James was bishop, was the mother and model church where all the Apostles met to decide hard issues (Acts 15). Their decisions were *"decrees for to keep"*; and were sent to all the existing churches to be obeyed (Acts 16). What they bound on earth, God bound in heaven; which can be seen in the rebukes sent to the churches in Asia Minor (Rev 2-3).

7

For the first **twelve years** after Pentecost **all** New Covenant Christians were Law abiding Jews faithfully practicing Judaism under Moses' Law; and the only way a Gentile could become part of the Christian Church at that time was to also become a proselyte to Judaism. From the time Moses' Law was established as a covenant until twelve years after Pentecost, the only way a Gentile could reconcile with God and be saved by grace through faith was to come under that covenant and become a practicing Jew obeying Moses' Law – like Rahab, Ruth, the Ethiopian Eunuch, etc. The term "Jew" included all those from any nationality who were practicing Judaism under Moses' Law. A converted Gentile who came under Moses' Law ceased to be called a *Gentile*.

After God grafted Gentiles (one not practicing Judaism) into the Jewish/Christian church, starting with Cornelius' conversion (Acts 10 – 12 yrs after Pentecost), you had Christian Gentiles and Christian Jews worshipping God in the same assembly. This challenging situation is a good part of the subject matter in many of the epistles. When this historic context is not recognized or understood, the epistles are wrongly interpreted and misunderstood. Much misinformation is taught as a result of the epistles being tortured out of their historic context.

The New Covenant was built upon the foundation of the Old, just like the Old Covenant was built upon the foundation of the covenants with Jacob, Isaac, Abraham, Noah, etc. So, as the covenant of circumcision through Abraham was continued under the newer Mosaic Covenant; the New Covenant, in being built on the foundation of the older covenants, continued many things

8

and modified others. What were these changes, and where do we draw the lines?

God Pardoning Repentant Sinners on the Basis of Christ's Atonement

God's Law of Love – Moral Law – Holiness – "Righteousness of the Law"

1868 BC	1462 BC		AD 29	AD 41	AD 70
▼	▼		▼	▼	▼
▲	▲		▲	▲	▲
Covenant of Circumcision	Sinai Moses' Law		Resurrection & Pentecost	Gentiles Grafted In	Jerusalem Destroyed

Abel, Enoch, Noah, Abraham, Isaac, Jacob (Offered Sacrifices)	Old Covenant	New Covenant

Not Required	Abraham's Children Required to be Circumcised		1Cor 7:18
	Israelites Required to Keep Ceremonial Law of Moses		?
Not Required	Believing Gentiles Required to be Circumcised		Not Required
	Believing Gentiles Required to Keep Ceremonial Law of Moses		

**Repentance and "Faith-full" Obedience
Required to receive the benefits of Christ's Atonement**

*Chronology from the Reese Chronological Bible

The diagram shows what principles are for **all time**, and which ones are **temporary**. The Gospel: "the good news of God's pardoning grace on the basis of Christ's atonement" has been relevant since the fall of man, and is God's **only** plan of salvation for repentant sinners. The transgression of God's Moral Law is why men are sinners from beginning to end. Mankind being required to respond to God with repentance and a humble obedient faith in order to be saved by grace is valid from Genesis to Revelation. Other matters, however, have only been relevant for a certain time period as part of a covenant arrangement.

9

Don't miss the fact that both Jews and Gentile converts were subject to circumcision and Moses' Law <u>in the New Covenant</u> until Cornelius (Ac 10). New Gentile converts were released from this obligation twelve years after Pentecost; but Jews were still under circumcision and ceremonial law <u>in the New Covenant</u> at least until the destruction of Jerusalem in AD 70. These are historical Biblical facts, not interpretations.

In A.D. 70 God used the Romans to destroy Jerusalem, lay the Temple waste, and disperse the unbelieving Jews throughout the world as bondmen, just as Jesus had predicted and warned. The believers followed Jesus' warnings and fled Jerusalem previous to its destruction. This destruction ended the believing Jew's obligations to the jurisdiction of the Sanhedrin, the Temple service, the priesthood, the sacrifices, i.e. every part of the Ceremonial Law that required Jerusalem and the Temple. It is debatable whether these Christian Jews were now released completely from circumcision and the ceremonial laws they could observe (Act 21:24-25; I Cor. 7:18); as not all of it is fulfilled – the fall feasts are prophetic of Christ's second coming. Obviously God didn't expect them to observe those ceremonies which were now impossible; and they were never to look at them for their justification; but only as types of Christ for edification. The believing Jews in the first century church understood that the ceremonial laws were just object lessons to teach mankind about Jesus' Priesthood in the heavens with His own perpetually meritorious sacrifice, and were not necessary or effective for justification in and of themselves.

Because of all these glaring facts of history, many need to rethink their theology. Were the Apostles "legalists" before Cornelius? Did they preach salvation by works before Cornelius? Were they saved by faith? Was the Gospel the same before and after Cornelius? Was the Gospel the same to both Jews and Gentiles? These questions and many others will be answered in the following pages if you pay close attention.

After AD 70, when Jerusalem was destroyed and most non-Christian Jews were carried away captive or killed, the Christian Church began to take on a more Gentile character and slowly moved away from its Hebrew roots due to more Gentiles coming into leadership. The Ante-Nicene writers are almost all Gentiles; and many of them misinterpret the Scriptures by wresting them from their Jewish context. The "church fathers" looked at the Bible through Gentile eyes; and this continual trend toward *Gentile thinking* eventually led to *Roman Catholicism* and many other errors.

Most denominations in Christendom today are ignorant of the Jewish context of the New Testament Scriptures, which we have mentioned in this chapter, and so continue to misinterpret them.   Has the teaching you've read in this chapter, concerning the historic context of the Christian Church, been taught to you in your modern church?   I speak with preachers who've been in ministry for many years, and they are misinformed!

Every heresy I know started early in the history of the church due to this issue. After AD 70 the wolves came in strong just like St. Paul had predicted; and the confusion is clearly seen in the Ante-Nicene writings with the trends and practices of those churches.

Ac 20:28 Take heed therefore unto yourselves, and to all the flock, over the which the Holy Ghost hath made you overseers, to feed the church of God, which he hath purchased with his own blood. 29 For I know this, that **after my departing (AD 67)** shall **grievous wolves enter in among you,** not sparing the flock. 30 **Also of your own selves shall men arise, speaking perverse things, to draw away disciples after them.** 31 Therefore watch, and remember, that by the space of three years I ceased not to **warn every one night and day with tears.**

Why Paul? Because God expected them (and us) to do something about it! We are responsible to contend for the *"faith once delivered to the saints"*. Approximately 30 years later we find this same church commended for battling against the onslaughts of Satan in their day.

Re 2:1 Unto the angel of the church of Ephesus write; These things saith he that holdeth the seven stars in his right hand, who walketh in the midst of the seven golden candlesticks; 2 I know thy works, and **thy labour,** and **thy patience**, and **how thou canst not bear them which are evil**: and thou **hast tried them which say they are apostles, and are not, and hast found them liars:** 3 And hast borne, and hast patience, and **for my name's sake hast laboured,** and **hast not fainted**.

Laboring for *"my name's sake"* against false apostles reminds us that they were fighting for Christ's proper identity against the False Christs being propogated. Changing anything about Jesus can change his identity to **another Jesus**.

2Co 11:2 For I am jealous over you with godly jealousy: for I have espoused you to **one** husband, that I may present you as a chaste virgin to Christ. 3 But I fear, *lest by **any** means, **as the serpent beguiled Eve** through his subtilty, so your minds should be corrupted from **[singlehearted devotion to]** Christ. 4 For if he that cometh preacheth **another** Jesus, whom we have not preached, or if ye receive **another** spirit, which ye have not received, or **another** gospel, which ye have not accepted, ye might well bear with him...13 For such are **false apostles**, deceitful workers, transforming themselves into the apostles of Christ. 14 And no marvel; for <u>Satan himself is transformed into an angel of light.</u> 15 Therefore it is <u>no great thing if his ministers also be transformed as the</u> **<u>ministers of righteousness...</u>***

The fact that the Ephesians were also reproved with *"leaving their first love"* could imply they were beginning to slip in this very area after so many years of faithfulness. Were they slipping into a false piety which could eventually redefine Jesus? For them to redefine Jesus by ignoring His Jewishness, and thereby misinterpreting His words, would definitely be "leaving their first love" and embracing "another Jesus". No wonder Jesus threatened to excommunicate them, which would be equivelant to divorce in the spiritual realm.

How sobering! Jesus has not changed. So, would our church meet the criteria of having a lamp in Jesus' lamp-stand if Ephesus failed? Since Jesus judges without partiality; and we have Revelation to read, are we not accountable to pass the same test? We had better put forth some effort to figure this out and make sure our definition of Jesus and our interpretation of His words are accurate.

Chapter Two
Firstborn Of Satan?

The renowned and aged bishop walked slowly along the ancient cobblestone street in Rome with a few of his fellow elders in serious discussion. The aged bishop had traveled to Rome for the express purpose of helping put down a heretical teaching threatening the preservation of truth in the church. As they moved slowly along the street, another teacher happened to be walking in the opposite direction with some companions and looking up recognized the well known bishop. Possibly resenting the fact that the bishop did not address or notice him as he drew nearer, the younger man spoke to the bishop thus, "Doest thou know me?" The aged bishop eyed the approaching men thoughtfully and said, "I do know thee, the first-born of Satan."

Wow! There must have been a serious clash of beliefs in this scenario. Who were these historic figures? What was happening in this dramatic encounter of two well known teachers? The story is told by Irenaeus concerning the renowned apostolic bishop, Polycarp (c69-156), who was probably the bishop of Smyrna during the time when the Book of Revelation was written. The church of Smyrna was free of heresy and error due to Polycarp's labors to contend for the "faith once delivered to the saints". As one can see from the Scriptures, there is no rebuke for the church at Smyrna during this time; so we need to pay attention to what they were so against!

Re 2:8 *And unto the angel of the church in Smyrna write; These things saith the first and the last, which was dead, and is alive; 9 I know thy works, and tribulation, and poverty, (but thou art rich) and I know the blasphemy of them which say they are Jews, and are not, but are the synagogue of Satan. 10 Fear none of those things which thou shalt suffer: behold, the devil shall cast some of you into prison, that ye may be tried; and ye shall have tribulation ten days: be thou faithful unto death, and I will give thee a crown of life. 11 He that hath an ear, let him hear what the Spirit saith unto the churches; He that overcometh shall not be hurt of the second death.*

Early in the second century the son of a Christian bishop became notorious for his innovations in doctrine and practice. He was excommunicated around the end of July 144 AD. He was a wealthy ship owner and didn't care if they excommunicated him. He started his own churches with his own philosophy to rival the Christian congregations of the day. His Gnostic heresy became wide spread; and Polycarp labored to squelch the rising error. The man that Polycarp termed the "firstborn of Satan" is none other than Marcion of Sinope, the leader of the heretical movement. Marcion Gnosticism plagued the church for centuries, and is still alive today in numerous, varied, and even some less obvious forms. Why did it catch on and flourish so? The same reason other heresies thrive: because of unlearned men trying to **teach** the Bible when they don't really **know** the Bible. They read into the Bible their own feelings while ignoring the historic Jewish context of Scripture. They jump to conclusions based on limited knowledge, emotion, and personal preferences; and then give over-simplified solutions to complex issues – thus drawing other gullible and unlearned people in to follow them.

2Pe 3:16 *As also in all his epistles, speaking in them of these things; in which are* **some things hard to be understood,** *which they that are* **unlearned and unstable wrest, as they do also the other scriptures,** *unto their own destruction.*

No doubt, Satan is helping this process as much as possible. Many in error are sincere but too impatient to learn the Bible well before they assume they know what it says. Marcionism, in all its forms, is due to this presumption of men thinking that they know what a passage means without studying carefully the whole revelation of an unchanging, consistent Heavenly Father. They come to the Scripture with their presuppositions and then assume the Bible agrees with them when they find a verse or two which can easily be twisted into their ideology. Marcionite influence is seen in doctrinal errors propagated by men who deny any connection with Marcion and would renounce much of what Marcion taught; yet fail to see they are building on the **same false premise** that Marcion built on. They reject the label of **Marcionite** while they insult God in the *same* fundamental way that Marcion did. They defend the fundamental principles of Marcionism with different arguments and theories; but this does not deliver them from being Marcionites; as Marcion's belief system was simply his desire to defend his fundamental argument that Jesus taught different ethics than the God of the Old Testament. Many claim to be defending the faith, as Marcion did, yet they reject the clear Word of God when it disagrees with them – as Marcion did. Marcion, in order to defend his error, rejected many portions of Scripture and designed his own canon with only the books and parts of the Scripture he liked. The men today, who support Marcionism while rejecting Marcionism, claim to believe all the Scripture; but indeed they do not accept the testimony of ALL the Scripture when it disagrees with their heresy – I've proved this to myself in debating with them. They are so sure their beliefs are right that they are not even open to consider the blatant and obvious facts proving them in error – *and have said so*! And so, just like Marcion, they abuse the Scripture and will not submit themselves to it. They would rather sacrifice the Scripture to save their "ism", than sacrifice their "ism" to be accurate with the Scripture. So...exactly what was this heresy?

Marcion's "way out" concepts were only his frenzied efforts to support his original premise that Jesus' teaching was contrary to God's Word through Moses and not consistent with it. Marcion, in order to support his claim that Jesus' teaching was contrary to God's inspired Word had to ignore many things. He knew that Jesus was God's WORD in the flesh; he knew that Jesus was supposed to be the Messiah of the Jews promised by the prophets; he knew that Jesus was said to be coming to write God's Law in the Jewish people's hearts and vindicate God's Law from all false teaching; he knew that the God of the Old Testament said He never changes; he knew that the Scriptures of the Apostles agree that God never changes, and that Jesus is the same yesterday, today, and forever; and he knew that if Jesus did teach contrary to God's Law, the Jews were commanded by God's own Law to kill him as a false prophet which would disqualify Him from being the Messiah by God's own WORD – **YES, he had heard all this**; yet he desired *more* to defend his own concept that Jesus did not consistently present the same moral ethic as the God of the Old Testament; but a higher and better "god" or ethic. In order for him to defend his error, he had to overcome all the Scriptural principles and facts that proved him to be wrong. Obviously he just wanted to employ Jesus to defend his own values and preferences, **which is true of all who defend Marcion's premise even today.**

NOW, it is important for you to understand that **anyone** who promotes the original premise of Marcion, even though they may defend it in different ways, is still siding with Marcion - the "First-born of Satan" in Polycarp's estimation. It is the *PREMISE* that is the *root of the heresy*, not just the different props to support it. Our books give overwhelming evidence, not only that Marcion was dead wrong and deserved to be renounced as Polycarp said; but that all who support his premise are equally supporting a doctrine of devils. Once you comprehend the infinite insult to YHVH (Jehovah or Yahweh), the God of the Hebrews who created the world and gave Moses' the Law, you will understand the gravity of this despicable error. Much of Christendom has been influenced by Gnostic doctrines and ideas since the times of the Apostles; and most heresies today began early in the history of the church.

Ac 20:28 Take heed therefore unto yourselves, and to all the flock, over the which the Holy Ghost hath made you overseers, to feed the church of God, which he hath purchased with his own blood. 29 For I know this, that after my departing shall grievous wolves enter in among you, not sparing the flock. 30 Also of your own selves shall men arise, speaking perverse things, to draw away disciples after them."

This treachery became a reality even while the Apostles were still living, and many of the *early church writings*, which usually are 100+ years removed from the Apostles, were tainted with error in some form – usually

19

because they divorced the Scriptures (Matthew through Revelation) from the Scriptures (Genesis through Malachi). There was much controversy with heretics of many sorts while the Apostles were still preaching, and it only became worse after they passed on. Just read Rev. 2 & 3.

The Marcionite Gnostics interpreted Jesus as correcting Moses and presenting a different standard of righteousness than the God of Moses. When Jesus said in the Sermon on the Mount, *"Ye have heard that it has been said by them of old time...but I say unto you."* They decided Jesus was correcting Moses...or actually Jehovah. Jesus would then actually be correcting Himself – The WORD OF GOD incarnate. However, Jesus was not correcting Moses, God, or Himself; but correcting the *abuse* of God's Word. The Jewish people and teachers had misunderstood and misused the Scriptures; and before Jesus could "write God's Law in our hearts" by the Holy Spirit, which **is** the "New Covenant", He had to correct the misinterpretations and misapplications of His Law. Before He could reconcile man to God, He had to clarify God's terms of reconciliation. This is so easy to prove from the Scriptures; but sadly most people love *their interpretation of Jesus* more than *the real Jesus*. Jesus' teaching is indeed antithetical to the Jewish abuse of God's Law, but **NEVER** antithetical to God's Law or any other part of the Scriptures.

The Marcionites were more logical than most today who teach Marcion's premise, because they concluded: If the God of the Old Testament says he is unchanging, and the God of the New Testament says he is unchanging; but they have different ethics, *then there must be two different gods!* Gods don't change their ethics and then

20

claim to never change unless they are liars.   There are scores of reasons straight from the Scripture why Jesus could not, did not, and would not speak anything contrary or inconsistent with the WORD of God already penned by Moses and the prophets. The fact that Jesus IS the WORD made flesh and thus the **author of all the Scriptures** is the most obvious reason; but there are many more which only an ism-ite could deny.

It has been my observation that many may believe the *premise* behind a heretical belief system; but not all are capable or willing to think this *premise* through to the logical conclusions. Those who *do* take the foundational thoughts to their logical conclusions are often renounced by those who only take the premise part way or to illogical conclusions. They don't realize they are all *really* in the SAME BOAT!   Let's have a short history lesson:

Marcionism
From Wikipedia, the free encyclopedia

"Marcionism was an Early Christian dualist belief system that originated in the teachings of Marcion of Sinope at Rome around the year 144.[1]   Marcion believed Jesus was the savior sent by God, and Paul the Apostle was his chief apostle, but he rejected the Hebrew Bible and the God of Israel. Marcionists believed that the wrathful Hebrew God was a separate and lower entity than the all-forgiving God of the New Testament. This belief was in some ways similar to Gnostic Christian theology; notably, both are *dualistic*,...**The premise of Marcionism is that many of the teachings of Christ are incompatible with the actions of the God of the Old Testament.** Focusing on the Pauline traditions of the Gospel, Marcion felt that all other conceptions of the Gospel, and especially any association with the Old

21

Testament religion, was opposed to, and a backsliding from, the truth. He further regarded the arguments of Paul regarding law and gospel, wrath and grace, works and faith, flesh and spirit, sin and righteousness, death and life, as the essence of religious truth. He ascribed these aspects and characteristics as two principles, the righteous and wrathful God of the Old Testament, who is at the same time identical with the creator of the world, and a second God of the Gospel, quite unknown before Christ, who is only love and mercy.

"Marcion is said to have gathered scriptures from Jewish tradition, and **juxtaposed these against the sayings and teachings of Jesus in a work entitled the *Antithesis*.**[16]"

"Historic Marcionism, and the church Marcion himself established, appeared to die out around the 5th century, although similarities between Marcionism and Paulicianism, a later heresy in the same geographical area, indicate that Marcionist ideas may have survived and even contributed to heresies derived from Paulicians in Bulgaria (Bogomilism) and France (Catharism) - *(Anabaptist groups).* Whether or not that is the case, Marcion's influence and criticism of the Old Testament are discussed to this very day.

"For some, the postulated problems of the Old Testament, and the appeal of Jesus are such that they identify themselves as modern day Marcionites, and follow his solution in keeping the New Testament as sacred scripture, and rejecting the Old Testament canon and practices. A term sometimes used for these groups is "New Testament Christians". Carroll R. Bierbower is a pastor of a church he says is Marcionite in theology and practice.[31] The Cathar movement *(Anabaptists)*, historically and in modern times, reject the Old Testament for the reasons Marcion enunciated. It remains unclear whether the 11th century Cathar movement is a continuation of earlier Gnostic and Marcion streams, or represents an independent re-invention."

(Comments in parenthesis and italics are mine)

It is very important to note that **where** the Marcionites **went** with their PREMISE is **not** the core of their wicked error; but the **PREMISE itself!** The main problem and slander upon God is the **PREMISE** that the ethics of the New Testament are opposite to the ethics of the Old Testament or at least incompatible and inconsistent. This is the heresy of Marcion and is seen in many denominations as well as modern Anabaptist groups (along with many of the ancient Anabaptists). Andrew Ste. Marie, in his attempt to defend Mennonite teaching against my expose', *The Alien Exposed*, only proves my case by demonstrating his alien agenda of attempting to reconstruct the entire Bible to his beliefs.

In the paragraphs below we are comparing the statements of modern Marcionites (The "Marcionite Church of Christ") with Ste. Marie's words. Judge for yourself. Ste. Marie denies being a Marcionite; but read this undeniable proof which reveals his true feelings, which are the foundations of his beliefs. Read the stated position of modern Marcionites who admit what they are; and then read Ste. Marie's sentiments that follow and compare:

Modern Marcionite Church Website
marcionitechurchofchrist.yolasite.com

"No good tree bears bad fruit, nor does a bad tree bear good fruit. Each tree is recognized by its own fruit." - Evangelion (aka Luke 6:43-44)

"With this verse Marcion began his central argument: that the God of the Old Testament is not and cannot be the same deity as the one revealed by Jesus Christ. To a modern Christian this may sound supremely strange. Weren't we all taught that the New Testament is the fulfillment of the Old?

"...So in the spirit of the Antitheses let's compare for a moment the fruit of Jehovah and the fruit of the Heavenly Father:

"Jehovah's "fruit":

"This is what the Lord of hosts has to say: 'I will punish what Amalek did to Israel when he barred his way as he was coming up from Egypt. Go, now, attack Amalek, and deal with him and all that he has under the ban. Do not spare him, but kill men and women, children and infants, oxen and sheep, camels and asses.' 1 Samuel 15:2-3

"I will make Mount Seir utterly desolate, killing off all who try to escape and any who return. I will fill your mountains with the dead. Your hills, your valleys, and your streams will be filled with people slaughtered by the sword. I will make you desolate forever. Your cities will never be rebuilt. Then you will know that I am the LORD. Ezekiel 35:7-9

"My angel will go before you and bring you to the Amorites, Hittites, Perizzites, Canaanites, Hivites, and Jebusites; and I will wipe them out. Exodus 23:23

"Anyone who is captured will be run through with a sword. Their little children will be dashed to death right before their eyes. Their homes will be sacked and their wives raped by the attacking hordes. For I will stir up the Medes against Babylon, and no amount of silver or gold will buy them off. The

attacking armies will shoot down the young people with arrows. They will have no mercy on helpless babies and will show no compassion for the children. Isaiah 13:15-18

"O Babylon, you will be destroyed. Happy is the one who pays you back for what you have done to us. Happy is the one who takes your babies and smashes them against the rocks! Psalms 137:8-9

"For the LORD your God is a consuming fire, a jealous God. Deuteronomy 4:24

"...and this is but a tiny sample of Jehovah's "fruit"!

"But what of the Heavenly Father? His fruit is clear:

"But I say to you who hear, love your enemies, do good to those who hate you, bless those who curse you, pray for those who mistreat you. "Whoever hits you on the cheek, offer him the other also; and whoever takes away your coat, do not withhold your shirt from him either.

"Give to everyone who asks of you, and whoever takes away what is yours, do not demand it back. Luke 6:27-30

"Love is patient, love is kind. It does not envy, it does not boast, it is not proud. It is not rude, it is not self-seeking, it is not easily angered, it keeps no record of wrongs. Love does not delight in evil but rejoices with the truth. It always protects, always trusts, always hopes, always perseveres. 1 Corinthians 13:4-7

"...again but a small taste of the fruit of the Father, revealed by his Son"

NOW COMPARE:

Mennonite Defender: Andrew Ste. Marie

"...So, we are back to our original question: Did the Old Testament **teach** hatred of enemies? My conclusion is that, although there are some glimpses of the bright new day to come, the Old Testament did indeed **teach** and exemplify the ill treatment – indeed, hatred – of enemies.

And **the LORD spake unto Moses, saying**, Vex the Midianites, and smite them: For they vex you with their wiles, wherewith they have beguiled you in the matter of Peor, and in the matter of Cozbi, the daughter of a prince of Midian, their sister, which was slain in the day of the plague for Peor's sake (Numbers 25:16-18).

And **the LORD spake unto Moses, saying**, Avenge the children of Israel of the Midianites: afterward shalt thou be gathered unto thy people. And Moses spake unto the people, saying, Arm some of yourselves unto the war, and let them go against the Midianites, and avenge the LORD of Midian. Of every tribe a thousand, throughout all the tribes of Israel, shall ye send to the war (Numbers 31:1-4).

When **the LORD** thy God shall bring thee into the land whither thou goest to possess it, and hath cast out many nations before thee, the Hittites, and the Girgashites, and the Amorites, and the Canaanites, and the Perizzites, and the Hivites, and the Jebusites, seven nations greater and mightier than thou; And when **the LORD thy God** shall deliver them before thee; thou shalt smite them, and utterly destroy them; thou shalt make no covenant with them, nor shew mercy unto them: Neither shalt thou make marriages with them; thy daughter thou shalt not give unto his son, nor his daughter shalt thou take unto thy son (Deuteronomy 7:1-3).

But of the cities of these people, which **the LORD thy God** doth give thee for an inheritance, thou shalt save alive nothing that breatheth: But thou shalt utterly destroy them; namely, the Hittites, and the Amorites, the Canaanites, and the Perizzites, the Hivites, and the Jebusites; **as the LORD thy God hath commanded thee** (Deuteronomy 20:16-17).

Remember what Amalek did unto thee by the way, when ye were come forth out of Egypt; How he met thee by the way, and smote the hindmost of thee, even all that were feeble behind thee, when thou wast faint and weary; and he **feared not God.** Therefore it shall be, when **the LORD thy God** hath given thee rest from all thine enemies round about, in the land which **the LORD thy God giveth thee** for an inheritance to possess it, that **thou shalt blot out the remembrance of Amalek from under heaven; thou shalt not forget it** (Deuteronomy 25:17-19).

So we have here the positive **words of God** regarding the Israelites' enemies, who were to be vexed, smitten, utterly destroyed, and have vengeance wreaked upon them – all without mercy. What could be more different from the teaching of the New Testament on the treatment of enemies?... I find it particularly hard to understand how someone could read in Numbers 31:2 that **God commanded** the children of Israel to take vengeance, and then compare it with Romans 12:19, where vengeance even for ourselves is forbidden, and argue that the ethics of the two covenants are the same. **They are opposites!**

...Now, to come all the way back to the Sixth Antithesis of the Sermon on the Mount, Jesus' quotation, "Thou shalt love thy neighbour, and hate thine enemy," is not a verbatim quotation of a specific Old Testament text, but is an accurate summary of the **teaching** and example of the Old Testament in its relationship to neighbors and enemies. **Jesus superseded this teaching and example,** *and replaced it with an ethic of absolute love for all – including enemies – in which every true Christian must follow the example of his Heavenly Father, Who is good to all – even His enemies."*

(emphasis mine)

Could any confession be clearer?? He is defending the SAME premise as the Marcionites. What **example** do "true Christians" have in "**Jesus' Father**", if *not* from the **God** of the Old Testament...the very God that the teaching and example of Jesus superseded?? Ste. Marie is essentially saying that Jesus led us *away* from the **example and teaching** of the **God of the Old Testament** to the **example and teaching of Himself and His Father** – *a different God? What else could this mean?!* What example do we have of Jesus' Heavenly Father? Only what He has told us in that one verse?? It seems so according to Ste. Marie. He **clearly denies** that the God of the Old Testament, who gave Moses the Law and commanded the war and killing, is Jesus' Father *OR* our example! He is a bonafide Marcionite heretic. This is sad, but true; and **everyone** who espouses his foundational argument falls into the **same camp**. Someday they will all hear God thunder from His throne, *"Wilt thou also disannul my judgment? wilt thou condemn me, that thou mayest be righteous?"* (Job 40:8). Everything Jesus taught was already taught in the Old Testament; but needed an authoritative clarification and application -- NOT CORRECTION. God is a just judge and everything He ever did or commanded was just, righteous, appropriate and YES....IT WAS LOVE; because God is LOVE. If you can't figure it out, then at least have enough fear of God to not charge Him with wrong doing.

28

As with all Marcionites, Ste. Marie doesn't understand or really believe in the immutability of God and of Christ. He hides behind the false front that Jesus is just *expanding* the law; but then states over and over that Jesus' teaching was the **antithesis of God's Law** – Just like Marcion did. He is just a grievous wolf hiding in sheep's wool trying to sound pious; and all true sheep need to beware. Before you die, you'd better make sure you are following the RIGHT JESUS. Go to www.TheRightJesus.com and you will find help. *See the full refutation of Ste. Marie's book on our website or order a free copy of our books by writing to us.*

The TRUTH is: WE, who are the TRUE Christians, **DO** believe we can follow the example of Jesus' Father concerning the **proper application and interpretation** of **ALL** Jesus' teaching; because it is **all** consistent with the revelation of Jesus' Father from Genesis to Revelation. True students of Scripture know the difference between the "governmental execution of the Law" upon those whom God has justly condemned to death, like the Amalekites; and the "interpersonal relationship", like what Jesus was dealing with in His preaching. We can see what Jesus and His Father have **done** to **define** their **terms** and **meanings.** They practice what they preach, and we are to follow their example. Jesus wanted us to act just like HIS FATHER, and live by the same principles.

*Mt 5:48 Be ye therefore perfect, **even as your Father** which is in heaven is perfect.*

*1Pe 1:15 But **as he which hath called you is holy, so be ye holy** in **all manner of conversation**; 16 Because **it is written**, Be ye holy; for I am holy.*

29

God has given us an *example* to *define* what He **means** by His *terms*. God's *actions* define His *terms*! We are to be holy in all our conduct **AS** HE IS HOLY in His conduct. We are to follow His example and interpret His Word by His example! This is so elementary; but vital to the foundation of right thinking and properly interpreting Jesus. Just because some of the unlearned cannot see the connection and consistency of God's will and Word, doesn't mean it is not there in plain sight. You won't see it, though, if you are *LOOKING FOR SOMETHING ELSE*.

Pr 28:5 *Evil men understand not judgment: but they that seek the LORD understand all things.*

Isa 8:20 *To the law and to the testimony: if they speak not according to this word, it is because there is no light in them.*

God IS LOVE. Do you believe that? Is the God of creation, the flood, and the Law, LOVE? Is God's Law the expression of His Love? **Jesus said so numerous times!** He clearly said that Moses' Law was God's Word and was ALL based on divine Love. All God's Laws were His love expressed in His moral judgments. Reread Deuteronomy in the light of God's love. **Every** law of God was **only** intended to be used by **sincere** believers to **maintain holy love in society. JESUS SAID SO!** He expects you to figure it out – not deny it.

Mt 7:12 *Therefore all things whatsoever ye would that men should do to you, do ye even so to them: <u>for this is the law and the prophets.</u>*

Mt 22:37 *Jesus said unto him, Thou shalt love the Lord thy God with all thy heart, and with all thy soul, and with all thy mind. 38 This is the first and great commandment. 39 And the second is like unto it, Thou shalt love thy neighbour as thyself. 40 <u>On these two commandments hang all the law and the prophets.</u>*

Does Jesus' and the Apostles' concept of LOVE **still** fulfill God's Law as given to Moses? **They said it did.**

Ro 13:10 *Love worketh no ill to his neighbour: therefore love is the fulfilling of the law.*

Ga 5:14 *For all the law is fulfilled in one word, even in this; Thou shalt love thy neighbour as thyself.*

Do you understand that God's love is not evolving, but was perfect before the world was created; and He has never manifested anything other than love. God could not manifest anything other than His love, because *He is love,* and cannot manifest anything else. If Jesus taught contrary to God's Law, then it couldn't also be love; but all God's revelation *is* love – and *LOVE* IS *LOVE* – God doesn't have two brands or standards of love. Every precept, law, statute, or principle taught in God's Word by God's inspired writers is a revelation of God's wise and perfectly appropriate Love. God has nothing else to manifest when He is giving a revelation of Himself and His ways. Jesus could not present anything contrary to God's inspired moral judgments without denouncing the love of His own Father! Every part of God's Law was the most appropriate and loving thing to do in that situation; *and* was intended to be used for that purpose alone! Any *other* use or representation of God's Law was and is abuse. God's Law is still the most wise, appropriate and loving thing to do. The **New Covenant was to be God's Law written in the hearts and minds** of His Jewish people by God's Spirit and *not* the changing of Gods' moral judgments (Jer 31:31-33).

Do you understand God's judgment? If you cannot understand how LOVE for truth and righteousness also necessitates HATE for iniquity, then you cannot understand God **or** Jesus – *and make sure you don't call*

the police when someone is trying to kill your children!
Listen to what GOD said about JESUS:

Heb 1:8 *But unto the Son he saith, Thy throne, O God, is for ever and ever: a sceptre of righteousness is the sceptre of thy kingdom. 9 Thou hast loved righteousness, and hated iniquity; therefore God, even thy God, hath anointed thee with the oil of gladness above thy fellows.*

Did Marcion ignore what is said about Jesus in **Luke 19:27** when he returns, or what Jesus said His Father would do to those who slew Him (**Luke 20:15-18**), and those who rejected His invitation (**Mt 22:1-7**)? What about what Paul says concerning Jesus when He returns:

2Th 1:8 *In flaming fire taking vengeance on them that know not God, and that obey not the gospel of our Lord Jesus Christ:*

I would rather side with the Apostle Paul in Romans where he is speaking about the moral judgments of the God of the Old Testament thus:

Ro 3:3 *For what if some did not believe? Shall their unbelief make the faith of God without effect? 4 God forbid: yea, <u>let God be true, but every man a liar;</u> as it is written, That thou mightest be justified in thy sayings, and mightest overcome when thou art judged.*

Marcionites labor to make God a liar concerning His testimony that He never changes! Jesus came to "justify" God in His sayings and overcome heretics who wrongly judged God because they didn't understand His judgment or believe His Word. Malachi and Isaiah expressly declare this! Just because people did not properly obey or understand God's Law, because they didn't "believe" it; their unbelief, which led to abuse, doesn't make God's Word wrong or ineffectual or imperfect (Heb 4:2; 1 Peter

32

1:25).   Just because some Marcionite doesn't define *LOVE* in the same terms as God, doesn't make God anything else but LOVE. Just because they **think** they see an inconsistency in God's directives, doesn't mean God has changed his Love or His Law – **"yea, let God be true, but every man a liar;"**

LOVE is only virtuous when LOVE is for RIGHT with hatred for iniquity (lawlessness), **because that is God's Love**. God **IS** love. He is the standard for righteous love; which is perfectly consistent with Him being the JUDGE who must justly deal out punishments and rewards impartially based on man's obedience or rebellion to the righteousness they know. God's judgments will actually come through the Lord Jesus whom God has appointed as the chief judge of mankind.

Ro 1:18 *For the wrath of God is revealed from heaven against all ungodliness and unrighteousness of men, who hold the truth in unrighteousness;...2:11 For there is no respect of persons with God. 12 For as many as have sinned without law shall also perish without law: and as many as have sinned in the law shall be judged by the law* **(Moses' Law)***; 13 (For not the hearers of the law are just before God, but the doers of the law shall be justified. 14 For when the Gentiles, which have not the law, do by nature the things contained in the law, these, having not the law, are a law unto themselves: 15 Which shew the work of the law written in their hearts, their conscience also bearing witness, and their thoughts the mean while accusing or else excusing one another;) 16 In the day when God shall judge the secrets of men by Jesus Christ according to my gospel.*

The LAW spoken of here is God's revelation of his moral judgments through Moses, which are consistent and unchanging because God's knowledge and holiness is consistent and unchanging.   What God gave through Moses is consistent with His entire Word **and His Spirit's**

conviction of men's hearts worldwide. This proves God's moral judgments are meant for all mankind, not just Israel.

Does God still feel and believe the same today about divorce and remarriage as He always has? Of Course! Everything the Bible says on the subject is consistent with God's Law. Does God still feel today the same about war, civil punishments, self defense, and the use of force as He always has? Yes, His feelings and opinions are based on eternal principles of LOVE. Does God still feel the same today about his people swearing oaths or being a part of the government as always? Most definitely. Does God ever misrepresent Himself or give direction contrary to His own holiness and wisdom and love? Absolutely not! If God never changes, which He clearly states, then could He give different judgments and verdicts at different times to the same people (Israel) on the same subject? If Jesus is the same yesterday, today, and forever; and He is the Word made flesh, thus being the author of the Scriptures from Genesis to Revelation – could He speak inconsistently and give different moral judgments at different times about the same issue to the same people? Never. Only a Marcionite would contrive such an insult to God's infinite holiness, love, and wisdom. To say God gave a **better** judgment **here** is to say He gave a **worse** judgment **there**; but that is not possible with an infinite, omniscient, and non-evolving God.

For intelligent people who are willing to listen, these truths should be enough to settle this matter without a large book to prove each point from the Scriptures. However, since there are those who labor to support Marcion's premise for the sake of their own false piety and personal pet doctrines, thus confusing the unlearned

34

and unaware, we will labor to unveil the serpent's lair more fully. Our books prove point by point the consistency of God's Word from Genesis to Revelation. They show clearly that Jesus never spoke inconsistent with the Scriptures or presented any "new ethic" contrary to God's Law.

The Marcionite-Centric Method

I recently received a letter from a Mennonite man trying to **deny** that Mennonites were Marcionite in doctrine. The only problem with his case is that over and over he proved he was indeed a Marcionite in doctrine. What follows is an important part of his case to "prove his doctrine and deny Marcionism". He is comparing what he believes are two different ways of looking at the Bible. See if you can recognize how he is simply proving himself to be what he is denying. He declares there is:

1. "A Torah-Centric interpretation: Under this method all the Scripture is held up to the Torah, the law given by God though Moses to the Children of Israel. Old Testament ethics are one and the same as New Testament ethics. New Testament teaching isn't any "higher" than the Old Testament teaching. The Scriptures are "flat", the law of God is unchanging and everything rests on the Torah — there is no higher revelation. The Torah is at the foundation and center of all of Scripture — hence the term "Torah Centric."

2. "A Christ-Centric interpretation. Under this method, Jesus Christ is considered God's highest revelation. The written Word is not an end in itself, but leads us to Jesus — the Living Word, the Word made flesh. (John 5:39-40) New Testament revelation is considered "higher" than OT revelation. The Sermon on the Mount is Jesus' higher ethical teaching for the regenerated People of God living under the New Covenant. Jesus towers over the

Scriptures; He stands with all authority in heaven and earth at the center of the Scriptures. Therefore, His life and teaching and the teaching of His apostles are at the center of everything, not the Torah. Hence the term Christ-Centric"

He also makes the following statement in all caps: *"WE MOST CERTAINLY BELIEVE AND CONFESS THAT JESUS CHRIST WHO IS LORD OF ALL, DID INDEED "CHANGE" THE WORD OF GOD BY SUPPLEMENTING IT, BY ADDING TO IT, AND IN THOSE ADDITIONS WE BELIEVE HE RAISED A MUCH HIGHER ETHICAL STANDARD FOR HIS FOLLOWERS."*

Now most likely you have received similar teaching from whatever denomination you are from. I say this because, once you understand the error of Marcionism, you will find it has affected most all of Christendom to some degree, without them even realizing it. Let's analyze the problems with these statements.

The core problem with this man's Torah-Centric VS Christ- Centric ideology is that he is declaring a **conflict** between Christ and His Law! Christ *is* the Word and the Law *is* His own sentiments. There is no conflict between Christ and His Word. The **written Word *is* Jesus on paper from Genesis to Revelation.** HOW can the written Word lead us to the Living Word, when, if this man is right, the written Word says we should stone the Living Word because He is leading us away from the written Word? What the sneaky snake philosophy of this man **really** means is this: *"We want everyone to interpret the entire Bible by OUR INTERPRETATION OF JESUS' WORDS, and **not** interpret Jesus' words in harmony with the rest of God's Word, which are JESUS' OWN WORDS."* This approach to interpretation would then really be **The Marcionite-Centric Method.**

36

*Pr 30:5 **Every word of God is pure**: he is a shield unto them that put their trust in him.*

*Lu 4:4 And Jesus answered him, saying, It is written, That man shall not live by bread alone, **but by every word of God.***

Here is a Bible Literacy Test:

1. In our New Testament in many Bibles there are words printed in **Black** and words printed in **Red**, which ones did Jesus author?

Answer: *Jesus didn't write any of them, but He authored ALL of them.*

2. We have an Old Testament and New Testament in our English Bible, which represents the teachings of Jesus?

Answer: *It all represents the teachings of Jesus who is the WORD OF GOD from Genesis to Revelation.*

Under the proper method of interpreting the Bible, **ALL** Scripture is held up to **ALL** other Scriptures and interpreted consistent with the **whole counsel of God**. This is the method God's expects us to use.

*2Ti 3:16 **All scripture** is given by inspiration of God, **and is profitable for doctrine**, for reproof, for correction, for instruction in righteousness: 17 That the man of God may be perfect (complete), throughly furnished unto **all** good works.*

Progressive revelation is not "EVOLVING REVELATION"; for God's wisdom, love, knowledge, and holiness **do not evolve;** and a further revelation of God's love, wisdom, holiness, and knowledge will ONLY CONFIRM what has already been revealed.

Notice how Marcionites have to demean the ***written Word*** in order to propagate *their* interpretation of Jesus' words. There is a big difference between a more glorious covenant and a more righteous law. There is a big difference between further revelation and "higher ethics". The further revelation of God is not a higher ethic, but only a confirming of the previous ethic. Listen to Jesus:

Mt 7:12 *Therefore all things whatsoever ye would that men should do to you, do ye even so to them: for* **this is the law and the prophets.**

Mt 22:37 *Jesus said unto him, Thou shalt love the Lord thy God with all thy heart, and with all thy soul, and with all thy mind. 38 This is the first and great commandment. 39 And the second is like unto it, Thou shalt love thy neighbour as thyself. 40* **On these two commandments hang all the law and the prophets.**

What "ethic" is higher than this?? Did Jesus teach anything higher than this?? IF He did, then why is He still teaching this?? Jesus says His teaching is the **same ethic** as the Law taught. The fact is that Jesus did not change anything about God's Law; but taught the people and His disciples to obey those in Moses' seat – Mat 23. This will be proven in the next chapters.

Jesus changed **nothing** concerning Jewish life, faith, and practice from what God's Word had already taught the people (Matt 5:17-20). Those who believed that Jesus was the Messiah kept right on obeying Moses with renewed zeal and better understanding (**Acts 21**), while they waited for the Messiah to return and set up His Kingdom on David's throne – Luke 19. Nothing outward changed concerning Jewish practice in the lives of those in the "New Covenant". Twelve years after Pentecost God revealed, through Peter and the pouring out of the Holy Spirit on Cornelius, that He would now accept believing

Gentiles in the church without them coming under Judaism. This "change" in the program was revealed directly from heaven; and was so documented in the OT Scriptures that the Apostles supported and defended it by quoting the OT (Acts 15 & Romans). It was not a change in moral judgment; but "plan A" of God's salvation program unfolding another page.

The Messianic Jews/disciples of Jesus kept right on obeying all that Moses taught with the only addition being that now they could eat and fellowship with believing Gentiles who became grafted members of the New Covenant with Israel (Acts 15 & 21). The New Covenant was WITH Israel; and it was the writing of **God's Laws** in their hearts by the indwelling Holy Ghost -- **NOT the undoing of God's Law**.

*Joh 5:46 For had ye believed Moses, ye would have believed me: for he wrote of me. 47 **But if ye believe not his writings, how shall ye believe my words?***

Does Jesus "tower above the Scriptures"?? If Jesus *is* the WORD of God in the flesh, then there is no competition or conflict between the two. God's Word *is* God's perspective – His opinion, His sentiments, His feelings, and thus we have the Holy Ghost declaring:

*Ps 138:2 I will worship toward thy holy temple, and praise thy name for thy lovingkindness and for thy truth: **for thou hast magnified thy word <u>above</u> all thy name.***

Listen to Jesus when Satan tempts Him to exert His rights and authority as the Son of God to meet His need of food and make the stones into bread:

*Mt 4:4 But he answered and said, **It is written**, Man shall not live by bread alone, **but by <u>every word</u> that proceedeth out of the mouth of God.***

Did Jesus exalt Himself above the Word of God?? NO, actually in all the temptations of the Devil we find Jesus **submitting Himself to God's Word** and quoting it against Satan's demand that Jesus *act in His own person,* and *not keep rank under God's Word.* Jesus had to keep the Law spotlessly to be the Lamb of God, and definitely didn't assume the right to disobey or change God's Word. Jesus' test as a faithful Son was to KEEP RANK under God's Law in doing "always" those things which pleased His Father — the God of the OT.

God doesn't give **LOW** revelations; so the false piety that says "Jesus is God's highest revelation" is a subtle insult to God whose revelations are always *His Holy Ways.* There is a difference between God's "greatest revelation" and His "highest revelation" of Himself. One deals with *magnitude* and the other with *altitude/quality.* For man to categorize God's Word as "important" and "not important" is the very thing Jesus is rebuking in the Sermon on the Mount (Mt 5:17-20). Jesus says those who do this and *teach men so* will not be allowed into the Kingdom of God.

Moses recorded God's Laws for the nation of Israel as they came into a covenant with God. The Bible record is basically the following: The recording of God's Law given to man in a covenant; the history behind this Law and covenant; the history of those who were supposed to be keeping this Law; the songs and proverbs about the glories of this Law; the prophets telling the people to return to this Law; Jesus coming to clarify and defend this Law; Jesus dying to make atonement for man's transgressions against this Law; the giving of the Holy Spirit to write this Law in our hearts; and the Apostles preaching and explaining how the goal of this Law is Love

40

and must be written in our hearts for us to reconcile with the God who wrote it. God's relationship with man has always included His Law – His Ways.

Jesus died to atone for our transgressions of God's Law and serves now as our High Priest to keep us clean before God if we transgress His Law while we are striving to walk in obedience. **It is all about God's Law and man being reconciled to it, so God can reinstate fellowship and take them to heaven.** Salvation is *man reconciling with God* by having God's Law written on our hearts so we can again be partakers of the divine nature; and thus have God's Love shed abroad in our hearts by the Holy Ghost. IT IS ALL ABOUT GOD'S LAW, BECAUSE THAT IS **GOD'S WAYS and God's LOVE**. Satan's prime jewel of deception is the changing of people's attitude and perception concerning God's Law, as though it is a negative and outdated concept which is not spiritual, nor meant to be loved and obeyed. All heresy is based on this false concept dressed in many different suits. **The Torah is God's Word!** Everyone who must demean it in order to promote their own doctrine are rank heretics and in danger of hellfire.

Ps 119:89 For ever, O LORD, thy word is settled in heaven.

Ro 3:31 Do we then make void the law through faith? God forbid: yea, **we establish the law.**

Ro 8:12 Wherefore **the law is holy, and the commandment holy, and just, and good.** 13 Was then that which is good made death unto me? God forbid. But sin, that it might appear sin, working death in me by that which is good; that sin by the commandment might become exceeding sinful. 14 **For we know that the law is spiritual**: but I am carnal, sold under sin.

41

1Jo 3:4 *Whosoever committeth sin* **transgresseth also the law:** *for* **sin is the transgression of the law.**

Chapter Three
Malachi's Introduction To Jesus

Malachi is the last word of God to the Jewish people before nearly 400 years of silence. This silence was finally broken by the preaching of John the Baptist as he introduces the Messiah. Malachi, along with addressing the sins of the people, gives them an introduction to the Messiah and His mission along with instructions to prepare them for this grand event. If one doesn't comprehend Malachi's prophecy then they will not rightly discern and evaluate Jesus.

In the book of Malachi we find God scolding Israel harshly for some misconceptions they had developed about God and His Laws due to elevating their own ideas and desires above God's Word. In chapter one, we see them as ungrateful and unbelieving in their treatment of God.

Malachi 1:6 A son honoureth his father, and a servant his master: if then I be a father, where is mine honour? and if I be a master, where is my fear? saith the LORD of hosts unto you, O priests, that despise my name. And ye say, Wherein have we despised thy name? 7 Ye offer polluted bread upon mine altar; and ye say, Wherein have we polluted thee? In that ye say, The table of the LORD is contemptible. 8 And if ye offer the blind for sacrifice, is it not evil? and if ye offer the lame and sick, is it not evil? offer it now unto thy governor; will he be pleased with thee, or accept thy person? saith the LORD of hosts.

In chapter two we see God's scathing rebuke for the misuse and misrepresentation of His Law and Ways.

*Malachi 2:1 And now, O ye priests, this commandment is for you. 2 If ye will not hear, and if ye will not lay it to heart, to give glory unto my name, saith the LORD of hosts, I will even send a curse upon you, and I will curse your blessings: yea, I have cursed them already, because ye do not lay it to heart. 3 Behold, I will corrupt your seed, and spread dung upon your faces, even the dung of your solemn feasts; and one shall take you away with it. 4 And ye shall know that I have sent this commandment unto you, that my covenant might be with Levi, saith the LORD of hosts. 5 My covenant was with him of life and peace; and I gave them to him for the fear wherewith he feared me, and was afraid before my name. 6 **The law of truth was in his mouth, and iniquity was not found in his lips: he walked with me in peace and equity, and did turn many away from iniquity.** 7 For the priest's lips should keep knowledge, and they should seek the law at his mouth: **for he is the messenger of the LORD of hosts.** 8 But **ye are departed out of the way; ye have caused many to stumble at the law; ye have corrupted the covenant of Levi, saith the LORD of hosts.** 9 Therefore have I also made you contemptible and base before all the people, **according as ye have not kept my ways, but have been partial in the law.***

Notice what the problem is and what it is not. Notice God's view of Moses' Law.

*...13 And this have ye done again, covering the altar of the LORD with tears, with weeping, and with crying out, insomuch that he regardeth not the offering any more, or receiveth it with good will at your hand. 14 Yet ye say, Wherefore? **Because the LORD hath been witness between thee and the wife of thy youth, against whom thou hast dealt treacherously: yet is she thy companion, and the wife of thy covenant.** 15 And did not he make one? Yet had he the residue of the spirit. And wherefore one? That he might seek a godly seed. Therefore take heed to your spirit, and **let none deal treacherously against the***

wife of his youth. *16 For the LORD, the God of Israel, saith that he* **hateth putting away:** *for one covereth violence with his garment, saith the LORD of hosts: therefore take heed to your spirit, that ye* **deal not treacherously.** *17 Ye have wearied the LORD with your words. Yet ye say, Wherein have we wearied him? When ye say,* **Every one that doeth evil is good in the sight of the LORD, and he delighteth in them***; or,* **Where is the God of judgment?**

We can gain a number of important insights from this inspired prophet of God:

1. God gave the tribe of Levi the priesthood and the Law. Moses and Aaron were of the tribe of Levi.

2. The Law given through Moses represented **God's Ways**. God's inspired Word is God's viewpoint and moral judgment on the issues addressed in the Law. This was God's revelation to mankind and the rest of the Bible is built around this. (The New Covenant is God's new method of writing THESE laws in Israel's hearts through Jesus and the Holy Ghost – Jer. 31:31-33)

3. The current priests were not properly representing God's Law, but corrupting His ways. He charges them with being **partial in the Law** – only taking what they liked and wanted. This **abuse of the Law** caused many to stumble by justifying sin.

4. One example given was their unlawful divorces which dealt treacherously against the bride of their youth. A divorce and remarriage dealt with according to God's Law was **not** *dealing treacherously* with the wife, because it was **only** allowed when sufficient "uncleanness" was found in her. **God's Laws were only intended to be used by sincere God fearing men under the oversight of righteous judges to maintain**

holiness in society, not to do damage (Ro 13:10, 1Ti 1:5). Therefore, these men who were rebuked were *putting away their wives* **unlawfully** and **not** according to Moses' Law; but probably just to obtain another wife. The priests, who were abusing God's Laws, justified this evil by saying they were still "good in the sight of the LORD" and that "he delighted in them". This is the situation that Jesus would confront according to Malachi's introduction. God's Laws were appropriate remedies for the problems sin caused in society; and they were always the wisest, most loving steps to take – and still are.

5. The priests were calling evil "good" and presenting a God who was not a God of judgment anymore or had changed His mind from what the Law said. They claimed to delight in God, but had forsaken His Law, and assumed God changed with the years just as they had. They viewed God as "evolving" and being more progressive in their days. They interpreted God's Laws according to "what worked for them", etc.

Now listen to God's reply to this:

Malachi 3:1 *Behold, I will send my messenger, and he shall prepare the way before me: and the **Lord, whom ye seek, shall suddenly come to his temple, even the messenger of the covenant**, whom ye delight in: behold, he shall come, saith the LORD of hosts.*

This is referring to John the Baptist's introduction of Christ; and also of Christ's coming to "his temple" 400 years later. They "delighted" in the coming Messiah, but they didn't understand that the Messiah was representing the same God who wrote the Law which they were abusing. They *thought* they wanted Jesus to come; but they didn't understand that Jesus would stand with His

46

Father against their abuses of God's Laws. Listen to what God says to them in response to their foolishness.

Mal 3:2 *But who may abide the day of his coming? and who shall stand when he appeareth? for he is like a refiner's fire, and like fullers' soap: 3 And he shall sit as a refiner and purifier of silver: and he shall purify the sons of Levi, and purge them as gold and silver, that **they** may offer unto the LORD an offering in righteousness. 4 Then shall the **offering of Judah and Jerusalem** be pleasant unto the LORD,* <u>*as in the days of old, and as in former years.*</u>

Jesus fulfilled this Beautifully; and we find in Acts 21 *(29 yrs after Pentecost)* that **thousands of Jews** believed on Jesus and were **zealous of the Law of God** (See Also Isa 42:21). Notice that it says, *"**as in the days of old**, and as in **former years**"*; which proves that **God doesn't change** and still meant what He had previously said. The Law God wanted them to obey, and which He wanted to write on their hearts, was the **same Law** they had obeyed and reverenced in **"former years"**. What else would God do in the person of Christ?

Mal 3:5 *And **I will come near to you to judgment**; and I will be a swift witness against the **sorcerers**, and against the **adulterers**, and against **false swearers**, and against **those that oppress the hireling in his wages, the widow, and the fatherless, and that turn aside the stranger from his right, and fear not me**, saith the LORD of hosts. 6 **For I am the LORD, I change not;** therefore ye sons of Jacob are not consumed. 7 Even from the days of your fathers ye are **gone away from mine ordinances**, and **have not kept them.** <u>**Return unto me,**</u> and I will return unto you, saith the LORD of hosts.*

Alright, what have we learned?

1. The Messiah will prove to them that God is a God of Judgment and has not changed His mind; but still sees the Law of Moses as HIS WAYS.

2. Jesus will preach against the **adulterers as defined by God's Law, not the Jews who were abusing God's Law.** They were abusing God's Law, and thus dealing treacherously against their wife by unlawful divorce and remarriage. Malachi labels them as adulterers in this.

3. Jesus will preach against **false swearers** (those swearing contrary to God's Law).

4. God's message through the Messiah would prove that He is a God of judgment that never changes concerning His moral judgments of right and wrong.

5. God, through Jesus, will call them to **return to His Law**, and promises that He will then return to them. They must return and be faithful to God's Law so they can recognize the Messiah and enter His Kingdom.

*Joh 1:45 Philip findeth Nathanael, and saith unto him, **We have found him, of whom Moses in the law, and the prophets, did write**,*

*Joh 5:46 For **had ye believed Moses, ye would have believed me:***

*Ac 26:22 Having therefore obtained help of God, I continue unto this day, witnessing both to small and great, **saying none other things than those which the prophets and Moses did say should come**: 23 That Christ should suffer, and that he should be the first that should rise from the dead, and should shew light unto the people, and to the Gentiles.*

Mt 5:19 Whosoever therefore shall break one of these least commandments, and shall teach men so, he shall be called the least in the kingdom of heaven: but whosoever shall do and teach them, the same shall be called great in the kingdom of heaven. 20 For I say unto you, That except your righteousness shall exceed the righteousness of the scribes and Pharisees, **ye shall in no case enter into the kingdom of heaven.**

Now, to complete Malachi's introduction to Messiah Jesus, and see God's will for these people in preparation for Him, we turn to Malachi chapter four.

Mal 4:4 *Remember ye the law of Moses my servant,* <u>which I commanded</u> *unto him in Horeb for all Israel, with the statutes and judgments.* *5 Behold, I will send you Elijah the prophet before the coming of the great and dreadful day of the LORD: 6 And he shall turn the heart of the fathers to the children, and the heart of the children to their fathers, lest I come and smite the earth with a curse.*

So, God is telling us that the Messiah will come to correct **misconceptions** about God and His Law in order to purify His people and get them back on track. The Messiah will call Israel back to a right conception of God and His laws in order to establish a firm foundation for the New Covenant where God has promised He would write THESE LAWS in our hearts and minds by the Holy Ghost indwelling us.

John the Baptist, who filled the role of Malachi's "Elijah", came calling Israel to repent and "prepare the way of the LORD". The only "Way of the LORD" they knew was the OT Scriptures. Gabriel told Zacharias about John, *"...he shall be filled with the Holy Ghost, even from his mother's womb. 16 And many of the children of Israel shall he* **turn to the Lord their God***. 17 And he shall go before him in the spirit and power of Elias, to turn the hearts of the fathers to the children, and* **the disobedient to the wisdom of the just; to make ready a people** *prepared for the Lord.*" *(Luke 1:15-17).* Turning the people to God meant turning them to God's Laws as Malachi prophesied. Now, if Jesus' message was morally different than what John the Baptist preached, then John would have been preparing a people to reject Jesus, not preparing a people "ready" and "prepared" for Jesus. If Jesus changed the Law, then what would the people *NOW* repent of? What was SIN *now*? What was "returning to the way of the LORD"? Malachi and John both introduced a Messiah that came to clarify Moses' Law, and thus bring men back to God's ways as contained in that Law.

Obviously God would have to clarify His law and rebuke misconceptions **before** He could make a New Covenant with Israel based on His laws being written in their hearts. The people would be sure to recognize the Messiah IF they were faithfully *tuned in* to Moses' writings, because the source for both were the same:

*De 18:18 I will raise them up a Prophet from among their brethren, **like unto thee**, and **will put my words in his mouth**; and he shall speak unto them **all that I shall command him**. 19 And it shall come to pass, that whosoever will not hearken unto my words which he shall speak in my name, I will require it of him.*

This applied to all the prophets with Jesus being the climax and ultimate prophet. All the prophets were recognized because their message aligned with God's Word through Moses. How could they hearken to any prophet if that prophet was telling them to disobey and live contrary to God's previous WORD? If any prophet spoke contrary to Moses' Law, they were at once noted as a false prophet and stoned (De 13 & 18).

De 13:1 If there arise among you a prophet, or a dreamer of dreams, and giveth thee a sign or a wonder, 2 And the sign or the wonder come to pass, whereof he spake unto thee, saying, Let us go after other gods, which thou hast not known, and let us serve them; 3 Thou shalt not hearken unto the words of that prophet, or that dreamer of dreams: for the LORD your God proveth you, to know whether ye love the LORD your God with all your heart and with all your soul. 4 **Ye shall walk after the LORD your God, and fear him, and keep his commandments, and obey his voice, and ye shall serve him, and cleave unto him.** 5 And that prophet, or that dreamer of dreams, shall be put to death; **because he hath spoken to turn you away from the LORD your God**, which brought you out of the land of Egypt, and redeemed you out of the house of bondage**, to thrust thee out of the way which the LORD thy God commanded thee to walk in.** So shalt thou put the evil away from the midst of thee.

Messiah Jesus would be recognized as a true prophet of God the same way; otherwise He would be rightfully rejected by the godliest of the Jews as an imposter. When a prophet presents "another way" he is presenting "another god", just as Paul had warned the Corinthians of (2 Cor 11:1-4). Messiah Jesus spoke so as to vindicate and defend God's ways as presented in His Word. God was IN CHRIST reconciling the world unto himself and His ways; not preaching a different law.

2Co 5:18 And all things are of God, **who hath reconciled us to himself by Jesus Christ,** and hath given to us the ministry of reconciliation; 19 To wit, that **God was in Christ, reconciling the world unto himself,** not imputing their trespasses unto them; and hath committed unto us the word of reconciliation. 20 Now then we are ambassadors for Christ, **as though God did beseech you by us: we pray you in Christ's stead, be ye reconciled to God.**

Jesus did not change ONE thing about God's revelation to mankind or what was previously expected of the Jews in faith and practice. Jesus re-established a right conception of God's Laws among those who had ears to hear so God could **reconcile** them to himself – *"as in the days of old, and as in former years."*

Heb 1:1 God, *who at sundry times and in divers manners* **spake** *in time past unto the fathers* **by the prophets,** *2 Hath in these last days spoken unto us* **by his Son,**

It was the SAME source, so it would be the same message and not a contradictory message. This is how the people could recognize their Messiah and any true prophet of God. The same applies today with teachers and preachers! Listen to Isaiah as he proclaims the same things concerning the coming Messiah:

Isa 42:1 *Behold my servant* **[Messiah]***, whom I uphold; mine elect, in whom my soul delighteth; I have put my spirit upon him: he shall bring forth judgment to the Gentiles. 2 He shall not cry, nor lift up, nor cause his voice to be heard in the street. 3 A bruised reed shall he not break, and the smoking flax shall he not quench: he shall bring forth judgment unto truth. 4 He shall not fail nor be discouraged, till he have set judgment in the earth: and the isles shall wait for his law. 5 Thus saith God the LORD, he that created the heavens, and stretched them out; he that spread forth the earth, and that which cometh out of it; he that giveth breath unto the people upon it, and spirit to them that walk therein: 6 I the LORD have called thee in righteousness, and will hold thine hand, and will keep thee, and give thee for a covenant of the people, for a light of the Gentiles; 7 To open the blind eyes, to bring out the prisoners from the prison, and them that sit in darkness out of the prison house....21 The LORD is* **well pleased for his righteousness' sake; he will magnify the law, and make it honourable.** *22 But this is a people robbed and spoiled; they are all of them snared in holes, and they are hid in prison houses: they are for a prey, and none delivereth; for a spoil, and none saith, Restore. 23 Who among you will give ear to this? who will hearken and hear for the time to come? 24 Who gave Jacob for a spoil, and Israel to the robbers? did not the LORD, he against whom we* *have sinned?* **for they would not walk in his ways, neither were they obedient unto his law.**

The *New Covenant* which God planned to make with the house of Israel was the **writing of God's Laws into their hearts in a new and living way.** His laws could be in their hearts previous to this; but not in the way God had now envisioned.

Ps 37:31 **The law of his God is in his heart**; *none of his steps shall slide.*

Ps 40:8 *I delight to do thy will, O my God: yea,* **thy law is within my heart.**

Isa 51:7 *Hearken unto me,* **ye that know righteousness, the people in whose heart is my law**; *fear ye not the reproach of men, neither be ye afraid of their revilings.*

Jer 31:31 *Behold, the days come, saith the LORD, that* **I will make a new covenant with the house of Israel, and with the house of Judah:** *32 Not according to the covenant that I made with their fathers in the day that I took them by the hand to bring them out of the land of Egypt; which my covenant they brake, although I was an husband unto them, saith the LORD: 33 But* **this shall be the covenant that I will make with the house of Israel; After those days, saith the LORD, I will put my law in their inward parts, and write it in their hearts;** *and will be their God, and they shall be my people. (Heb 10:16)*

This new way was a more powerful and effective writing of God's Laws in man's hearts. God is love and His Law is love.

Ro 5:5 *...***the love of God is shed abroad in our hearts by the Holy Ghost which is given unto us.**

2Co 3:3 *Forasmuch as ye are manifestly declared to be the epistle of Christ ministered by us,* **written not with ink, but with** *the Spirit of the living God; not in tables of stone, but in fleshy tables of the heart.*

The shedding abroad of God's Love in our hearts by the Holy Ghost indwelling us is the new and living way of putting God's Law in our hearts. The Spirit of God had been WITH them, but now He would be IN them.

Joh 14:17 Even the Spirit of truth; whom the world cannot receive, because it seeth him not, neither knoweth him: but ye know him; for he dwelleth with you, and shall be in you.

With all this clear in your mind, let's establish some foundation stones of sound doctrine. God's Laws were meant to make us wise in recognizing and appreciating Jesus. All God's Word is necessary for men to understand and properly interpret Jesus.

2Ti 3:15 And that <u>from a child thou hast known the holy scriptures</u> (Old Testament)*, <u>which are able to make thee wise unto salvation through faith which is in Christ Jesus</u>. 16 <u>All</u> scripture <u>is</u> given by inspiration of God, and <u>is</u> profitable for doctrine, for reproof, for correction, for instruction in righteousness:*

*Ga 3:24 Wherefore the law was our schoolmaster **to bring us unto Christ*** (It taught us all about atonement, priesthood, etc.)

*2 Pe 1:21 For the **prophecy*** (Old Testament) ***came not in old time by the will of man: but holy men of God spake as they were moved by the Holy Ghost.***

*Joh 1:1 In the beginning was **the Word,** and the Word was with God, and the Word was God...**14** And the **Word** was made **flesh**, and **dwelt among us**, (and we beheld his glory, the glory as of the only begotten of the Father,) full of grace and truth.*

*Heb 13:8 Jesus Christ the same **yesterday**, and **to day,** and for ever.*

Jas 1:17 *Every good gift and every perfect gift is from above, and cometh down from the Father of lights,* **with whom is no variableness, neither shadow of turning.**

All true students of the Scripture believe that Jesus is the Word of God; that He never changes; that all the Old Testament Scriptures were inspired by Him; and therefore Jesus never did preach anything contrary or contradictory to the Scriptures previously penned. Moses' words were Jesus' words! To teach otherwise is due to that Gnostic dualism that we spoke of earlier, and will be explained in the next chapter.

The false teaching that Jesus, in the Sermon on the Mount, was correcting or changing Moses' Law is a doctrine of devils to destroy important truths in the Word of God.

1. It destroys the immutability of God in saying that He changed His mind on a moral issue or improved His moral judgments.

2. It presents Jesus, the Word in the flesh, as coming to correct His own inspired Word and thus dishonor His Father.

3. It destroys the inspiration of the Old Testament Scriptures by implying God's Law was in error or that Moses made a mistake. It demands that God's Word through Moses was a concession to sin, rather than a solution from God for the problems sin causes in a fallen society. This charges God with doing something unrighteous and unloving.

4. It makes Moses, Malachi, and Isaiah false and misled prophets in their presentation of the Messiah and His message.

5. It makes Jesus a false prophet in that His preaching is against the written Word of God that existed in His day, and therefore He could not be the pure, spotless Lamb of God; but an imposter.

Isa 8:20 To the law and to the testimony: if they speak not according to this word, it is because there is no light in them.

6. It would justify the Jew's rejection of Christ by the very commands of Scripture.

*De 13:1 If there arise among you a prophet, or a dreamer of dreams, and giveth thee a sign or a wonder, 2 And the sign or the wonder come to pass, whereof he spake unto thee, saying, Let us go after other gods, which thou hast not known, and let us serve them; 3 Thou shalt not hearken unto the words of that prophet, or that dreamer of dreams: for the LORD your God proveth you, to know **whether ye love the LORD your God with all your heart and with all your soul. 4 Ye shall walk after the LORD your God, and fear him, and keep his commandments, and obey his voice,** and ye shall serve him, and cleave unto him. 5 And **that prophet, or that dreamer of dreams, shall be put to death; because he hath spoken to turn you away from the LORD your God,** which brought you out of the land of Egypt, and redeemed you out of the house of bondage, **to thrust thee out of the way which the LORD thy God commanded thee to walk in. So shalt thou put the evil away from the midst of thee.***

7. It fosters the idea that we can improve on the Word of God; that our ways are wiser than His ways; or that God's holiness is evolving.

8. It represents Jesus as not reconciling the world unto God; but away from God to himself as a better leader.

9. It destroys the core of God's revelation to mankind – His Law. In reality, the rest of the Bible is a commentary on and exhortation to keep God's Laws.

Every covenant between God and man was to establish God's Laws in our hearts and make atonement for our trespasses; which two issues must be set in order for us to reconcile with God and thus be saved from His wrath.

10. It produces a number of contradictions and inconsistencies between Jesus and the apostle's *teaching* and their actual *practice*. This will be demonstrated as we go along.

If you really care about truth and righteousness, I ask you to continue with an open heart to the clear Word of God.

Chapter Four
Did Jesus Correct Moses' Law?

Well, in order to have a *"Christ-Centric"* view of this topic we need to listen to Jesus' own words, right? The introduction that Jesus gives in the **Sermon On The Mount** leaves Marcionites with NO EXCUSE for their error. No doubt, Jesus foresaw the snake's lies and made ample provision for lovers of truth to be delivered from confusion.

Matt 5:17 <u>**Think not that I am come to destroy the law, or the prophets:**</u> *I am not come to destroy, but to fulfil. 18 For verily I say unto you, Till heaven and earth pass, one jot or one tittle shall in no wise pass from the law, till all be fulfilled.*

What does "destroy" and "fulfill" involve? These terms are meant to be opposite options in this context. If we follow the thought on through by **actually listening** to what Jesus is saying rather than trying to force our own beliefs upon His words, then it is undeniably clear. Jesus defines His terms in the next verse!

5:19 Whosoever therefore shall break one of these least commandments, and shall teach men so (destroy), *he shall be called the least in the kingdom of heaven: but* **whosoever shall do and teach them** (fulfill)**, the same shall be called great in the kingdom of heaven**. *20 For I say unto you, That except your righteousness shall exceed the righteousness of the scribes and Pharisees* (to fulfill God's Law)*, ye shall in no case enter into the kingdom of heaven* (destroyed).

59

Don't think what? Jesus clearly said before correcting the misconceptions of the Jews that His purpose was not to correct or overthrow the Law of God, but to fulfill it – to properly interpret and satisfy the purpose of the Law. **YES, actually He came to write it on our hearts!!** Verses 18-20 prove that every jot and tittle as well as the least commandments were still relevant and must be obeyed by all those who heard Jesus. Obviously the Pharisees were abusing the law by not obeying certain commands. They cast them aside as "least" or "insignificant". Jesus said those who treated God's law in such a way, would themselves be treated so – They would not enter into the kingdom of heaven. Four hundred years previous to this, God had charged the religious leaders with being "partial" in His Law. Obviously the problem still existed.

The word "fulfill" in Matt 5:17 is the same as in Romans 8:4 – *"That the righteousness of the law might be __fulfilled__ in us, who walk not after the flesh, but after the Spirit."* The meaning is to "satisfy the purpose of the Law". When we walk in the Spirit – *the Holy Spirit who writes God's Laws in our hearts* – the righteousness of the Law (the moral principles of the Law) is "fulfilled", is "satisfied", is "lived out", is "demonstrated" in our actions, attitudes, and words. What moral principle did Jesus say was behind ALL and Every Law of God? **LOVE!** This must be fulfilled in our lives according to God's definition.

I used to say that when you fulfill a type or shadow it loses relevance; as when Jesus fulfilled the role of the sacrificial Lamb – the natural lamb for sacrifice then not being necessary. However, it is more correct to realize the ceremonial law was still practiced by all believing Jews with a **greater relevance** and meaning than ever before!

Jesus didn't change the Jew's obligation to practice God's Law at all. The sacrifices were seen as only a type of Christ and not a true atonement; but that is what made them infinitely more special! They had **always** been just *types and shadows*; and the only thing that made it necessary at *any* time was God's command, which still existed and was still in full force for all Jews until the Temple was destroyed making it impossible. Malachi said that the Messiah would purify the priesthood so the sacrifices of the sons of Levi would be pleasing to God as in former years; and in Acts 21 we find thousands of believing Jews zealously observing the Law with the types and shadows – Why? Because now it had much more meaning! They understood and saw that Lamb as representing JESUS! So, Yes, Jesus fulfilled the types; but that did not make them obsolete, but actually made them **more relevant**.

In order to fulfill a moral precept it must be obeyed and therefore will remain obligatory through eternity. "Thou shalt not bear false witness" will never lose its relevance, but must be **fulfilled continually**. The laws of God were the basis for the New Covenant as they were written on the hearts of all true believers by God's Spirit and the preaching of the Word. This was a necessary step for them to be partakers of the divine nature and be able to reconcile with God and dwell with Him! His Laws had to become their *modus operandi* – mode of operation, and their very character and sentiments. Two cannot walk or dwell together except they be agreed. In order for the world to be reconciled to God, they had to repent of transgressing His Laws and submit themselves to His Laws again – Romans 8:1-8.

The New Covenant was all about helping us to love and obey God's Laws in a better way than possible under the Old Covenant. Just think how opposite this is of most people's thinking! Most believe the New Covenant was *doing away* with God's Law; but the Bible clearly tells us that the whole purpose of the New Covenant was to write God's Laws in our hearts in a new a living way (Heb 8:8-10).

The point you cannot miss is this: Jesus says clearly that, if you disregard one of the least commandments of God's Law, and teach men so, you will be disregarded, and not enter Christ's kingdom. This **proves** that Jesus is only correcting men's view of God's Law; but **not** correcting God's Law. He could not be doing the very thing He is condemning! He compares the "righteousness" of the scribes and Pharisees with the true righteousness of the Law of God, which exceeded the interpretations and hypocritical practices common among the Jews. Jesus said we must obey God's Law without partiality or we cannot live in His Kingdom!

Chapter Five
What is Moses' Law?

The Law of Moses is the first five books of the Bible, called the Pentateuch: Genesis, Exodus, Leviticus, Numbers, and Deuteronomy. The Law of Moses was a covenant between God and Israel; and contained both moral Laws, and also ceremonial laws. The entire Old Covenant scriptures were combined with Moses' five books; and the whole was considered as the complete covenant and also referred to as "the Law" at times. Sometimes the word "law" is specifically referring to the ceremonial aspects, and sometimes it is referring to the moral aspects; and this must be determined by the context in which it is used. The difference between a law and the covenant based on that law is the same difference as a real estate contract based on the laws of the state and a *new real estate contract* in the same state with the *same laws; but with some different particulars*. The different provisions in the new real estate contract cannot violate the state laws; but must work within those laws. People who do not understand this often confuse "the Law" with "the Covenant"; but they are two different things; and any covenant God makes will be based on His eternal and unchanging Law of Love.

All the Old Covenant Scriptures are the inspired Word of God and were intended for all mankind. All nations were to look at Israel and see what God had said the same way they should look to the church to find God's will and salvation today. God's judgments were a witness unto all nations and anyone wishing to have a relationship with the true God had to come into this covenant and join with Israel. This was God's offer of salvation to all the world, just as Noah's Ark had been. No one could be saved outside God's covenant arrangements.

He 1:1 _God,_ who at sundry times and in divers manners spake in time past _unto the fathers by the prophets, 2 Hath in these last days spoken unto us by his Son,_

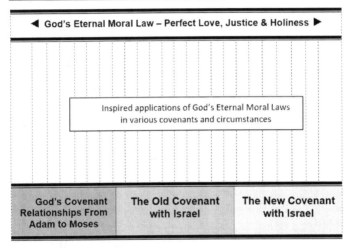

◀ **God's Eternal Moral Law – Perfect Love, Justice & Holiness** ▶

Inspired applications of God's Eternal Moral Laws
in various covenants and circumstances

God's Covenant Relationships From Adam to Moses	The Old Covenant with Israel	The New Covenant with Israel

If the Gospels and epistles are for the whole world's salvation and reconciliation with God, then so were all the OT writings in the same sense and manner. It is God who spoke in the past **and** through Christ. The _same_ God speaking to **all** mankind through His ordained channels can only speak consistent with himself. He could not be speaking contrary or contradictory to His own Word; and men who understand this will only interpret Christ consistent with Moses and the prophets. You can replace

"Moses said" with "Jesus said" every time Moses was giving God's Word to the people.

If one wishes to see how God felt about His laws given through Moses, just read Deuteronomy chapter 4 & 5.

*De 4:1 Now therefore hearken, O Israel, unto the statutes and unto the judgments, which I teach you, for to do them, ...2 Ye **shall not add** unto the word which I command you, **neither shall ye diminish** ought from it, that ye may keep the commandments of the LORD your God which I command you.... 5 Behold, **I have taught you statutes and judgments, even as the LORD my God commanded me**, that ye should do so in the land whither ye go to possess it. 6 **Keep therefore and do them; for this is your wisdom** and your understanding in the sight of the nations, which shall hear all these statutes, and say, Surely this great nation is a wise and understanding people....8 And what nation is there so great, that hath **statutes and judgments so righteous as all this law,** which I set before you this day?...5:29 **O that there were such an heart in them, that they would fear me, and keep all my commandments always, that it might be well with them, and with their children for ever!***

God's Law in every respect is the proper application of Love – so if the circumstances are the same, the same expression of love is still appropriate. God's nature of universal benevolence or unselfish love is the basis of all that He does or ever has done. God's moral laws have always existed right along with God. The moral precepts of Moses' Law are simply the inspired applications of God's eternal moral standards.

As long as **"Thou shalt love the Lord thy God with all thy heart, and with all thy soul, and with all thy mind"** and, **"Thou shalt love thy neighbour as thyself"** are still relevant, then the whole Moral Law of God is still relevant, for it only expresses these two commands according to what God judges proper.

Isa 51:6 *Lift up your eyes to the heavens, and look upon the* *earth beneath: for the heavens shall vanish away like smoke,* *and the earth shall wax old like a garment, and they that dwell* *therein shall die in like manner: but my salvation shall be for* *ever,* **and my righteousness shall not be abolished.**

The Law of Moses was in full force when Jesus gave the Sermon on the Mount and continued to be the church standard for all believers for the first twelve years after Pentecost. Cornelius was the first to be baptized without coming under the ceremonial law/Judaism. No Gentile could be baptized without coming under circumcision and the Law of Moses for twelve years after Pentecost! Jesus did not liberate his disciples from obeying Moses' Law (Matt 23); but only allowed Gentile converts to start being accepted without the ceremonial law and circumcision **after** Peter's vision concerning Cornelius. Jesus did not change his Jewish disciple's practice, beliefs, or lifestyle from what God's Word had already commanded them.

New Covenant believers are not under the Old **Covenant**, but still under the **same God** with the **same** **morals**. Just like a new real estate contract must be according to the same state and federal laws, so any new covenant God makes will still be according to His eternal WAYS. The New Covenant is the Law of Moses/of God written on our hearts by the Holy Ghost. Just as the covenant of circumcision was continued under the newer Mosaic Covenant, so many components of what we call the Old Covenant are still relevant in what we call the New Covenant. There were parts of the Old Covenant that were temporary and parts that were eternally relevant. There is a definite difference between the ceremonial laws of the Old Covenant which dealt with sacrifices, temple service, priesthood, and ceremonial

66

cleanliness; and the moral laws of God which were given in the Old Testament and are also the basis of the new covenant as they are now written on all believers' hearts and called **the righteousness of the Law** -- LOVE.   **See Romans 8:1-13**

Do Gentile converts like Cornelius now have to obey God's **moral laws** or are they free from these also? The events of Acts 21 are about **29 years after Pentecost**, and we find the believing Jews, including Paul, still being faithful to the Law of Moses – and they continued so until at least AD 70 when Jerusalem and the Temple were destroyed. After reading Acts 21:25 some assume the Gentiles only had to observe "the necessary things" decided on in Acts 15; but these were only "entrance requirements" to be sure the newly converted Gentiles made a clean break with old pagan idolatrous practices. These entrance requirements took the place of the Jewish entrance requirements of circumcision and submission to Moses' Law concerning all the ceremonies, diets, holy days, temple service, etc. This kept the Gentile believers from having to come under the jurisdiction of the Sanhedrin; and helped them focus on Christ's administration instead of becoming enthralled with Judaism. The converted Gentiles still had to follow Christ, obey the moral laws of God, obey the Apostle's decisions, and obey the local bishop's teaching, etc.   All Christians must obey the "righteousness of the Law" which is also called the Moral Law – The Law of God's Love.

Ro 2:25 *For circumcision verily profiteth, if thou keep the law: but if thou be a breaker of the law, thy circumcision is made uncircumcision. 26 Therefore if the <u>uncircumcision</u> <u>keep</u> the <u>righteousness of the law</u>, shall not his uncircumcision be counted for circumcision? 27 And shall not uncircumcision which is by nature, **if it fulfil the law**, judge thee, who by the <u>letter and</u>*

circumcision dost transgress the law? *28 For he is not a Jew, which is one outwardly; neither is that circumcision, which is outward in the flesh: 29* **But he is a Jew, which is one inwardly; and circumcision is that of the heart, in the spirit, and not in the letter; whose praise is not of men, but of God.**

These very arguments which show that New Testament Gentile converts had to obey God's Moral Law also prove beyond doubt that **there is a difference between the moral and ceremonial aspects of God's Law**, and, furthermore, that a New Testament Gentile convert could be fulfilling the moral law and be pleasing to God while still considered as an uncircumcised Gentile – not keeping the ceremonial law.

So... can it be said that the "uncircumcised" or "man who does not obey the ceremonial law" is at the same time keeping "the righteousness of the law" (moral law)? Yes, the whole point here is that one can keep the moral law and be a Jew **inwardly** while not keeping the ceremonial law and being a Jew **outwardly**. Can anything be clearer? This means he was not circumcised, did not obey the dietary laws, washings, temple service, Sabbaths, feasts, etc. The New Covenant Gentile convert had the circumcision of the heart, but not the outward circumcision of the flesh. (**Col. 2:11**)

Paul's whole argument about faith imputed for righteousness in Romans 4 is to show that justification by *God graciously imputing our living faith to us for righteousness* was known to Abraham **before** circumcision and to David **under** Moses' Law; and is therefore valid to both those who are under Moses' Law as well as the Gentile convert who *walks in the righteous faith that Abraham exercised.* Abraham obeyed God by faith before the laws given by Moses were ever written.

Ro 4:12 *And the father of circumcision to them who are not of the circumcision only, but* **who also walk in the steps of that faith of our father Abraham, which he had being yet uncircumcised.**

Ge 26:5 *Because that Abraham obeyed my voice, and kept my charge, my commandments, my statutes, and my laws.*

This obedient faith that Abraham exercised was counted to him for righteousness just as it will be for the New Testament Gentile converts who *"walk in the steps of that faith of our father Abraham, which he had being yet uncircumcised." (Romans 4:12)*

Abraham had to follow the morals or ways of God as much as he knew, and so do we. We learn God's moral opinions and judgments through the **written Word**. Even the civil and ceremonial laws which may not directly affect us have a moral lesson or principle which we must follow. We should love and desire to follow every gold nugget of God's wisdom and righteousness that we can glean from His encounters with man. We should thirstily absorb every aspect of the mind of God we can decipher from His actions and judgments – THIS IS THE FAITH OF ABRAHAM!

Again, in Romans 8 the apostle Paul makes it clear that a New Testament convert – whether Jew or Gentile – must be characterized by submission to God's moral laws which the carnal lost man is at enmity against and not subject to.

Ro 8:1 *There is therefore now* **no condemnation to them which are in Christ Jesus, who walk not after the flesh, but after the Spirit.** *2 For the law of the Spirit of life in Christ Jesus hath made me free from the law of sin and death. 3 For what the law could not do, in that it was weak through the flesh, God sending his own Son in the likeness of sinful flesh, and for sin,* *condemned sin in the flesh: 4 **That the righteousness of the law might be fulfilled in us, who walk not after the flesh, but after the Spirit.** 5 For they that are after the flesh do mind the things of the flesh; but they that are after the Spirit the things of the Spirit.   6 For to be carnally minded is death; but to be spiritually minded is life and peace.   7 **Because the carnal mind is enmity against God: for it is not subject to the law of God, neither indeed can be.   8 So then they that are in the flesh cannot please God**. 9 But ye are not in the flesh, but in the Spirit, if so be that the Spirit of God dwell in you. Now if any man have not the Spirit of Christ, he is none of his. 10 ¶ And if Christ be in you, the body is dead because of sin; but the Spirit is life because of righteousness.   11 But if the Spirit of him that raised up Jesus from the dead dwell in you, he that raised up Christ from the dead shall also quicken your mortal bodies by his Spirit that dwelleth in you.   12 Therefore, brethren, we are debtors, not to the flesh, to live after the flesh. 13 **For if ye live after the flesh, ye shall die: but if ye through the Spirit do mortify the deeds of the body, ye shall live.***

Yes, the Gentile converts had to obey the righteousness of God's Law or all Paul's arguments for why the Gentiles are justified before God without the ceremonial laws would fall flat. Jesus never compromised or changed God's moral judgments. The whole doctrine of **Justification through faith in Christ** demands that the **righteousness of the Law** is fulfilled in those who walk by this faith.   Jesus clearly said that the "Law and the prophets" were summed up in the word *LOVE*.   The Apostles continued to teach that we are to fulfill God's Law, and that **Love** was the **goal** of the Law.

*Ga 5:6 For in Jesus Christ neither circumcision availeth any thing, nor uncircumcision; but **faith which worketh by love.***

*1Ti 1:5 Now the **end** (goal) of the commandment is charity out of a pure heart, and of a good conscience, and of faith unfeigned:*

70

Does the New Testament command us to walk in LOVE? Yes, of course. Well, it also says that this LOVE fulfills the Old Testament law. God's Love fulfills the moral aspects of God's Law which are a manifestation of God's heart and mind; and, according to Jesus, are built upon the two greatest commandments concerning loving God and loving our neighbor. The **same** love fulfills **both** the Old and New Testament moral obligations, which proves there is no difference in God's moral requirements in the two covenants. The New Covenant simply being God's Law written in our hearts, or said in another way; *"...the love of God is shed abroad in our hearts by the Holy Ghost which is given unto us."* Ro 5:5

The Bible is a progressive revelation in many areas, but it never contradicts itself. Circumstances change, and covenant arrangements change; but God never changes. Progressive revelation is simply the unfolding of one and the same picture, which only adds beauty and clarity to the first scenes and never contradicts them. Genesis 1:1 says, "In the beginning God..." The Bible teaches that God pre-dates the world; and that God's nature, purpose, views, opinions, and standards are unchanging.

God's Law is always the best, wisest, most appropriate, and most LOVING thing to do under the circumstances – Always. The Bible says "God is Love" and that to obey his commandments is to act in His love:

1Jo 4:7 Beloved, let us love one another: for love is of God; and every one that loveth is born of God, and knoweth God. 8 He that loveth not knoweth not God; for God is love.

*1Jo 5:2 By this we know that we love the children of God, when we love God, and keep his commandments. 3 For **this is the love of God, that we keep his commandments**: and his commandments are not grievous.*

God is Love; and He is the only one qualified to dictate **what is** and **what is not** a proper expression of benevolence. Therefore, because God is the creator, owner, and only qualified judge; He is also obligated to teach and enforce the law of benevolence on all moral beings. His moral precepts, statutes, commands, etc. found in the Bible, and more particularly in the Law of Moses, are God's Word teaching us to obey the Law of Love, which He applies to many aspects of life. Jesus declared that the "law and the prophets" (meaning all the Old Covenant teaching) hung from this divine principle of love.

Mt 22:34 But when the Pharisees had heard that he had put the Sadducees to silence, they were gathered together. 35 Then one of them, which was a lawyer, asked him a question, tempting him, and saying, 36 Master, which is the great commandment in the law? 37 Jesus said unto him, **Thou shalt love the Lord thy God with all thy heart, and with all thy soul, and with all thy mind. 38 This is the first and great commandment.** *39 And the second is like unto it,* **Thou shalt love thy neighbour as thyself.** *40* <u>**On these two commandments hang all the law and the prophets.**</u>

Jesus didn't say it would be this way **"from now on"**; but that it **had always been this way**. Jesus wasn't presenting a higher plain of ethics than the Word of God; but defending and clarifying the Word He gave to Moses! Jesus never said**, *From this day forward these two commandments replace the Law and the Prophets;*** but rather He was saying**, *The law and the prophets have* <u>*always*</u> *and* <u>*only,*</u> <u>*from the beginning,*</u> *expressed these two great commandments.* Everything they said can be summed up in these two great commandments – which can be summed up in the word LOVE -- God's very nature of benevolence – <u>LOVE in its proper definition and</u>

expression. God cannot manifest anything else!! If God manifested anything other than divine love, then HE WOULD CEASE TO *BE* LOVE.

When the New Testament says that "love fulfills the law" it is saying that THE SAME LOVE THAT FULFILLS THE NEW TESTAMENT MORAL REQUIREMENTS ALSO FULFILLS THE OLD TESTAMENT MORAL REQUIREMENTS SIMULTANEOUSLY; WHICH PROVES JESUS WASN'T CORRECTING MOSES' LAW. God's Law in every respect is the proper application of Love — so if the circumstances are the same, the same expression of love is still appropriate.   God's nature of universal benevolence or unselfish love is the basis of all that He does or ever has done. God's moral laws have always existed right along with God. The moral precepts of Moses' Law are simply the inspired applications of God's eternal moral standards.   Have you ever considered what John said around A.D. 95?

1Jo 3:4 *Whosoever committeth sin **transgresseth also the law**: for **sin is the transgression of the law.** 5 And ye know that he was manifested to take away our sins (transgressions of the Law); and in him is no sin (transgression of the Law).   6 Whosoever abideth in him sinneth not: whosoever sinneth hath not seen him, neither known him.*

Jesus came to vindicate and teach God's Law properly. SIN is still the transgression of God's Laws! Jesus' blood was shed to cover the transgressions of God's Laws. Jesus is our High priest TODAY to cover the transgressions of God's Laws. Love TODAY fulfills God's Laws when understood according to God's Word.   Those who are not subject to God's Law TODAY are not of God — they haven't been born again and are not walking in the Spirit (Rom 8:1-7).

Is the "Golden Rule" still relevant?

Mt 7:12 <u>*Therefore all things whatsoever ye would that*</u> <u>*men should do to you, do ye even so to them:*</u> **for this is the law and the prophets.**

Do you live by the golden rule? Does Christ expect you to? Is it sin if you don't? *Need we say more?*

If you really do live by the "golden rule" in God's definition, **then you live by the Law and the prophets as well**. If you truly live by God's Law and prophets, then you really live by the golden rule. So, is God's Law still relevant? If Jesus commanded the golden rule, which is the principle on which all the Law and the prophets are built, then Jesus is teaching and commanding the spirit and righteousness of God's Law – just as He plainly said in Matthew 5:17-20 where we began this chapter.

When Studying the Scripture we must build from these clear and undeniable foundation stones. We cannot look at a passage of Scripture and say that God seems to have changed his mind about "right and wrong"; but we must first say, "God is immutable, and therefore we must interpret this passage in light of God's unchanging standards of morality"; and thus find out the true meaning which God intended. To interpret Scripture as to overthrow God's immutability, or the principles so clearly discussed in this chapter, is to create heresy. Some will say, "But God changed His mind many times, like when He decided not to destroy Nineveh". God warning a city, and then having mercy on them when they repent is a part of God's unchanging ways. This is how God always operates (Ez 18 & Jer 18). **A word of wisdom:** Don't be so foolish as to try and seek out some place where you can write to me and say, "See! God changed his mind!" You will only be revealing your low level of Marcionite discernment; and setting yourself up for a well deserved humbling reproof.

Jesus was definitely different in the manger than he was on the cross; yet Jesus is the same yesterday, today, and forever (Heb. 13:8) – So **what** is the same? When He was in the manger, He was a baby; and when He was on the cross, He was a man; but His moral judgments, values, opinions, etc. as the Son of God are eternal and unchanging.

So, again let's ask the question, "Did Jesus Correct or Change Moses' Law in the Sermon on the Mount?" Of course He didn't! It is impossible to reconcile such a false charge with the Scriptures Jesus inspired!

Mt 5:17 *Think not that I am come to destroy the law, or the prophets: I am not come to destroy, but to fulfil. 18 For verily I say unto you, Till heaven and earth pass, one jot or one tittle shall in no wise pass from the law, till all be fulfilled. 19 Whosoever therefore shall break one of these least commandments, and shall teach men so, he shall be called the least in the kingdom of heaven: but whosoever shall do and teach them, the same shall be called great in the kingdom of heaven. 20 For I say unto you, That except your righteousness shall exceed the righteousness of the scribes and Pharisees, ye shall in no case enter into the kingdom of heaven.*

After Matthew 5:17-20 in the Sermon on the Mount, Jesus proceeds to **show the differences between what the Jews had taught or lived; and what the Law actually meant**. **He is showing them what it means to exceed the righteousness of the scribes and Pharisees.** Let's analyze the times Jesus compared the Jews teachings with His own interpretation of God's Laws. Obviously "His own interpretation" was the "original intent" because He was the Word of God incarnate when speaking those words.

Chapter Six
Thou Shalt Not Kill

Mt 5:21 Ye have heard that it was said by them of old time, Thou shalt not kill; and whosoever shall kill shall be in danger of the judgment: 22 But I say unto you, That whosoever is angry with his brother without a cause shall be in danger of the judgment: and whosoever shall say to his brother, Raca, shall be in danger of the council: but whosoever shall say, Thou fool, shall be in danger of hell fire. 23 Therefore if thou bring thy gift to the altar, and there rememberest that thy brother hath ought against thee; 24 Leave there thy gift before the altar, and go thy way; first be reconciled to thy brother, and then come and offer thy gift. 25 Agree with thine adversary quickly, whiles thou art in the way with him; lest at any time the adversary deliver thee to the judge, and the judge deliver thee to the officer, and thou be cast into prison. 26 Verily I say unto thee, Thou shalt by no means come out thence, till thou hast paid the uttermost farthing.

"Thou shalt not kill" means "thou shalt not murder or shed innocent blood." God commanded killing, but only by those who had proper jurisdiction and only upon principles of justice. Killing according to principles of justice is actually an expression of love – not to the criminal, but to society as a whole - especially toward the victims and the "innocent blood". God's love is never to love the evil at the expense of the good. God IS LOVE; and God's Law is an expression of divine LOVE to man. It is best for man to obediently maintain this law and order, which demands the execution of penalties upon lawbreakers. God's love for mankind as a whole demands the lawful killing of those worthy of death. From the very beginning, after the fall, God commanded men to execute those who shed innocent blood.

Ge 9:5 And surely your blood of your lives will I require; at the hand of every beast will I require it, and at the hand of man; at the hand of every man's brother will I require the life of man.

Killing in and of itself is sad and distasteful; but not wicked or evil when the execution is according to justice and righteousness. Like many other "hard truths", *killing* is due to the presence of sin; **but when it is right and just it is not sin**. God's destruction of the world with a flood, upon Sodom, through God ordained governments, etc. was due to the presence of sin; but God's actions were holy, righteous, just, wise and **loving**. Pacifists have a hard time understanding these principles, but it is high time they awake out of sleep and realize **there is no pacifism in the Bible**. Jesus is continually called the "Son of David" the greatest warrior hero in Israel's history. How could he be a pacifist and accept this title as heir to David's throne?

The purpose for Jesus contrasting His Law with the "righteousness of the scribes and Pharisees" in this matter is because of the Jews allowing malice and hatred with the justification that, after all, "they didn't kill them". If the Jews thought that their interpersonal relationships were alright as long as they didn't kill, they were greatly mistaken. Jesus gives them the spirit of God's commandments, which prohibits injustice and hatred in the heart towards your fellow man (Lev 19:18). Jesus said you could not be angry or unkind to your fellow man without a just cause. God's Law is full of commands and precepts about having proper relationships with others just as Jesus himself declared: *"Therefore all things whatsoever ye would that men should do to you, do ye even so to them: **for this is the law and the prophets"** (Mt 7:12).*

Jesus goes on to say that if you are not right in your relationships with people, God will not have a relationship with you. God doesn't even want your gift at the altar until you have made things right with your fellow man as far as you have fault in the matter. If you are angry or accusing toward your brother without sufficient cause, then you are jeopardizing your own soul before God. You cannot be right with God and wrong in your relationship with any man on earth. *This is the Law and the Prophets; and this is the message of Jesus – the Word made flesh.*

When Jesus said, "By them of old time" He wasn't seeking to correct Moses, but rather the "righteousness of the scribes and Pharisees" as He told us in His introduction to these precepts. In this passage He did not say, *"It is written"*; however, when contending with Satan he always said, *"It is written"* (Matt. 4). Saying, *"It is written"* means we are speaking of this passage in it's *original and proper context, application, and intent*; however, saying, *"Ye have heard that it was said by them of old time,"* refers to the **application and usage of those teaching,** which in this case was wrong or insufficient. For one to use *"it is written"* when speaking of errors in doctrine would be to blame the problem on the Scriptures rather than on the teachers. Even if Jesus said something that the law had also said, His correction has to do with the **context** and **usage** of that statement, which in this case came from the interpreters, not from Moses. We cannot hear the tone or see the expressions of Jesus speaking when quoting portions of the Law *"as the* *teachers used them"*; but I'm sure that would make a difference in how we perceived the statement. Those who understand the passage can well imagine the tone and expressions most likely used. He was dealing with the **common misconceptions about the Law.** Remember how God through Malachi rebuked them for being "partial" in the Law and causing many to stumble 400 years previous to this? 400 years would qualify for "them of old time". The following quote will show how widespread Marcionism has become in Christendom.

Jamieson, Fausset, and Brown Commentary: "Nearly all who would translate "to the ancients" take the speaker of the words quoted to be Moses in the law; "the ancients" to be the people to whom Moses gave the law; and the intention of our Lord here to be to contrast His own teaching, more or less, with that of Moses; either as opposed to it--as some go the length of affirming--or at least as modifying, enlarging, elevating it. **But who can reasonably imagine such a thing, just after the most solemn and emphatic proclamation of the perpetuity of the law, and the honor and glory in which it was to be held under the new economy? To us it seems as plain as possible that our Lord's one object is to contrast the traditional perversions of the law with the true sense of it as expounded by Himself."**

When Jesus says, "...but I say", He is saying, "But **The Word of God** says..." and this could not be contradictory to *what the written Word of God says*. He is preaching the spirit or "original intent" of the Law, which is the essence of "fulfilling the Law" – if you don't have the right spirit or intent, then you are not fulfilling the righteousness of the law. If you just rest in the "letter" and ignore the spirit or intent of any law, you are missing the point and using it out of context. Obviously anyone who obeys the spirit of the Law will also be obeying the letter of that law. The spirit of the law says, *"If you don't have a right relationship with your fellow man, don't even come and offer a gift to God until you have made it right"*. God will not have a relationship with you, nor accept your gift until you have a right relationship with your brother. Keep your heart and life right, and then God will accept your gift.

"Agree with thine adversary quickly..." (Vs 25,26) is a further application of the same principle for when someone is rebuking you for misconduct; and it underscores your need to humbly own your trespass before they have to drag you into court. It has to do with not determining right and wrong according to what is *best for me in this situation* or *what I can get by with*; but according to truth and righteousness. If you have done wrong, don't hold out hoping to get by with it; but agree – own your trespass and make it right before you have to be proven wrong – in court. In Luke, Jesus applies this principle to the Jews due to their stubborn resistance of the truth He is preaching. He warned them that if they held out until judgment day when they are brought before the judge, it will then be too late to recant. They needed to repent before the one confronting them brought his case before the Judge of all the earth. One who has a proper relationship with God and His Law will be more concerned with truth and righteousness than their own personal image and agenda.

I say to the Marcionites that I am confronting, "Pay attention", for this principle is for you too. You need to face the fact that your denomination is tainted with Marcion's error, and you need to repent before we go to

God's court and you are proven to be in error. It will be too late to get things right on that day.

I said that there is no pacifism in the Bible. Pacifists imagine that they have found their pet sentiments in the teaching and example of Jesus Christ; but this is one of the most reckless misinterpretations that there is in Marcionism. Jesus, after three years of instruction and example to His chosen leaders, tells them during His last supper with them that times are going to get tough and there is coming a day when it would be better for them to have a sword than their shirt. The context is that of defending one's life against criminal action, which is in perfect harmony with the righteousness of God's Law. The disciples, who after three years of hearing and watching Jesus did not think this was strange or out of character; but promptly took inventory to see how many swords they had among them at that moment. Yes, two of them were at that time, during the Passover meal, wearing a sword. Evidently Peter was one of them. Yes, Peter, the head apostle and the one to whom Jesus gave the Keys of the Kingdom. Peter had a sword with full intention to use it in self defense.

You say, "But Jesus rebuked him for using it". Typical pacifist response! Jesus never intended to be an insurrectionist or lead an insurrection. He did not want His testimony tainted with revolt against the authorities. His rebuke to Peter and all that He said on that occasion was in this context! Peter was using the sword inappropriately because those who came to arrest Jesus were their God-ordained authorities and not just common criminals. Peter acted out of rashness and panic, and not according to God's Law in this situation. It was also Jesus' time to be delivered up so He didn't escape as He had done previously (Jn 10:39). This also confused Peter, who was caught up in his zeal to protect Jesus.

If I gave my adult son a 9mm pistol to carry for protection against criminals, but then he acted like he was going to pull it out when a police officer approached, I would rebuke him in the **same context** that Jesus rebuked Peter. It was not the time! Does this mean there was *never* a time? Does this mean Peter should *never* carry a sword? Obviously Jesus did think there was an appropriate time for He told them to carry a sword. ASK PETER! He had been with Jesus for three years and knew Him better than YOU EVER WILL! He knew that carrying a sword and using it for self defense was not against what Jesus taught and lived. Jesus told them all just hours previous to sell their shirt and buy a sword in the context of self defense. Jesus was not, however, referring to their use of the sword *that night*; for the "shirt buyers" and "sword sellers" were not even open at that time of night during the Passover; but He was referring to future events. Jesus' life and teachings do not support pacifism in the slightest! Jesus agreed 100% with God's Law which demanded that the weak and innocent blood be protected and avenged according to God's rules of appropriateness.

A man defending his home and family is part of this appropriate use of force as well as a person defending their own life against bloodshed and criminal action; which is why Jesus used that example to illustrate His principle that a kingdom cannot be divided against itself and still stand (Mt 12:29). Pacifists who don't defend their homes are violating this principle and are thus divided against themselves. Jesus would not use an illustration of something He believed was wrong to defend the principle He was teaching. It was such a "no brainer", which everyone accepted as true and appropriate that it perfectly defended His point about a kingdom divided against itself as well as the importance of "watching" (Lu 12:39). Don't think you are smarter or more spiritual than the Apostles because *you read their book*! More on this later.

*Lu 12:39 And this know, that if the **goodman** of the house had known what hour the thief would come, **he would have watched, and not have suffered his house to be broken through.***

Chapter Seven
Thou Shalt Not Commit Adultery

Mt 5:27 *Ye have heard that it was said by them of old time,* **Thou shalt not commit adultery:** *28 But I say unto you, That whosoever looketh on a woman to lust after her hath committed adultery with her already in his heart. 29 And if thy right eye offend thee, pluck it out, and cast it from thee: for it is profitable for thee that one of thy members should perish, and not that thy whole body should be cast into hell. 30 And if thy right hand offend thee, cut it off, and cast it from thee: for it is profitable for thee that one of thy members should perish, and not that thy whole body should be cast into hell. 31 It hath been said, Whosoever shall put away his wife, let him give her a writing of divorcement: 32 But I say unto you, That whosoever shall put away his wife, saving for the cause of fornication, causeth her to commit adultery: and whosoever shall marry her that is divorced committeth adultery.*

Notice Jesus is showing that the teachers of the Law stopped short with "not committing adultery" according to their definition and application. The people in Malachi's day didn't think they were committing adultery either; but that was due to being *partial in the Law (Mal 2:9)*. Jesus is preaching against the adultery of these who denied they were committing adultery due to their partiality in applying God's Law. Malachi said Jesus would preach against adulterers in the same message where he tells the people to obey God's Law through Moses, so there is no doubt or debate on this issue — Jesus is not teaching contrary to God's Law; but against the abuse of God's Law.

When Jesus applies His own Law we learn that, not just the outward act, but **the attitude and spirit of adultery are prohibited.** Did Moses' Law forbid such? Of course it did – it was Jesus' Law.

Ex 20:17 *Thou shalt not covet thy neighbour's house, thou shalt* **not covet thy neighbour's wife,** *nor his manservant, nor his* **maidservant,** *nor his ox, nor his ass, nor any thing that is thy neighbour's.*

Living by the spirit and righteousness of the Law prohibits adultery in the heart as well as the abuse of Deut. 24:1-4. What God commanded Moses in Deut. 24 was to protect the purity of the home and marriage, not destroy it. What God commanded Moses was the very best thing to do under the circumstances; and under the same circumstances it is still the best thing to do. God's Laws are always and only supposed to be used by sincere God loving people for the maintenance of love and holiness in society. Any other use of God's Laws is contrary to the law-giver's intent.

Unjust divorce and evil desires both violate the spirit of the seventh commandment. The exception clause that Jesus gives in Matt. 5:32 and 19:9 is a clarification of Moses' exception given for "some uncleanness" (Deut. 24:1-4) which means a "matter of nakedness". The word "uncleanness" is the Hebrew term `**Ervah** (#6172 – Strong's); and literally means, "nakedness", or "something shameful or repulsive". `**Ervah** is translated 51 times as "nakedness" in the Old Covenant, once as "shame", and once as "uncleanness".

Jesus, in opposing the Jew's abuse in making divorce lawful for "every cause", brings back the original intent of the Law – divorce and remarriage only when the marriage covenant has been duly violated by some type of immorality. **Jesus did not say, "from now on it will be this way"; but is telling them the crime committed when they abused what God and Moses intended from times immemorial.** The Jews were abusing Deut. 24:1-4 in a terrible way according to Josephus, their own historian:

Adam Clarke: That the Jewish priesthood was exceedingly corrupt in the time of the apostle, and that they were so long before, is fully evident from the sacred writings and from Josephus. The high-priesthood was a matter of commerce, and was bought and sold like other commodities. Of this Josephus gives many instances. ...They were guilty of adultery by unjust divorces, Matthew 19:9. Their polygamy was scandalous: even their rabbins, when they came to any place, would exclaim, Who will be my wife for a day?

They assumed that as long as they went through the proper *paper-work* of marriage and divorce it was all lawful and pleasing to God for *any cause*.

Remember what Malachi said?

Mal 2:16 - *God hates men putting away their wives unjustly so they can marry another one.*

Mal 3:1-6 - *Messiah will preach against adulterers as defined by Moses' Law; and God says, "I am the Lord, I change not"*

Mal 4:4 "*Remember ye the law of Moses my servant, which I commanded unto him in Horeb for all Israel, with the statutes and judgments.*"

Do you believe God is consistent?

Have you ever asked yourself the reason God inserted, *"I am the Lord, I change not"*? It relates back to the statement, *"And I will come near to you to judgment"* at the beginning of the previous verse. The Jews were acting as though God was far off and not really involved – listen to Malachi 2:17,

Mal 2:17 Ye have wearied the LORD with your words. Yet ye say, Wherein have we wearied him? When ye say, Every one that doeth evil is good in the sight of the LORD, and he delighteth in them; or, **Where is the God of judgment?**

God, through Malachi, is rebuking them for questioning whether God really means what He says and whether He is truly a God of judgment. His answer to them is that He will come near to them in judgment in the person of the Messiah and they will find that He means what He has said, and **HAS NOT CHANGED!**

Jesus was to preach against adulterers – not just what the Jews thought was adultery, but what the true spirit of the Law called adultery. Jesus' teaching was not contrary to the Law. The God, who never changes, commanded them to keep it in the same message where he tells of the Messiah preaching against adulterers! What the Law of God taught could not have been called adultery by the Messiah – the Word in the flesh. The Jews never accused Jesus of contradicting Moses' Law; and Jesus expressly declared that He was not seeking to destroy Moses' Law, but to fulfill or confirm it. Jesus said that not one little command could be cast aside or whoever did it would also be cast aside and not enter His Kingdom – remember?

Ps 19:7 The law of the LORD is **perfect**, converting the soul: the testimony of the LORD is **sure**, making wise the simple. *8* The statutes of the LORD are **right**, rejoicing the heart: the commandment of the LORD is **pure**, enlightening the eyes. *9 The fear of the LORD is* **clean, <u>enduring for ever</u>**: the judgments of the LORD are **true and righteous altogether.** *10 More to be desired are they than gold, yea, than much fine gold: sweeter also than honey and the honeycomb. 11 Moreover by them is thy servant warned:* **and in keeping of them there is great reward.**

In this matter of divorce there is much confusion due to people not giving God's Word its due respect. "Adultery" in Bible usage would be better understood as "breaking wedlock" or committing "advoutry", (breaking vows). William Tyndale understood this, and translated the New Testament in this very way. The crime was not "committing adultery **with** the second wife" but rather "committing adultery **against** the first wife". The reason we know this is because it is not the obtaining of the second person that created the adultery, but the putting away of the first wife unjustly. Polygamy was never called adultery by God's Law, by Jesus, or the Apostles who allowed men with two wives to be church-members, but not leaders. Did Abraham commit adultery with Hagar? No, it was not the second marriage, but the unjust treatment towards the first marriage which caused the problem that Jesus is dealing with.

Mk 10:11 And he saith unto them, Whosoever shall put away his wife, and marry another, **committeth adultery <u>against</u> her.**

In Mark where people say, "there is no exception clause", we actually have an "understood exception clause" or a "built in exception clause"; because it is impossible to commit adultery against the wife who committed adultery against you when you put her away for such. Thus the exception is understood by those who pay attention. Jesus also makes it clear that in His understanding the "adultery" was the "breaking of wedlock" against the first wife, not the taking of the second. Jesus knew that if the man had kept both wives there would be no charge of adultery according to God's Word. Jesus had told the Jewish leaders:

Mk 10:6 *But from the beginning of the creation God made them male and female. 7 For this cause shall a man leave his father and mother, and cleave to his wife; 8 And they twain shall be one flesh: so then they are no more twain, but one flesh. 9 What therefore God hath joined together, let not man put asunder.*

Breaking wedlock without God's approval and contrary to His Law is "man putting asunder" what God joined. How did "God join it"? Not personally, but by MEN joining them ACCORDING TO GOD'S LAW! In the SAME way, divorce **according to God's Law** is not "man putting asunder" but "God putting asunder". It is "God putting asunder" when men are following God's Law. Jesus was too smart to charge men of putting asunder what God joined when they were simply following God's own Laws correctly. The fact is that the Jews were **not** following God's Laws correctly and therefore **they** were **not** putting asunder with God's approval. THIS was the issue! Any clear thinking person can see this.

Jesus uses the word "porneia", as the only legitimate reason for allowing divorce and remarriage in the context of the Deut 24 precept. This includes immorality of many sorts: Moral perversion, incest, homosexuality, prostitution, adultery, bestiality, etc. He clearly says that the only "matter of nakedness" that God accepts as a sufficient ground for divorce, in this context, is moral or sexual impurity which would fall under the classification of fornication and therefore be a breach of the marriage covenant. God definitely would not accept "every cause" like the Jews settled for as their interpretation of the "matter of nakedness" – Moses' condition for divorce. Thus Jesus is giving the original intent of God's Law, and vindicating Moses. In our day we use the same Greek word to speak of matters of nakedness when we speak of "pornography" – from the Greek "porneia". Jesus is simply defining the terms of HIS OWN LAW for us.

It is vital to note that Moses' Laws were **part of a system** of Laws, Judges, Religious observances, and social order. You could not use God's Laws apart from the whole system without causing abuse. The Law was not intended to be used by someone outside the program God arranged. There were judges in every city who sat in the gates; and the marriages, divorces, and all legal and civil transactions were overseen by them. They were often Levites and knew God's Law better than most of us today. They are the ones who were supposed to define "uncleanness" and decide if this was important enough to allow divorce. Moses' Laws were a ground-work of principles upon which the judges were to make decisions, not exhaustive lists of do's and don'ts for every possible situation. The same is true in the program and organization of the New Testament church – the Bible was written for those in God's program and meant to be obeyed **within** the program. It must be interpreted in this context to be rightly understood and obeyed. Church leaders are to use the groundwork of principles in the Word to make decisions in the regulation and guidance of the church much like the Levites were supposed to. The

Bible was not meant to cover every possible scenario, but give us guidelines and principles to work from.

Jesus is rebuking the religious leaders and judges for watering down God's laws they were to uphold. He tells them that when men abuse Deut 24 they are "breaking wedlock" or breaking vows before God. Just doing the paperwork for the bill of divorce is not enough; you must also have a just and righteous reason and motive in God's opinion. The man who puts away his wife without God's approval is not only breaking wedlock unlawfully, but causing the man who might marry his wife to be an accomplice in this sin as well as causing his wife to be unlawful if she remarries this man. As long as they were still obligated to reconcile the first covenant which they were unlawfully breaking, none of them were free to marry another without the guilt of enabling the sin. The sin is that of unlawfully breaking wedlock – putting asunder what God joined without His permission. **This** is what needs to be repented of and thus never committed again if one has done this in their past.

The early Christians did not believe that Jesus was correcting Moses; but early Marcionite heretics did believe and teach this; and they eventually affected most of Christendom to this day. Listen to Tertullian as he argues this point against Marcion. Tertullian (160-230 AD), a Gentile Christian, said this of the words of Christ when contending with Marcion.

"But, observe, if this Christ be yours when he teaches contrary to Moses and the Creator, on the same principle must He be mine if I can show that His teaching is not contrary to them. I maintain, then, that there was a condition in the prohibition which he now made of divorce; the case supposed being, that a man put away

92

his wife for the express purpose of marrying another. His words are: "Whosoever putteth away his wife, and marrieth another, committeth adultery; and whosoever marrieth her that is put away from her husband, also committeth adultery," -- "put away," that is, for the reason wherefore a woman ought not to be dismissed, that another wife may be obtained. For he who marries a woman who is unlawfully put away is as much of an adulterer as the man who marries one who is undivorced. Permanent is the marriage which is not rightly dissolved; to marry, therefore, whilst matrimony is undissolved, is to commit adultery. Since, therefore, His prohibition of divorce was a conditional one, He did not prohibit absolutely; and what He did not absolutely forbid, that He permitted on some occasions, when there is an absence of the cause why He gave the prohibition. In very deed His teaching is not contrary to Moses, whose precept he partially defends, I will not say confirms. If, however, you deny that divorce is in any way permitted by Christ, how is it that you on your side destroy marriage, not uniting man and woman, nor admitting to the sacrament of baptism and of the eucharist those who have been united in marriage anywhere else, unless they should agree together to repudiate the fruit of their marriage, and so the very Creator Himself? Well, then, what is a husband to do in your sect, if his wife commit adultery? Shall he keep her? But your own apostle, you know, does not permit "the members of Christ to be joined to a harlot." Divorce, therefore, when justly deserved, has even in Christ a defender. So that Moses for the future must be considered as being confirmed by Him, since he allows divorce in the same sense as Christ does, if any unchastity should occur in the wife. For in the Gospel of Matthew he says, "Whosoever shall put away his wife, saving for the

93

cause of fornication, causeth her to commit adultery."
...The Creator, however, except on account of adultery, does not put asunder what He Himself joined together....He prohibits divorce when He will have the marriage inviolable; he permits divorce when the marriage is spotted with unfaithfulness." Tertullian 3.404,405

Tertullian, though stating the truth concerning Jesus and Moses, still seemed to have some hang-ups in his own prejudices and reveals some ignorance of the Hebrew roots of the teachings of Christ. Some other early Christian writers show their departure from the Scriptures and go completely contrary to Moses and Paul in making marriage after the death of one's spouse a "species of adultery"; so you cannot build your doctrine on early church writings that were not inspired by God. Early church writings are just men who share their opinions and some valuable historical information; but are not to be trusted in matters of doctrine as they leaned strongly toward Romanism and it superstitious rites.

Neither Jesus nor the Apostles taught anything about marriage that was contrary to Moses' Law. Everything taught on marriage in the New Testament is based on Moses' Law. In Romans 7 Paul says he is speaking to them that "know the Law" and speaks perfectly consistent with God's Law. In I Cor. 7 we find that the wife is "bound by the Law" – this means Moses' Law was still regulating marriages in the New Covenant. Of course it was; because the New Covenant was God's Laws written on our hearts, not some new and different laws. Nothing in the New Testament Scriptures contradicts Moses' Law concerning Marriage. When the noble Bereans searched the OT scriptures, they didn't find Jesus or Paul heretical, but found them consistent with God's Holy Inspired Word.

The Modern Mennonite position on this subject is a mess. They believe Jesus is correcting Moses, but in what way? There are numerous conflicting and contradicting interpretations full of strange and silly stretches of logic and grammar -- and all are allowed as long as they end up concluding that remarried people cannot be accepted into the church. It seems that it really doesn't matter how one arrives at that conclusion, as long as they get there. The duplicity of doctrine on this subject is quite amazing and shameful. Their tenacity to force the Scriptures into their own mold is even more shameful. The more I debate with them, the more disappointed I am. They consistently interpret Jesus' words to mean the exact opposite of what He said – THEY create an opposite ethic:

Jesus said: *"Whosoever shall put away his wife, **except it be** for fornication, and shall marry another, committeth adultery:"*

THIS IS THE OPPOSITE OF:

*"Whosoever shall put away his wife, **even if it be** for fornication, and shall marry another, committeth adultery:"*

When you interpret Jesus' words to mean the exact opposite of what He said, *HOW CAN YOU EVER FIND THE TRUTH?*

What did the Anabaptists believe on this issue?

Anyone who has studied the Pilgrim Church smiles at such a question, because among the ancient groups of Christians and also among the later Anabaptists/nonconformists there were a variety of opinions and differences as they grew and changed; but the ancient Anabaptists consistently rejected the false doctrine which placed Jesus in conflict with God's Law on this issue at least. They held firm to the correct teaching that divorce and remarriage in the case of immorality, apostasy or death is lawful.

In Peter Allix's The Ecclesiastical History of the Ancient Churches of Piedmont and of the Albigences, he states about St. Chromatius (one of those who never supported papal dominion), that, **"He plainly asserts, that marriage is so wholly dissolved by adultery, that it is lawful for the innocent party to marry again".** This Allix says was also, **"...the opinion of the Romish Church till after the tenth century."**

Let us hear what Menno Simons (the ordained bishop of the majority movement of Anabaptists during reformation times) has to say about divorce and remarriage due to immorality or the unbelieving one departing (Complete Writings – Herald Press):

"We acknowledge, teach, and assent to no other marriage than that which Christ and His apostles publicly and plainly taught in the New Testament, namely, of one man and one woman (Matt. 19:4), and that they may not be divorced except in case of adultery (Matt. 5:32); for the two are one flesh, but if the unbelieving one depart, a sister or brother is not under bondage in that case. I Cor. 7:15." pg. 200 (Pathway – pg. 83 part one)

"For divorce is not allowed by the Scriptures except for adultery." pg.479 (Pathway – pg. 277 part 2)

"These two, one husband and one wife, are one flesh and can not be separated from each other to marry

again otherwise than for adultery, as the Lord says. Matt. 5:19; Mark 10; Luke 16." pg. 561 (Pathway – pg. 311 part 2)

"We know too that the bond of undefiled, honorable matrimony is so firm and fast in the kingdom and government of Christ, that no man may leave his wife, nor a wife her husband, and marry another (understand rightly what Christ says), except it be for adultery. Paul also holds the same doctrine that they shall be so bound to each other that the man has not power over his own body, nor the woman over hers." pg.970 (Pathway – pg. 247 part 1)

Notice that Menno is not sheepishly defending what he considers the liberal view, but speaking with earnest about the strength of the marriage bond.

Now listen to Menno on the matter of past sin in one's life. This is about those who have "shacked up" unmarried, and then left and later married another. The law says they should have married the one they first violated, but what about when it is already done in the past?

"I do not mean to say that a person who has in days gone by ignorantly done this thing must leave the wife whom he afterwards married and take in her stead the violated one. Not at all, for I doubt not but that the merciful Father will graciously overlook the errors of those who have ignorantly committed them, and who will now fear and gladly do what is right." pg. 379 (Pathway – pg. 145 part 1)

Menno Simons, Dirk Philips, Leonard Bouwens, Gillis of Aachen, and three other Anabaptist leaders made this statement in 1554:

"If an unbeliever wishes to separate for reasons of the faith, then the believer shall conduct himself honestly. He shall not marry again as long as the unbeliever remains unmarried. But if the unbeliever marries or commits adultery, then the believing mate may also marry, subject to the advice of the elders of the congregation..."

In 1571, Anabaptist leader, Rauff Bisch said:

"We believe that nothing may terminate a marriage except adultery. But if the unbelieving wants to divorce because of the faith, we would let him go as Paul says in I Cor. 7. We believe that the cause for divorce should never be found in the believer."

On page 401 in the Martyr's Mirror we find in an early Anabaptist confession of faith these words:

"...Christ the perfect Lawgiver...referring all that heard and believed him to the original ordinance of his heavenly Father...and thus re-establishing marriage between one man and one woman, and so inseparably and firmly binding the bond of matrimony, that they might not, on any account, separate and marry another, except in case of adultery or death."

Many of the Anabaptist leaders could read the Greek, Latin, German, and sometimes Hebrew. Many were well read and studied men; having access to the early church writings, and apocryphal writings. They believed in divorce and remarriage in the case of immorality as Jesus and the Law of Moses taught. **See our book "What The Bible Really Teaches About Divorce And Remarriage" for a fuller discussion of this important issue.**

So how did it happen that modern Mennonites are nurturing this false doctrine so vigorously? Why do we find them rejecting new converts due to divorce and remarriage in their past when Jesus and God's Law taught differently? Why are they trying to split up marriage covenants and calling them "continued adultery", when it is Biblically impossible to live in continued adultery with the person you are in a marriage covenant with? <u>There is absolutely *no* evidence in the Bible or early church history of new converts being rejected from the church due to divorce and remarriage in their past.</u> This horrendous and foolish teaching which has damaged and destroyed so many seeking souls is due to the effects of wicked Marcionism!

Chapter Eight
Swear Not At All

Mt 5:33 Again, ye have heard that it hath been said by them of old time, Thou shalt not forswear thyself, but shalt perform unto the Lord thine oaths: 34 But I say unto you, Swear not at all; neither by heaven; for it is God's throne: 35 Nor by the earth; for it is his footstool: neither by Jerusalem; for it is the city of the great King. 36 Neither shalt thou swear by thy head, because thou canst not make one hair white or black. 37 But let your communication be, Yea, yea; Nay, nay: for whatsoever is more than these cometh of evil.

At this point some people really think they can prove that Jesus is correcting and changing the commandments of God in the Old Covenant; but it can be shown that this is again, not the case; but that Jesus is clarifying the Law. The big question is, "Why are they so intent on trying to set Jesus against the Scriptures?" The Jews would have loved to have accomplished such so they could justly condemn Jesus in court; but as you can read, they did not have any charges of this sort in court against Jesus. Surely, if **they** couldn't set Jesus' teachings against Moses' Law, no man today can do so.

Remember Malachi?

Mal 3:1 Behold, I will send my messenger, and he shall prepare the way before me: and the Lord, whom ye seek, shall suddenly come to his temple, even the messenger of the covenant, whom ye delight in: behold, he shall come, saith the LORD of hosts. 2 But who may abide the day of his coming? and who shall stand when he appeareth? for he is like a _refiner's fire_, and like _fullers' soap:_ 3 And he shall sit as a refiner and purifier of silver: and he shall purify the sons of Levi, and purge them as gold and silver, that they may offer unto the LORD an offering in righteousness. 4 Then shall the offering of Judah and Jerusalem be pleasant unto the LORD, as in the days of old, and as in former years. 5 **And I will come near to you to judgment;** and I will be a _swift witness_ against the sorcerers, and against the adulterers, and against **_false swearers_**, and against those that oppress the hireling in his wages, the widow, and the fatherless, and that turn aside the stranger from his right, and fear not me, saith the LORD of hosts. **6** For I am the LORD, _I change not_; **therefore ye sons of Jacob are not consumed.**

Jesus came to preach against false swearers – the Sermon on the Mount is vindicating the Moral Law -- preaching the Spirit and righteousness of the Law against the abuse of the letter of the Law. What is false swearing?? Listen to Jesus' use of qualifying statements and you will learn what false swearing the Jews were guilty of. Jesus never taught against lawful swearing; but against man's innovations. **Lawful swearing is simply calling God to witness and judge our words**.

Mt 23:16 _Woe unto you, ye blind guides, which say, Whosoever shall swear by the temple, it is nothing; but whosoever shall swear by the gold of the temple, he is a debtor! 17 Ye fools and blind: for whether is greater, the gold, or the temple that sanctifieth the gold? 18 And, Whosoever shall swear by the altar, it is nothing; but whosoever sweareth by the gift that is upon it, he is guilty. 19 Ye fools and blind: for whether is greater, the gift, or the altar that sanctifieth the gift? 20 Whoso therefore shall swear by the altar, sweareth by it, and by all things thereon. 21 And whoso shall swear by the temple, sweareth by it, and by him that dwelleth therein. 22 And he that shall swear by heaven, sweareth by the throne of God, and by him that sitteth thereon._

Malachi says Jesus would preach against those who swore contrary to the Law – false swearers or unlawful swearers. Did Jesus then come to preach against lawful swearers or unlawful swearers? Will you allow the Bible to answer this question for you? Do you believe Malachi was inspired by God?

It seems clear to me that Jesus is saying, ***"Ye have heard that it hath been said by them of old time, Thou shalt not forswear thyself*** (Don't take God's name in vain by perjuring yourself), ***but shalt perform unto the Lord thine oaths; but I say unto you beyond this to not use any vain or man-made oaths, such as swearing by heaven; for it is God's throne: nor by the earth; for it is his footstool: neither by Jerusalem; for it is the city of the great King. Neither shalt thou swear by thy head, because thou canst not make one hair white or black...etc."*** Or more simply, ***"Ye have heard by them of old time not to perjure yourself; but I say beyond that don't use any common oaths such as swearing by heaven...etc."***

He declares that simply performing the promise of man-made oaths was not enough, but that we should not use them at all – "Swear not at all with man-made oaths". This is consistent with Malachi and the immutability of God. The interpretation that says Jesus corrected the Law makes Malachi a liar, and destroys God's immutability. Jesus says, "let your ***communication*** be..." – He is speaking about their common conversations, and not about the special and sacred use of lawful swearing as used in the New Testament inspired Scriptures several times as we will demonstrate. **Malachi's prophecy demands that Jesus was not rebuking lawful oaths, but unlawful ones.**

Do you understand that if Jesus is speaking against lawful swearing commanded by God, that He is also calling God or Himself evil? Jesus said, **"But let your communication be, Yea, yea; Nay, nay: for <u>whatsoever is more than these cometh of evil.</u>"** If Jesus is including lawful swearing as commanded by God, which is more than "Yea, yea" and "Nay, nay", then He is calling Himself and His Father evil, because God inspired the OT Law, and that is where lawful swearing **came from**! How could LOVE fulfill the law if it is now wrong to swear lawfully as the law commanded? How could the righteousness of the law be fulfilled in believers who are walking in the Spirit, if part of the law is now sin?

The Jews were notorious for their swearing in common conversation with many different oaths which they saw as more or less binding. It was a system of "lawful lying" depending upon what oath they used. We can see this in Peter's life when he became angry.

Mt 26:72 And again he denied with an oath, I do not know the man.

Mt 26:74 Then began he to curse and to swear, saying, I know not the man. And immediately the cock crew.

Obviously Peter at this time had slipped back into his old ways, and wasn't *calling GOD to witness*, but some other common Jewish oath – the kind Jesus is forbidding. What oath do you suppose Peter used to convince them that he was telling the truth and didn't know Jesus? Was he swearing according to God's Law? No way.

What the Law commanded can be seen in the following verses:

Ex 22:11 Then shall an oath of the LORD be between them both, that he hath not put his hand unto his neighbour's goods; and the owner of it shall accept thereof, and he shall not make it good.

Le 19:12 And ye shall not swear by my name falsely, neither shalt thou profane the name of thy God: I am the LORD.

De 6:13 Thou shalt fear the LORD thy God, and serve him, and **shalt swear by his name.**

De 10:20 Thou shalt fear the LORD thy God; him shalt thou serve, and to him shalt thou cleave, and **swear by his name.**

De 23:23 That which is gone out of thy lips thou shalt keep and perform; even a freewill offering, according as thou hast vowed unto the LORD thy God, which thou hast promised with thy mouth.

To "swear by His name" was to call God as a witness of your words and deeds and thus put yourself directly under God's judgment if you were not telling the truth. This was a godly and biblical way to settle disputes as Paul tells us.

Heb 6:16 For men verily swear by the greater: and an oath for confirmation is to them an end of all strife.

Albert Barnes on Matthew 5:33-37: "An oath is a solemn affirmation, or declaration, made with an appeal to God for the truth of what is affirmed, and imprecating his vengeance, and renouncing his favour, if what is affirmed is false. A false oath is called perjury; or, as in this place, forswearing.

It appears, however, from this passage, as well as from the ancient writings of the Jewish Rabbins, that while they professedly adhered to the law, they had introduced a number of oaths in common conversation, and oaths which they by no means considered as binding. For example, they would swear by the temple, by the head, by heaven, by the earth. So long as they kept from swearing by the name Jehovah, and so long as they observed the oaths publicly taken, they seemed to consider all others as allowable, and allowedly broken. This is the abuse which Christ wished to correct. It was the practice of swearing in common conversation, and especially swearing by created things. To do this, he said that they were mistaken in their views of the sacredness of such oaths. They were very closely connected with God; and to trifle with them was a species of trifling with God. Heaven is his throne; the earth his footstool; Jerusalem his peculiar abode; the head was made by him, and was so much under his control, that we could not make one hair white or black. To swear by these things, therefore, was to treat irreverently objects created by God; and could not be without guilt

Our Saviour here evidently had no reference to judicial oaths, or oaths taken in a court of justice. It was merely the foolish and wicked habit of swearing in private conversation; of swearing on every occasion, and by everything, that he condemned. This he does condemn in a most unqualified manner. He himself, however, did not refuse to take an oath in a court of law, Matthew 26:63,64. So Paul often called God to witness his sincerity, which is all that is meant by an oath. See Ro 1:9; 9:1; Ga 1:20; Heb 6:16. Oaths were, moreover, prescribed in the law of Moses, and Christ did not come to repeal those laws. See Ex 22:11; Le 5:1; Nu 5:19 De 29:12,14."

When one swears before the court, he is simply binding himself before God to tell the truth of what he knows concerning things that have already happened –

and this is within his power. It is also within his power if he swears by calling God to witness and hold him accountable for what he promises concerning the future. It is within his power to genuinely intend and do his best to perform what he promised; though he could still fail to perform the promise by circumstances beyond his control.   If we call God to witness, then God also witnesses that we did all we could do to perform our oath.

When Jesus forbids oaths, He is speaking of man-made oaths which claim ability beyond our power; not just calling God to witness our sincere efforts. To say, "As the temple stands, I will pay the money back in a week" is more than I can guarantee; and the temple isn't going to hold me accountable or be a true witness. If I can't make one hair white or black, then I shouldn't be promising or guaranteeing what I may not have ability to deliver – for I know not what a day may bring forth. Thus Jesus is rebuking them for taking something that is logical and righteous (calling God to witness), and turning it in to something foolish and unrighteous (boasting of tomorrow).

Heb 6:16 For men verily swear by the greater: and an oath for confirmation is to them an end of all strife.

Neither God, Jesus, nor the Apostles would practice or commend something that "cometh of evil"!   Who would ever be so foolish and arrogant as to think they would, and then interpret the Word of God in such a way.

God Swearing:

You can be sure that Jesus isn't condemning that which God not only commanded, but exemplified.

Lu 1:73 The oath which he sware to our father Abraham,

Ac 2:30 Therefore being a prophet, and knowing that God had sworn with an oath to him, that of the fruit of his loins, according to the flesh, he would raise up Christ to sit on his throne;

Heb 3:11 So I sware in my wrath, They shall not enter into my rest.)

Heb 3:18 And to whom sware he that they should not enter into his rest, but to them that believed not?

Heb 6:13 For when God made promise to Abraham, because he could swear by no greater, he sware by himself,

Heb 6:17 Wherein God, willing more abundantly to shew unto the heirs of promise the immutability of his counsel, confirmed it by an oath:

Jesus was made priest by God swearing an oath:

The priests under the law (Mosaic Covenant) were not made with an oath; **but Jesus was**; and by *SO MUCH (the very oath of God)* He was declared to be the priest after the order of Melchisedec of a better and greater covenant.

Heb 7:20 **And inasmuch as <u>not without an oath</u> he was made priest: 21 (For those priests <u>were made without an oath;</u> but this <u>with an oath</u> by him that said unto him, The Lord sware and will not repent, Thou art a priest for ever after the order of Melchisedec:) 22 <u>By so much</u> was Jesus made a surety of a better testament. ...28 For the law maketh men high priests which have** *infirmity; but the word of the oath, <u>which was since the</u> <u>law</u>, maketh the Son, who is consecrated for evermore.*

Even though the priests under Moses' Law were appointed without an oath of confirmation; God chose to confirm Jesus as the Priest of the New Covenant after the order of Melchisedec **with an oath – the very oath of God.** You can be sure Jesus was not teaching that **this type** of an oath **was evil or** *came of evil*.

Jesus answered under oath when on trial

*Mt 26:63 But Jesus held his peace. And the high priest answered and said unto him, **I adjure thee by the living God,** that thou tell us whether thou be the Christ, the Son of God. 64 Jesus saith unto him, Thou hast said:*

William Burkitt: "Yea, farther observe, That as Christ answered directly and plainly at his trial, so he did not refuse to answer upon oath; I adjure thee by the living God, says the judge of the court, that thou tell us whether thou art the Christ; that is, I require thee to answer this question upon oath; for adjuring a person, or requiring him to answer upon oath, was the manner of swearing among the Jews. Now to this adjuration our Saviour answered plainly and directly, I am,

Hence learn, That swearing before a magistrate, upon a just and great occasion, is lawful; if Christ in the fifth of St. Matthew forbid all oaths, then here his practice was contrary to his own doctrine; but it is evident that Christ answered the magistrate upon oath, and so may we."

Adam Clarke: *I adjure thee by the living God]* "I put thee to thy oath. To this solemn adjuration Christ immediately replies, because he is now called on, in the name of God, to bear another testimony to the truth."

A. T. Robertson: "So Caiaphas put Jesus on oath in order to make him incriminate himself, a thing unlawful in Jewish jurisprudence. He had failed to secure any accusation against Jesus that would stand at all. But Jesus did not refuse to answer under solemn oath, clearly showing that he was not thinking of oaths in courts of justice when he prohibited profanity."

The Apostle Paul Practiced Lawful Swearing in His Holy Ghost inspired writings

You can be sure that Paul understood Jesus better than you or anyone today. Marcionism cannot gain ground with those who properly honor and believe God's Word through His chosen messengers. Those who demean Moses and the Apostles are arrogant fools who "professing themselves to be wise" become fools by setting themselves up to condemn God's vessels. They think they understand Jesus' words better than the Apostles who gave us Jesus' words. If Paul was in the practice of swearing according to the Law of God, then we can **know** this is **not** what Jesus or James was condemning. Here are **nine examples** of Paul's swearing.

1. *Ga 1:20 Now the things which I write unto you, behold, before God, I lie not.*

Albert Barnes: *Verse 20. Behold, before God, I lie not.* "This is an oath, or a solemn appeal to God. See Note, Ro 9:1. The design of this oath here is to prevent all suspicion of falsehood.

2. *Ro 9:1 I say the truth in Christ, I lie not, my conscience also bearing me witness in the Holy Ghost,*

Adam Clarke: *Verse 1. I say the truth in Christ, I lie not]* "This is one of the most solemn oaths any man can possibly take. He appeals to Christ as the searcher of hearts that he tells the truth; asserts that his conscience was free from all guile in this matter, and that the Holy Ghost bore him testimony that what he said was true. Hence we find that the testimony of a man's own conscience, and the testimony of the Holy Ghost, are two distinct things, and that the apostle had both at the same time."

3. *2Co 1:23 Moreover I call God for a record upon my soul, that to spare you I came not as yet unto Corinth.*

Albert Barnes: The phrase, "I call God for a record upon my soul," is, in the Greek, "I call God for a witness against my soul." It is a solemn oath, or appeal to God; and implies, that if he did not in that case declare the truth, he desired that God would be a witness against him, and would punish him accordingly. The reason why he made this solemn appeal to God, was the importance of his vindicating his own character before the church, from the charges which had been brought against him."

Wesley: *V. 23. I call God for a record upon my soul-* "Was not St. Paul now speaking by the Spirit? And can a more solemn oath be conceived? Who then can imagine that Christ ever designed to forbid all swearing?"

William Burkitt: "Here observe the apostle's manner of speech, it is by way of adjuration: I call God to record upon my soul, &c. The words are an assertory and execratory oath, wherein God is called to witness the truth of what he said.

Learn hence, That it is lawful for Christians under the gospel to swear upon a necessary and great occasion."

4. *Php 1:8 For God is my record, how greatly I long after you all in the bowels of Jesus Christ.*

Barnes *Verse 8. For God is my record.* "My witness; I can solemnly appeal to him."

5. *Ro 1:9 For God is my witness, whom I serve with my spirit in the gospel of his Son, that without ceasing I make mention of you always in my prayers;*

William Burkitt: "Observe, 2. That because the apostle was yet a stranger to them, had never seen them, and it was impossible for them to know the outgoings of his heart toward them, he solemnly appeals to the heart-searching God, calls him to witness how affectionately he loved them, and how frequently he prayed for them; God is my witness. The words have the force, if not the form of an oath, and teach us, that it is unquestionably lawful in important affairs to swear, to appeal to God, and call him to be a witness of what we either say or do. We find St. Paul did it often, and our Saviour himself did not refuse to answer upon oath, when solemnly adjured.

Observe, 3. How the apostle swears by God, not by the creatures, which is the swearing condemned by our Saviour and by St. James, Matthew 5:1-48 and Jas 5:1-20."

6. *1 Th 2:5 For neither at any time used we flattering words, as ye know, nor a cloke of covetousness; God is witness:*

Albert Barnes: *God is witness.* "This is a solemn appeal to God for the truth of what he had said. He refers not only to their own observation, but he calls God himself to witness his sincerity. God knew the truth in the case. There could have been no imposing on him; and the appeal, therefore, is to one who was intimately acquainted with the truth. Learn hence,

(1.) that it is right, on important occasions, to appeal to God for the truth of what we say.

(2.) We should always so live that we can properly make such an appeal to him."

Robertson: "Paul feels so strongly his innocence of this charge that he calls God as witness as in 2Co 1:23; Ro 9:1; Php 1:8, a solemn oath for his own veracity."

7. *2 Co 11:10 As the truth of Christ is in me, no man shall stop me of this boasting in the regions of Achaia.*

Adam Clarke: *Verse 10.* *"As the truth of Christ is in me]* estin alhyeia cristou en emoi. The truth of Christ is in me. That is: I speak as becomes a Christian man, and as influenced by the Gospel of Christ. It is a solemn form of asseveration, if not to be considered in the sense of an oath."

Albert Barnes: *Verse 10. As the truth of Christ is in me.* "That is, I solemnly declare this as in the presence of Christ. As I am a Christian man; as I feel bound to declare the truth; and as I must answer to Christ. It is a solemn form of asseveration, equal to an oath. See Barnes for Ro 9:1. Comp. 1Ti 2:7."

8. *2 Co 11:31 The God and Father of our Lord Jesus Christ, which is blessed for evermore, knoweth that I lie not.*

Adam Clarke: *Verse 31.   The God and Father of our Lord]* "Here is a very solemn asseveration; an appeal to the ever blessed God for the truth of what he asserts. It is something similar to his asseveration or oath in ver. 10 of this chapter; {2Co 11:10} see also Ro 9:5, and Ga 1:20. And from these and several other places we learn that the apostle thought it right thus to confirm his assertions on these particular occasions.   But here is nothing to countenance profane swearing, or taking the name of God in vain, as many do in exclamations, when surprised, or on hearing something unexpected, &c.; and as others do who, conscious of their own falsity, endeavour to gain credit by appeals to God for the truth of what they say. St. Paul's appeal to God is in the same spirit as his most earnest prayer. This solemn appeal the apostle makes in reference to what he mentions in the following verses. This was a fact not yet generally known."

Albert Barnes: *Verse 31.   The God and Father*, etc. "Paul was accustomed to make solemn appeals to God for the truth of what he said, especially when it was likely to be called in question. See 2Co 11:10. Comp. Ro 9:1.

...This passage proves that an appeal to God on great occasions is not improper; it proves also that it should be done with profound veneration."

Robertson: *I am not lying* (ou pseudomai). The list seems so absurd and foolish that Paul takes solemn oath about it (cf. 2Co 1:23). For the doxology see Ro 1:25; 9:5."

9. *1Ti 2:7 Whereunto I am ordained a preacher, and an apostle, (I speak the truth in Christ, and lie not;) a teacher of the Gentiles in faith and verity.*

Albert Barnes: *I speak the truth in Christ, and lie not.* "That is, by Christ; or I solemnly appeal to Christ--a form

114

of an oath. See Barnes for Ro 9:1. Paul makes a solemn declaration similar to this in regard to his call to the apostleship, in Ga 1:20. For the reasons why he did it, See Barnes for Ga 1:20. It is probable that there were those in Ephesus who denied that he could be an apostle, and hence his solemn declaration affirming it."

Does this mean anything to Marcionites?? No they deny, fight, squirm, and lie to themselves to avoid the undeniable truth I am presenting them. If they would listen to Jesus, they would "agree with their adversary" before I drag them into court before God. I will be a witness against them someday, which is a sad reality. I am laboring in these books to make the arguments clear and plain so as to save as many from error as possible. I ask you reader to humble yourself before the facts.

Holy angels swearing in Revelation:

Re 10:5 And the angel which I saw stand upon the sea and upon the earth lifted up his hand to heaven, 6 And sware by him that liveth for ever and ever, who created heaven, and the things that therein are, and the earth, and the things that therein are, and the sea, and the things which are therein, that there should be time no longer:

Albert Barnes: *Verse 5. And the angel which I saw stand,* etc. Re 10:2. "That is, John saw him standing in this posture when he made the oath which he proceeds to record.

Lifted up his hand to heaven. The usual attitude in taking an oath, as if one called heaven to witness. See Ge 14:22; De 32:40 Eze 20:5-6. Compare Barnes on "Da 12:7".

I am sure the Apostles understood Jesus' words better than any today; and what is righteous for angels, Apostles, and God, cannot be sin for saints if used in the same sense.

If you understand the style or method of Jesus' speaking, you can see that *"Swear not at all"* would be in the same sense as *"Take no thought for your life"*, which obviously needs qualifying statements; *"Take no thought for the morrow"*, which needs qualifying statements; *"Judge not,"* which must be taken in context with the qualifying statements; *"Labor not for the meat which perisheth"*, which needs qualifying statements; and *"Resist not evil"* which needs qualifying statements. People who properly understand Jesus' style of teaching will not use His words superstitiously so as to: *only pray in a closet with the door shut, pluck out their eye, cut off their hand, never think about your food or clothes or tomorrow,* etc. **Jesus always gave qualifying statements so the people who were listening to Him were not confused.** If you really want to "take Jesus at face value" or "interpret Jesus' words literally" as some Marcionites spout out, then you must also take what Jesus said **with** His qualifying statements. Misinterpreting Jesus is NOT taking Jesus at face value; and interpreting Jesus contrary to His own Word by ignoring the complete statement is SIN.

In what Jesus said of swearing... **"neither by heaven; for it is God's throne: 35 Nor by the earth; for it is his footstool: neither by Jerusalem; for it is the city of the great King. 36 Neither shalt thou swear by thy head, because thou canst not make one hair white or black"...are the qualifying statements** used by Jesus and James; and they do not forbid what the Law of God commands – swearing by God in a holy and reverent way.

116

James never intended for his statements to correct or condemn God's Law. James is very intent on telling men to be "doers of the Word, and not hearers only". What Word is James speaking of? Listen:

*Jas 1:22 But be ye doers of **the word,** and not hearers only, deceiving your own selves. 23 For if any be a hearer of the word, and not a doer, he is like unto a man beholding his natural face in a glass: 24 For he beholdeth himself, and goeth his way, and straightway forgetteth what manner of man he was. 25 But whoso looketh into the **perfect law of liberty**, and **continueth therein,** he being not a forgetful hearer, **but a doer of the work**, this man shall be blessed in his deed.*

*Jas 2:8 If ye fulfil the royal law **according to the scripture,** Thou shalt love thy neighbour as thyself, ye do well: 9 But if ye have respect to persons, **ye commit sin, and are convinced of the law as transgressors.** 10 For whosoever shall keep the whole law, and yet offend in one point, he is guilty of all. 11 For he that said, Do not commit adultery, said also, Do not kill. Now if thou commit no adultery, yet if thou kill, thou art become a transgressor of the law. 12 **So speak ye, and so do, as they that shall be judged by the law of liberty.***

*Jas 4:11 Speak not evil one of another, brethren. He that speaketh evil of his brother, and judgeth his brother, speaketh evil of the law, and judgeth the law: **but if thou judge the law, thou art not a doer of the law, but a judge.** 12 **There is one lawgiver**, who is able to save and to destroy: who art thou that judgest another?*

Jas 5:12 But above all things, my brethren, swear not, neither by heaven, neither by the earth, neither by any other oath: but let your yea be yea; and your nay, nay; lest ye fall into condemnation.

James was the bishop of Jerusalem where thousands of Jews had believed and were all zealous of the Law of Moses as they should have been as Jews – Read Acts 21

117

which occurs 29 years after Pentecost. James certainly believed that Jews were not to "forsake Moses" and live contrary to God's Law, which He calls the Law of Liberty, because with Jesus as our atonement and High Priest it was not to be looked upon as bondage or condemning, but as Liberating and blessed. James commands people to be doers of the Word, which he reveals as the Scriptures of his day, which comprised what we call the Old Testament! He makes it clear that they were to be obedient to God's Laws or they would be in trouble with the ONE lawgiver to whom they would give account. Now for us to think that he then turns around and contradicts himself by saying they should not obey God's Word about lawful swearing is silly and foolish. He gives the same qualifying statements as Jesus does and is speaking of man's innovations – not the calling of God to witness as Paul practiced while inspired by the Holy Ghost!

Consider the following:

Ro 14:11 For it is written, *As I live, saith the Lord, every knee **shall** bow to me, and every tongue shall **confess** to God.*

Where is it written?

Isa 45:23 *I have **sworn** by myself, the <u>word is gone out of my mouth in righteousness</u>, and shall not return, That unto me every knee shall bow, every tongue shall **swear**.*

This will yet be fulfilled! This means an oath of allegiance that Jesus is LORD. So, again we see that everything must be understood in the context of Jesus' purpose of clearing misconceptions about God's Law and showing its purity and excellence. Interpreting the Bible in a way that produces a contradiction or sets God against himself is error and misinterpretation! This is what the

Gnostics did in their dualism, and as it was then called heresy, it is still heresy now.

You may say, "Well, we know Menno was against swearing oaths". Yes, but did Menno even understand oaths? When writing to the magistrates (Complete Writings, Herald Press, pg 554) He says this: *"**God is my witness** that I desire nothing but that you all may actually be what you are acclaimed to be – noble lords and Christian magistrates..."* Do you see anything strange about what he is saying to the government? He calls God to be his witness, which is the same as swearing by God – Menno is speaking under oath to the authorities! Hmmm...do you think Menno understood the difference between lawful and unlawful swearing? Listen to Menno explain his position.

"This is our position and understanding in regard to this matter. Inasmuch as the Lord has forbidden us to swear at all (understand in temporal matters) neither sincerely nor falsely...We say, in temporal matters, and for this reason: Because Christ sometimes in His teachings makes use of the word verily and because Paul called upon the Lord as a witness of his soul. For this some think that swearing is allowable; not observing that Christ and Paul did not do this in regard to temporal matters as in matters of flesh and blood or money or property but in affirmation of the eternal truth to the praise of God and to the salvation and edification of their brethren" (Complete Writings, Herald Press, page 521).

Now, listen closely: Menno has just admitted that he understands that Jesus using "verily", and Paul calling God as his witness are **both** a type of oath and are exceptions to Christ's teaching in the Sermon on The Mount; but he excuses them by saying they only did it in matters of eternal truth and not in temporal matters. So, he KNEW that Christ and Paul both practiced what Jews understood as lawful swearing by God's Law. Instead of realizing that Jesus could not be condemning this TYPE of swearing, Menno excuses them as using it only in eternal matters and not temporal; but this is sadly lacking. Why would it be OK to do that which "cometh of evil" in regards to eternal truth, but not in regards to legitimate matters of this life?? If it "cometh of evil" it would be even more profane to use it in matters of eternal truth than in earthly matters. Sadly Menno didn't know what he was talking about.

Jesus also answered under oath in court. So, is this merely a temporal matter, or is God ordained government when operating as the "ministers of God" (Romans 13) to punish the evil and reward the good also of eternal importance? **Besides this, Jesus did not even teach against lawful oaths in temporal matters; but taught against man-made oaths in any matters – temporal or eternal.** Menno could see that there were exceptions to Jesus' words, but by missing what Malachi had said, and not considering that Jesus would never correct His own inspired Word, he missed the mark in his reasons for the exceptions. The Marcionite influence was strong among those he was associated with and it stumbled him.

Later, Menno, in his reply to Martin Micron, tries to make a distinction between an oath and an affirmation, and says that Jesus and Paul were simply affirming, but not swearing. This shows further that he did not understand the Jewish mode of swearing; because "affirming" anything *before God as witness* was swearing by their definition and practice. Let's see what is considered as swearing from the Scriptures.

Nu 32:10 *And the LORD'S anger was kindled the same time, and he* **sware,** *saying,* **Surely** *none of the men that came up out of Egypt, from twenty years old and upward, shall see the land which I sware unto Abraham, unto Isaac, and unto Jacob; because they have not wholly followed me:* **(also Deut. 1:34,35)**

Jer 51:14 *The LORD of hosts hath* **sworn** *by himself, saying,* **Surely** *I will fill thee with men, as with caterpillers; and they shall lift up a shout against thee.*

This is similar to Jesus using, "verily" or "verily, verily" which means, "surely, surely". Jesus was using a form of swearing when He highlighted his words with "verily, verily". Just because you never considered this as a form of swearing doesn't mean ANYTHING. You need to learn the ways of the ones who penned the Scriptures and spoke the language! Let the Bible define its own terms or you will end up in error every time. Next, see that calling God to be witness is swearing.

Jg 11:10 *And the elders of Gilead said unto Jephthah,* **The LORD be witness between us,** *if we do not so according to thy words.*

1Sa 20:42 *And Jonathan said to David, Go in peace, forasmuch as we have* **sworn** *both of us in the name of the LORD, saying,* **The LORD be (witness) between me and thee,** *and between my seed and thy seed for ever. And he arose and departed: and Jonathan went into the city.*

Compare with Paul's swearing:

Ro 1:9 For God is my witness, *whom I serve with my spirit in the gospel of his Son, that without ceasing I make mention of you always in my prayers;*

1 Th 2:5 *For neither at any time used we flattering words, as ye know, nor a cloke of covetousness;* **God is witness:**

Here is another form of calling God to witness and be the judge of what is said and done.

1Sa 19:6 *And Saul hearkened unto the voice of Jonathan: and Saul* <u>**sware**</u>, <u>**As the LORD liveth**</u>, *he shall not be slain.*

1Ki 1:29 *And the king* **sware**, *and said,* **As the LORD liveth**, *that hath redeemed my soul out of all distress, 30* **Even as I sware** *unto thee by the LORD God of Israel,* **saying, Assuredly** *Solomon thy son shall reign after me, and he shall sit upon my throne in my stead; even so will I certainly do this day.*

2Ch 18:13 *And Micaiah said,* **As the LORD liveth**, *even what my God saith, that will I speak.*

Jer 38:16 *So Zedekiah the king* **sware** *secretly unto Jeremiah, saying,* **As the LORD liveth that made us this soul**, *I will not put thee to death, neither will I give thee into the hand of these men that seek thy life.*

There is no real difference in the essence of these oaths with those of Paul:

2 Co 1:23 *Moreover* **I call God for a record upon my soul,** *that to spare you I came not as yet unto Corinth.*

2 Co 11:10 **As the truth of Christ is in me**, *no man shall stop me of this boasting in the regions of Achaia.*

Ga 1:20 *Now the things which I write unto you,* **behold, before God, I lie not.**

I greatly appreciate Menno, but I'm afraid in this case he was wrong as were the Anabaptist peoples in general on this subject. It is easy to see how they could be confused, and their confusion should not have been rewarded with persecution and bloodshed as it was. Their confusion was due to Marcionite influence and their own ignorance of Jewish ways and thoughts; which was also partly due to a wrong attitude toward the Old

Testament. Though professing Christians did not agree on this point, they still could have loved and cared for one another's souls. A stubborn and unteachable spirit always compounds problems.

Again we have loaded on the clear and undeniable evidence that Jesus was not teaching in conflict with God's Holy Word, because He **was** God's Holy Word.

Joh 1:1 In the beginning was the Word, and the Word was with God, and the Word was God...14 And the Word was made flesh, and dwelt among us..."

Chapter Nine
Resist Not Evil

Mt 5:38 Ye have heard that it hath been said, An eye for an eye, and a tooth for a tooth. 39 But I say unto you, That ye resist not evil: but whosoever shall smite thee on thy right cheek, turn to him the other also. 40 And if any man will sue thee at the law, and take away thy coat, let him have thy cloke also. 41 And whosoever shall compel thee to go a mile, go with him twain. 42 Give to him that asketh thee, and from him that would borrow of thee turn not thou away.

Jesus is here speaking of "resisting evil" in the context of *personal retribution* or *avenging one's self* with the concept of an "eye for an eye" as their justification. In the matter of an "eye for an eye" Jesus is correcting a misconception that arose due to a **wrong application** of God's Law. This command was given to the **magistrates and judges** as part of the just process of law. It was never intended to be a principle for interpersonal relationships or personal vengeance as the Jews were using it! Remember I said that God's Laws were a part of an overall program and social order. The principle of "eye for eye" is a principle of justice, but not a principle of interpersonal relationships. How do we know this is the case Jesus is dealing with?

1. The command is given in Moses' Law as part of the civil law to judges in the course of their duty.

2. Jesus is speaking about interpersonal relationships, because His words, *"But I say unto you, That ye resist not evil: but* **whosoever shall smite thee** *on thy right cheek,* **turn to him** *the other also."* has never applied to the magistrates on duty who "bear not the sword in vain". Jesus is not speaking to judges and magistrates; but to individuals and their relationships with others. Jesus is not even speaking about an attack on one's life; but about personal insult from another individual – *a slap in the face*. Rulers are commanded to punish the evil and reward the good. If they **resist not evil men**, they are violating God's design expressed by Paul in Romans 13. Jesus is therefore showing that "eye for an eye" was being misapplied.

Ex 21:22 *If men strive, and hurt a woman with child, so that her fruit depart from her, and yet no mischief follow: he shall be surely punished, according as the woman's husband will lay upon him; and he shall pay as the* **judges** *determine. 23 And if any mischief follow, then thou shalt give life for life, 24 Eye for eye, tooth for tooth, hand for hand, foot for foot, 25 Burning for burning, wound for wound, stripe for stripe.*

Le 24:20 *Breach for breach, eye for eye, tooth for tooth: as he hath caused a blemish in a man, so shall it be done to him again.*

Clarke on _Ex. 21:22_ "This is the earliest account we have of the lex talionis, or law of like for like, which afterwards prevailed among the Greeks and Romans. Among the latter, it constituted a part of the twelve tables, so famous in antiquity; but the punishment was afterwards changed to a pecuniary fine, to be levied at the discretion of the praetor. It prevails less or more in most civilized countries, and is fully acted upon in the canon law, in reference to all calumniators: Calumniator, si in accusatione defecerit, talionem recipiat. "If the calumniator fail in the proof of his accusation, let him suffer the same punishment which he wished to have inflicted upon the man whom he falsely accused." Nothing, however, of this kind was left to private revenge; the magistrate awarded the punishment when the fact was proved, otherwise the lex talionis would have utterly destroyed the peace of society, and have sown the seeds of hatred, revenge, and all uncharitableness."

*De 19:18 And the **judges** shall make diligent inquisition: and, behold, if the witness be a false witness, and hath testified falsely against his brother; 19 Then shall ye do unto him, as he had thought to have done unto his brother: **so shalt thou put the evil away from among you**. 20 **And those which remain shall hear, and fear, and shall henceforth commit no more any such evil among you**. 21 And thine eye shall not pity; but life shall go for life, eye for eye, tooth for tooth, hand for hand, foot for foot.*

There is no question that this principle was given to the civil magistrates who were responsible before God to uphold righteousness in society. There is also no question that Jesus was rebuking the abuse of this principle in being used for interpersonal relationships where it was not meant to apply.

Clarke on Matthew 5:38: "It seems that the Jews had made this law (the execution of which belonged to the civil magistrate) a ground for authorizing private resentments, and all the excesses committed by a vindictive spirit. Revenge was often carried to the utmost extremity, and more evil returned than what had been received. This is often the case among those who are called Christians."

Jesus' examples had to do with personal insult, not an attack on one's life. This does not forbid self-defense or defending the weak when life is at stake. You cannot apply "resist not evil" to any and every evil, or untold foolishness would result. Jesus is teaching the spirit of God's Law concerning interpersonal relationships, and self defense against criminal action or defending the weak is never condemned in the Old Testament or New Testament; it was actually commanded. The Apostles declare along with Jesus that LOVE fulfills the law and that the Law was based on appropriate and godly love. This proves that Jesus and the Apostles would have fulfilled every obligation the law commanded concerning delivering the damsel or defending the weak.

De 22:24 Then ye shall bring them both out unto the gate of that city, and ye shall stone them with stones that they die; the damsel, because she cried not, being in the city; and the man, because he hath humbled his neighbour's wife: so thou shalt put away evil from among you. 25 But if a man find a betrothed damsel in the field, and the man force her, and lie with her: then the man only that lay with her shall die: 26 But unto the damsel thou shalt do nothing; there is in the damsel no sin worthy of death: for as when a man riseth against his neighbour, and slayeth him, even so is this matter: 27 For he found her in the field, and the betrothed damsel cried, and there was none to save her.

It is clear that the damsel was expected to "resist evil" and defend herself in this situation; and if she cried, God expected the person who heard her to deliver her. Has this changed? NO, absolutely not. This has not changed, and Jesus is not condemning this type of resisting evil, but only in the context of personal insult. He is not speaking contrary to God's perfect Law. If Jesus or the Apostles had heard a damsel cry, they would have delivered her or they would have been sinning against the "righteousness of the Law of God".

Pr 24:11 *If thou forbear to deliver them that are drawn unto death, and those that are ready to be slain; 12 If thou sayest, Behold, we knew it not; doth not he that pondereth the heart consider it? and he that keepeth thy soul, doth not he know it? and shall not he render to every man according to his works?*

For Jesus to be the perfect Lamb of God without sin, He would have had to fulfill this part of God's righteousness as well; and NEVER taught anything contrary to it. The same godly love fulfills both the Old Testament and the New Testament moral obligations, because the New Covenant is the SAME Law written in our hearts.

Pacifists cry, "We just need to trust God". They think that unless you are a pacifist you are not really trusting God. Abraham had trained all 318 of his servants in warfare along with making and storing up enough weapons to arm all of them. Read the account when he went to deliver Lot from the invaders. Did he trust God in this? Yes, the father of the faithful was known for his faith in God and was called the Friend of God! Your salvation is connected with Abraham having faith in God (Gal. 3:6-9). He did indeed trust in God or he would not have attacked those four kings who had just conquered five kingdoms at once. This faith and effort was so pleasing to God as a "just war" that God not only helped and blessed Abraham, but received tithes of the spoils. This was not Israel as a nation; but Abraham, the friend of God, before Israel was established as a nation. We are to follow the Faith of Abraham and the God of Abraham. Jesus is a priest after the order of Melchizedek; and this

Melchizedek could have even been an appearance of Jesus to Abraham. God is not a pacifist; Jesus is not a pacifist; and only a Marcionite can find pacifism in the Bible.

After hearing all of Jesus' teaching and understanding it better than YOU, Peter was wearing a sword in the Garden and intended to use it for self defense. Jesus only rebuked him for using it against the authorities; but knew he had it for self defense and hadn't forbidden it. Why did Peter have a sword and intend to use it for self defense? Because Jesus had told His disciples there was coming a day soon where it would be better to have a sword than their shirt; and this was in the context of self defense. Everything Jesus said against the use of the sword in the Garden of Gethsemane was in the context of not using it for insurrection against God ordained authorities. He was not contradicting himself. He did not tell his disciples to carry a sword as a "set up" just so He could rebuke them! Some pseudo "Bible scholars" actually teach such foolishness to defend their Marcionism.

Jesus was no pacifist and never taught pacifism. Listen to Jesus in Luke 19 as He describes His own future plans:

Lu 19:11 And as they heard these things, he added and spake a parable, because he was nigh to Jerusalem, and because they thought that the kingdom of God should immediately appear. 12 He said therefore, A certain nobleman went into a far country to receive for himself a kingdom, and to return. 13 And he called his ten servants, and delivered them ten pounds, and said unto them, Occupy till I come. 14 But his citizens hated him, and sent a message after him, saying, We will not have this man to reign over us. 15 And it came to pass, that when he was returned, having received the kingdom, then *he commanded these servants to be called unto him, to whom he had given the money, that he might know how much every man had gained by trading... 27 But **those mine enemies, which would not that I should reign over them, bring hither, and slay them before me.***

Now, who was supposed to slay these enemies? The same servants who were to "occupy till Jesus returns", which are the Christians who follow and obey Jesus. Listen again to Jesus describe His own Father:

Mt 22:7 *But when the king heard thereof, he was wroth: and he sent forth his armies, and destroyed those murderers, and burned up their city.*

In the context this king is Jesus' Father acting in reaction to the fact that the Jews rejected the invitation for His Son's wedding and slew His servants. This same reaction is taught in the King's reaction to the keepers of the vineyard slaying His Son (Mk 12). This was all fulfilled in AD 70 when God used the Roman armies to punish the Jews for killing Jesus. There is no pacifism taught in the Bible. James tells us to take the OT prophets as an example of suffering affliction:

Jas 5:10 *Take, my brethren, the prophets, who have spoken in the name of the Lord, for an example of suffering affliction, and of patience.*

The prophets were not pacifists! Nobody is silly enough to even argue that they were, yet they were martyrs. Can one be a martyr without being a pacifist? I say this because some think that just because someone got burned at the stake or such like, they must have been a pacifist. When the government arrests you and then executes you unjustly it doesn't mean you were a pacifist.

What was Jesus teaching?

1. **KEEP RANK**: Stay within the bounds of jurisdiction and righteousness – no matter how unjust the situation. Every police officer and soldier knows they cannot avenge themselves with their own hand or retaliate against personal insult; **but must keep rank**, and only do what is within the realms of their duty and jurisdiction. Christians are ambassadors on duty at all times, and we must respond according to our vocation, not our personal feelings.

2. Don't stoop to the level of those opposing you! Seek only righteousness even in conflict or litigation. Show that you are not motivated by selfish and evil motives. You are called to demonstrate God's righteousness and not your own ends and ways. If you have trespassed, and the judge awards the other person your coat as payment, give him also your cloke to show you are truly sorry and truly want to make it right. Jesus may have been referring to God's Law in Exodus 22, where it says the offender must restore *double*; so, even if the ruling government didn't require it, you should do it anyways for God.

3. Be prepared to help, serve, and give with an unselfish spirit when it can be done to the glory of God. Don't keep score; but serve and help willingly. This is opposite the Jewish misconception of using "eye for eye" as a guide to personal relationships.

Mt 5:41 "And whosoever shall compel thee to go a mile, go with him twain."

The Word "compel" refers to the government's practice of "commandeering" service for government's causes. This is referring to government and military service. There are those who take the "resist not evil" teaching to an extreme which says a Christian can never serve in the government or military; but this verse could be taken to the opposite extreme to show they can and must serve when asked in whatever the military does – even to the second mile! **Extremes are dangerous things, and Christians cannot afford to be so rash with Jesus' words.** The following commentary sums it up nicely.

Liberty Bible Commentary: "In ancient times government agents were in a position to compel forced service upon a subjugated people. A Roman soldier, for example, could compel a Jewish native to carry his armor or materials for one mile, in order to relieve the soldier. Jesus now states that if someone compels you to walk a mile, go with him twain. The believer is to be willing to "go the extra mile". Doing double our duty not only proves the loyalty and faithfulness of our cooperation to human authority, but likewise proves the spiritual intention of our heart. It also provides an opportunity of conviction in order to witness effectively out of our life message. It would have been foolish for the believer of Jesus' day to reluctantly go only a mile with a Roman official and then attempt to share the gospel with him. By going the second mile he proved the innermost intention of his heart."

Jesus had no problem with military and government service as a principle. Was it serving two masters? No! Was it compromising with evil? No! Jesus was telling his disciples that if a Roman soldier commandeered their service for the extent the law allowed, they should render more service than required for a testimony. Jesus would have done what He was teaching others to do.

Mt 8:10 When Jesus heard it, he marvelled, and said to them that followed, Verily I say unto you, I have not found so great faith, no, not in Israel. 11 And I say unto you, That many shall come from the east and west, and shall sit down with Abraham, and Isaac, and Jacob, in the kingdom of heaven. 12 But the children of the kingdom shall be cast out into outer darkness: there shall be weeping and gnashing of teeth.

Jesus had no problem with this man's position as a Centurion; but declares that men **like him** would be in heaven while others missed out. The Apostles unhesitatingly baptized soldiers, governors, centurions, Jailers, chamberlains, tax collectors, and other state officials and received them into communion. **Would your church?** Do you remember Cornelius, Zaccheus, Sergius Paulus, Erastus, the Philippian Jailor, the publicans, and the Ethiopian Eunuch? As soon as these men were baptized they were eligible for communion. There is no pacifism or "non-participation in government" taught in the Bible anywhere. It is simply not there – only imagined by Marcionites. The Apostles all believed and adhered to Moses' Law their whole life and saw it as the Word of God which was to be written on their hearts by the Holy Ghost. Pacifism is not taught in the Bible anywhere!

Did all the Anabaptists believe in the pacifist non-resistance and non-participation in government that the Mennonites hold today? Did they believe that you could not be a Christian following Christ and also be part of the sword bearing state? It is sure that some did in varying degrees, but the fact that they were under a state church system which tried to enforce their "gospel" with the sword really helped confuse the issue.

Balthasar Hubmaier and others with him believed Scripturally on this issue. If you read the writings of Menno Simons, you will find he doesn't believe in this modern Mennonite position. He believed magistrates could be Christians and saved without stepping down or becoming a pacifist. He was much against the Church government acting as a civil government as the state churches were doing; but he was much for having Christian magistrates who used the sword in a just and righteous way, according to Romans 13. The following quotes are from The Complete Writings Of Menno Simons published by Herald Press.

"Therefore, dear sirs, take heed; this is the task to which you are called: namely, to chastise and punish, in the true fear of God with fairness and Christian discretion, manifest criminals, such as thieves, murderers, Sodomites, adulterers, seducers, sorcerers, the violent, highwaymen, robbers, etc. Your task is to do justice between a man and his neighbor, to deliver the oppressed out of the hand of the oppressor... Such rulers were Moses, Joshua, David,..O highly renowned, noble lords, believe Christ's Word, fear God's wrath, love righteousness, do justice to widows and orphans....bow to the scepter of him who called you to this high service. Then shall your throne stand firm forever." Pg. 193

'Do not boast that you are mighty ones upon the earth, and have great power, but boast in this rather if so be you rule your land in the true fear of God with virtuous wisdom and Christian righteousness to the praise of the Lord...For if you are such kings, then you are not only kings according to the flesh, but also according to the spirit;" Pg. 206

"Be pleased, in godly fear, to ponder what it is that God requires of your Highnesses. It is that without any respect of persons you judge between a man and his neighbor, protect the wronged from him who does him wrong, even as the Lord declares, Execute judgment and justice, Assist, against the violent, him that is robbed, Abuse not the stranger, the widow, the orphan, Do violence to no man, and shed no innocent blood, so that your despised servants and unhappy subjects,

having escaped the mouth of the lion, may in your domain. ...serve the Lord in quietness and peace..." Pg. 526

"Dear sirs, seek God; fear God; serve God with all your might; do justice to widows, orphans, strangers, the sad, and the oppressed; wash your hands of blood; rule your lands with wisdom and peace. Train yourselves in thought, word, and deed upon the crucified Christ Jesus, follow his steps, and then, though your sins be red as blood they shall be white as snow, though they be red as crimson they shall be as wool!" Pg. 529

"Paul says, Rulers are not a terror to good works, but to evil...But if thou do that which is evil, be afraid; for he beareth not the sword in vain; for he is the minister of God, a revenger to execute wrath upon him that doeth evil...you may understand from these Scriptures that you are called of God and ordained to your offices to punish the transgressors and protect the good..." Pg. 550-551

"He that saith he abideth in Christ, he, whether he be emperor or king, ought himself also so to walk, even as he walked. I John 2:6. Beloved lords, this is God's Word. This is the prize and standard after which we should strive...We teach and direct you in the right way which you should walk if you wish to be saved...God is my witness that I desire nothing but that you all may actually be what you are acclaimed to be noble lords and Christian magistrates..." Pg. 553-554

It is obvious from the Scriptures and thoughts Menno employs that he didn't believe what modern pacifists believe. Menno, who was chosen as head bishop over the Anabaptist movement, should be a good representation of what they believed. Is there such a thing as a **Christian magistrate** who **follows Jesus**? Menno thought so.

Did you notice that Menno's understanding of "Do violence to no man" in John the Baptist's exhortation to the soldiers is simply "don't shed innocent blood or abuse your office" (Pg. 526)? Of course that is what John meant, for he clearly tells them afterward, **"Be content with your wages"**.   He would never tell them to take wages for being a soldier without intending to actually do what they were hired to do. *Being content with your wages* is **NOT** stepping down; but this was preparation for the Messiah, Jesus!

How is it that Mennonites today have veered so far from the common sense and Scriptural understanding of their forefathers?   Menno believed that when a magistrate rightly and fairly executed his office to protect the innocent and punish the wicked that he was "following Jesus"! He uses Old Testament examples to teach what New Testament state officers were to be like! He teaches that emperors and kings can walk as Jesus walked, even in their positions!   How different from modern day Mennonites; **BUT HE WAS RIGHT**.

Balthasar Hubmaier, an Anabaptist minister and martyr for the faith, strove to correct his Anabaptist brothers on this issue. Here he writes concerning Romans 13:1-7:

"...everyone should be subject to the government. Believing or unbelieving, we should be obedient and subject to it. He points out the reason. For there is no government which does not come from God. Therefore obedience consists in all that which is not against God, for God has not ordered the government against himself. Now if the government wants to punish the evil ones-as it should for the sake of their soul's salvation-and is yet not strong enough to deal with the evil ones, then it is now to command its subjects through bells and various alarm signals, letters, or through other summons. Subjects are obligated for the sake of the salvation of their souls to sustain and help their superiors so that the evil ones are annihilated and rooted out according to the will of God. Nevertheless, subjects should first test well the spirit of their

governments, as to whether they are not moved and compelled more out of arrogance, rather than out of love of the common good and territorial peace. For that would not be to use the sword according to the order of God. However, if you recognize that the government punishes the evil only so that the righteous remain at rest and unharmed, then help, counsel, and sustain it, as often and as much as you are commanded. Thereby, you fulfill the order of God and do his work and not a human work. However, if a government is childish or foolish, yea, perchance it is not competent at all to reign, then you may escape from it legitimately and accept another, if it is good. For on account of an evil government God has often punished an entire land. If the seeking of another cannot be done lawfully and peacefully, and not also without great damage and rebellion, then one must endure it, as the one which God has given us in his wrath, and as if he desires to chastise us on account of our sins, as those who deserve no better.

Whoever now does not want to help the government save widows, orphans, and other oppressed ones, as well as to punish vandals and tyrants, resists the order of God and will receive a judgment from him, for he acts against the mandate and order of God, who wants the righteous to be protected and the evil punished. However, if you are obedient you should truly know that you are obedient not to the government or to people but to God himself, and you have become a special servant of God just as the government itself also is nothing other than a servant of God.

However, Paul testifies openly that the government has the power and authority to kill the evil when he says: "The authority does not bear the sword in vain." If now the government did not have the authority to kill, why should the sword then hang at its side? It would then bear it in vain, which Paul cannot bear. He also explicitly adds that the authority is the servant of God. Where are now those who say a Christian cannot use the sword? For if a Christian could not be a servant of God, could not fulfill the mandate of God *without sinning, then God would not be good. He would have made an order which a Christian could not fulfill without sin. That is blasphemy.*

Accordingly I counsel you faithfully, dear brothers, return and repent. You have stumbled badly and produced much trash everywhere against God and against brotherly love under the appearance of spirituality and the pretense of humility. God knows whom I mean." Balthasar Hubmaier, pgs. 520,521.

Here, Balthasar is writing to correct other Anabaptists. He also says that **if** the judge is righteous to condemn the criminal to death, then the executioner is no less righteous to fulfill the order of the judge. He points out faithful men like Benaiah, in the Old Testament, who fulfilled the orders of King Solomon. Then he adds:

"Therefore the judges, governments, and executors of justice are called servants of God in the Scripture and not murderers, Rom. 13:4. God judges, sentences, and kills through them, and not they themselves. From this it follows that those who do not want to kill the evildoer but let them live, are acting and sinning against the commandment: "You should not kill." For whoever does not protect the righteous kills him and is guilty of his death as much as the one who does not feed the hungry."

Hear the response of a modern Anabaptist pacifist, and you will understand why they *cannot see the truth.*

"My own views of how the exact details of nonresistance should look in our daily lives are open to be influenced, but the basic principles are not. For me to accept the belief in Just War would require such a huge leap in logic that I would basically need to embrace a different Jesus, an altogether different gospel. I have no interest in that and am willing to engage in the discussion only as an attempt to help others better understand.

On subjects like these, I make no claims to open- mindedness. Because of that, we need to be careful to limit our discussions of this nature and not allow them to become emotionally charged. We need to see these as opportunities to contend for the faith, but not imagine that we ourselves should be coming into the discussion with a willingness to be persuaded. I am not." A.S.

This subject is dealt with more thoroughly in our book, "RESIST NOT EVIL??"

Chapter Ten
Love Your Enemies

*Mt 5:43 Ye have heard that it hath been said, Thou shalt love thy neighbour, and hate thine enemy. 44 But I say unto you, **Love your enemies**, bless them that curse you, do good to them that hate you, and pray for them which despitefully use you, and persecute you; 45 That ye may be the children of your Father which is in heaven: for he maketh his sun to rise on the evil and on the good, and sendeth rain on the just and on the unjust. 46 For if ye love them which love you, what reward have ye? do not even the publicans the same? 47 And if ye salute your brethren only, what do ye more than others? do not even the publicans so? 48 **Be ye therefore perfect, even as your Father which is in heaven is perfect.***

Being **perfect,** in this context, means living by an unselfish love like God's divine nature. Living not for selfish motives; but according to justice, righteousness, and mercy; which are all summed up in one word, **Love**. God is LOVE and all His laws and motives are from this divine benevolence. We are to live by this same principle, which is what the Law of God is trying to accomplish in our lives. The same preacher who said **love your enemies** above also said, *"Therefore all things whatsoever ye would that men should do to you, do ye even so to them: **for this is the law and the prophets".*** Yes, and Jesus also said that the whole law of God hung from the two greatest commandments: *"Thou shalt love the Lord thy*

God with all thy heart, and with all thy soul, and with all thy mind." and, *"Thou shalt love thy neighbour as thyself."*

Now, if God's Law is LOVE, God's nature is Love, God's example is Love; and we are to be perfect *even as He is perfect*; then we are to define and practice Love according to God's Law and example. If we are supposed to love like God loves, then we are to love our enemies in the context that God loves His enemies – this is clearly stated when Jesus said, *"Be ye therefore perfect, even as your Father which is in heaven is perfect."* Marcionite interpreters choke at this point, because they don't want us being perfect as Jehovah was perfect, and loving as Jehovah's Law teaches love; but they want us to love with some love they dream up where you put your enemies at the highest level and sacrifice your life and family to them; which is something neither Jehovah nor Jesus ever intended. There is a major difference in Governmental obligation to destroy the life threatening enemies of the innocent people in order to preserve society in righteousness; and the way individuals are to conduct their interpersonal relationships with neighbors who may hate them, be an enemy to them, but not be threatening their life. Jesus was teaching individuals how to deal with their personal enemy in the home-town, at work, at school, or that neighbor that didn't like them.

Did the Law of God teach the Jews to hate their enemies?

The Jews were indeed abusing God's Laws for carnal selfish retaliation and unkindness toward those they didn't like.

Adam Clarke: "The Jews thought themselves authorized to kill any Jew who apostatized; and, though they could not do injury to the Gentiles, in whose country they sojourned, yet they were bound to suffer them to perish, if they saw them in danger of death. Hear their own words: "A Jew sees a Gentile fall into the sea, let him by no means lift him out; for it is written, Thou shalt not rise up against the blood of thy neighbour:-but this is not thy neighbour." Maimon. This shows that by neighbour they understood a Jew; one who was of the same blood and religion with themselves."

God had told them not to make a league with any of the nations of Canaan, but destroy them. This was an act of God's judicial decree and was meant for the government to fulfill, not a command for personal hate; and did not include all non-Jews. God had commanded them to keep themselves separate from sinners – This He also commands us. This is not hate of the person, but hate of their sinful way; and while we are trying to reach them for God, we are thus avoiding the same pitfalls in our own life. We cannot love enemies to the sacrifice of pleasing God!

2Co 6:14 Be ye not unequally yoked together with unbelievers: for what fellowship hath righteousness with unrighteousness? and what communion hath light with darkness? 15 And what concord hath Christ with Belial? or what part hath he that believeth with an infidel? 16 And what agreement hath the temple of God with idols? for ye are the temple of the living God; as God hath said, I will dwell in them, and walk in them; and I will be their God, and they shall be my people. 17 Wherefore come out from among them, and be ye separate, saith the Lord, and touch not the unclean thing; and I will receive you, 18 And will be a Father unto you, and ye shall be my sons and daughters, saith the Lord Almighty. Having therefore these promises, dearly beloved, let us cleanse ourselves from all filthiness of the flesh and spirit, perfecting holiness in the fear of God.

Our *perfect* Father in heaven demands we live separated lives and obey His laws of holiness while we are, "loving our enemies". There are **priorities** in all Love and we learn these priorities by studying God's Laws, Ways, and example. If we are to be *perfect as He is,* then we are to follow His examples and commands just as Jesus taught us to do. Jesus and the Apostles warned against wicked people with terms that could be abused by carnal men too.

Mt 7:6 *Give not that which is holy unto the dogs, neither cast ye your pearls before swine, lest they trample them under their feet, and turn again and rend you.*

Mk 7:27 *But Jesus said unto her, Let the children first be filled: for it is not meet to take the children's bread, and to cast it unto the dogs.*

1Co 5:13 *...therefore put away from among yourselves that wicked person.*

Php 3:2 *Beware of dogs, beware of evil workers, beware of the concision.*

Ga 5:12 *I would they were even cut off which trouble you.*

2Jo 1:10 *If there come any unto you, and bring not this doctrine, receive him not into your house, neither bid him God speed:11 For he that biddeth him God speed is partaker of his evil deeds.*

Does this justify a haughty, hateful spirit?? Of course it doesn't. God expected the nation of Israel to be a light to the World and keep themselves clean; but not to be hateful to the lost or heathen man. This is the same ethic we are to observe. There is a difference between a policy of separation or national security and a policy of seeking to evangelize the heathen – Israel as a nation needed all three; and so do we. Had they obeyed God's

Laws they would have been representing God and demonstrating HIS WAYS to the world around them; instead, God says they profaned His name among the heathen (Ezekiel 36). They actually "loved" their enemies in a carnal way instead of a spiritual way. They worshipped with them and copied them, but didn't keep separate and evangelize them.

Did the O.T. teach the principle of loving our fellow man, even when he was an enemy to us? Yes, God hasn't changed, evolved, or improved. **How else could love fulfill the law? How else could Jesus say that the "golden rule" or "royal law" was the Law and the prophets? (Mt 7:12)**

Ex 23:4 If thou meet thine enemy's ox or his ass going astray, thou shalt surely bring it back to him again.

Ex 23:5 If thou see the ass of him that hateth thee lying under his burden, and wouldest forbear to help him, thou shalt surely help with him.

Le 19:18 Thou shalt not avenge, nor bear any grudge against the children of thy people, but thou shalt love thy neighbour as thyself: I am the LORD.

Le 19:34 But the stranger that dwelleth with you shall be unto you as one born among you, and thou shalt love him as thyself; for ye were strangers in the land of Egypt: I am the LORD your God.

De 10:17 For the LORD your God is God of gods, and Lord of lords, a great God, a mighty, and a terrible, which regardeth not persons, nor taketh reward: 18 He doth execute the judgment of the fatherless and widow, and loveth the stranger, in giving him food and raiment. 19 Love ye therefore the stranger: for ye were strangers in the land of Egypt.

De 23:7 *Thou shalt not abhor an Edomite; for he is thy brother: thou shalt not abhor an Egyptian; because thou wast a stranger in his land*

Pr 24:17, 18 *Rejoice not when thine enemy falleth, and let not thine heart be glad when he stumbleth: lest the LORD see it, and it displease him, and he turn away his wrath from him.*

Pr 25:21, 22 *If thine enemy be hungry, give him bread to eat; and if he be thirsty, give him water to drink: for thou shalt heap coals of fire upon his head, and the LORD shall reward thee.*

Ps 35 *"Plead my cause, O LORD, with them that strive with me: fight against them that fight against me...for without cause have they hid for me their net in a pit, which without cause they have digged for my soul...False witnesses did rise up; they laid to my charge things I knew not. They rewarded me evil for good to the spoiling of my soul. But as for me, when they were sick, my clothing was sack-cloth: I humbled my soul with fasting; and my prayer returned into mine own bosom. I behaved myself as though he had been my friend or brother: I bowed down heavily, as one that mourneth for his mother. But in mine adversity they rejoiced, and gathered themselves together: yea, the abjects gathered themselves together against me, and I knew it not; they did tear me, and ceased not...Lord, how long wilt thou look on? rescue my soul from their destructions...Let not them that are mine enemies wrongfully rejoice over me- For they speak not peace: but they devise deceitful matters against them that are quiet in the land...This thou hast seen, O LORD: keep not silence: O Lord, be not far from me...*

Ps. 69:1-4 *Save me, O God; for the waters are come in unto my soul...I am weary of my crying: my throat is dried: mine eyes fail while I wait for my God. They that hate me without a cause are more than the hairs of mine head: they that would destroy me, being mine enemies wrongfully, are mighty:* **then I restored that which I took not away.**

Have you ever noticed that when the apostle Paul is teaching these principles in Romans 12 that **he quotes the Old Testament as his authority on the subject?** Listen! This can *only* mean Paul is speaking in the *same context* and *same spirit* as the Old Testament Scriptures! Did Paul understand Jesus as teaching a different ethic? If he did he would not be quoting the OT to teach the "new" ethic!

Ro 12:19 Dearly beloved, avenge not yourselves, but rather give place unto wrath: <u>for it is written</u>, Vengeance is mine; I will repay, saith the Lord. 20 Therefore if thine enemy hunger, feed him; if he thirst, give him drink: for in so doing thou shalt heap coals of fire on his head.

"For it is written" produces the reason for Paul's teaching – it was commanded and taught in the Scriptures already! The Jews were to love the nations around them and testify the truth of God for the salvation of their souls. Christians are to love other people in general, and strive to bring them to the truth. This is the teaching Jesus gives; not that we should allow a criminal intruder to molest our wife and daughter just because we are to "love our enemies". This is foolishness, and proves the foolish extremes that men go to when they ignore solid Bible principles for interpreting Jesus' words. They sacrifice all logic and common sense in their ditch effort to defend their Marcionite ism. What a shame!

***God so loved the world*...while we were enemies!** (Romans 5:10, Col 1:21) This means He pitied our blindness and certain destruction; and He made a way for us to escape; but he does not compromise right or capitulate to evil. God has priorities in His love, and so must we. *Loving our enemies* doesn't demand they be *first priority* over loving God, our family, neighbors, truth, and righteousness. We must "wish for their salvation" like God does; but Jesus wept over Jerusalem while condemning them to desolation! Jesus loved the people He scourged out of the temple – didn't He? Was He "resisting evil"? We must resist evil every day in numerous ways to be right with God and defend the faith; but Jesus was only using these words in a specific context which we stated earlier.

In the Laws of God, a rapist, murderer, and similar crimes deserved the death penalty; so for us to love with God's love and "be partakers of the divine nature" (2Pe1:4), we must have the same moral opinion of one who is trying to commit such a crime. Of course we can only act upon this if we have the jurisdiction to do so. Jesus was once asked to judge in an inheritance dispute between two brothers; but He declined, saying, *"Who made me a judge or a divider over you?"(Lu 12:14)*. Jesus, no doubt, agreed with the judgment God would give in this matter; but had not the jurisdiction to enforce it. People don't just appoint themselves as judge; but must be appointed according to the law. When we do have jurisdiction and lawful obligation, then we are to perform the judgment of God as our duty before Him. This is God's will clearly stated in His inspired Word. The following principle would apply to murder, rape, or any injustice against an innocent victim. If you are aware of it, then you have jurisdiction and moral obligation to deliver the victim.

Pr 24:11 If thou forbear to deliver them that are drawn unto death, and those that are ready to be slain; 12 If thou sayest, Behold, we knew it not; doth not he that pondereth the heart consider it? and he that keepeth thy soul, doth not he know it? and shall not he render to every man according to his works?

148

There is no contradiction in this and what Paul quoted from the SAME book in Romans 12:19-20. God expects us to use the brain He gave us and figure it out, not charge Him with changing his mind or sending His Son to correct His inspired laws!

Can you love, while defending yourself or keeping peace and order? Yes, it is the same principle as God loving the world and yet judging it; Jesus loving the churches, yet removing their *candlestick* if they don't repent; as a parent loving the child they are spanking, the goodman of the house defending his beloved household against the criminal intruder; the King loving his people while he upholds law and order in his kingdom; and God loving the world while he sends a flood or burns up Sodom. What if you are the Sheriff and your son becomes a criminal? You love your son, but you must do your duty and bring him to justice. What if you are the judge and your son commits murder? You love your son, but you must do your duty. God loves truth, righteousness, and the common good of all more than a rebellious individual; and we must love with God's priorities. God's love cannot compromise righteousness or it ceases to be love. God cannot love a rebel man over the righteous man without showing ungodly partiality and respect of persons. The same applies to a Christian loving his enemy, yet doing his duty in the realm of his jurisdiction.

"But, you will send the person to hell!" cries the pacifist. NO, I am obeying God and sending them to God if necessary; and He can take it from there. I don't need to disobey God **or** protect Him from making a bad decision. Where did Ananias and Sapphira go? Where do excommunicated people go?

Did Jesus correct Moses and the Law of God in The Sermon On The Mount? No! Impossible! Of course He didn't. He cleared the Law of misinterpretations and man's corruptions. Jesus consistently sided with Moses against the apostate Jews and consistently upheld the Scriptures as inspired, valid, and necessary.

*Jn 5:37 And the Father himself, which hath sent me, hath borne witness of me. Ye have neither heard his voice at any time, nor seen his shape. 38 **And ye have not his word abiding in you**: for whom he hath sent, him ye believe not.*

(If you had the Old Testament in your heart and mind, you would immediately recognize and receive the Messiah)

*39 **Search the scriptures**; for in them ye think ye have eternal life: and they are they which testify of me...*

*...46 For **had ye believed Moses, ye would have believed me**: for **he wrote of me**. 47 But **if ye believe not his writings, how shall ye believe my words?***

If you would search the Scriptures, especially Moses' writings, and believe them, you would also receive and believe Jesus' words – can there then be any contradiction? If we teach that Jesus corrected Moses, then those who had a problem with Moses would be in a *better* frame of mind to receive Jesus?? **Could anyone seriously accept such a belief?**

On one hand modern Mennonites claim that Jesus took us to a higher and more strict morality (in not allowing divorce and remarriage for any reason and condemning remarried people as adulterers), yet on the other hand they say Jesus taught us to love and forgive sinners (in not condemning the woman taken in adultery)? First they say that the law was not loving, and

Jesus taught us to love more and not condemn the adulteress; then they say the Law was more compromising with divorce and remarriage, and Jesus raised the bar of morality to a stricter level -- which is it?? They say the Jews could divorce because they were under God's grace; but now God expects more from Christians – then they turn around and say the Jews were under the Law and we are under Grace so we don't have to obey the Law. Talk about confusion!! God says He would write His laws -- not new and different laws -- in our hearts as the foundation of the New Covenant. How sad they will not accept the obvious truth of God's Word that the only NEW thing said about the New Covenant was God's better method of putting His Laws in our hearts and minds!

Mt 4:1 *Then was Jesus led up of the Spirit into the wilderness to be tempted of the devil. 2 And when he had fasted forty days and forty nights, he was afterward an hungred. 3 And when the tempter came to him, he said, If thou be the Son of God, command that these stones be made bread. 4 But he answered and said, It is written, Man shall not live by bread alone, but* **by every word that proceedeth out of the mouth of God.**

How could we live by every word that proceedeth out of the mouth of God if Jesus corrects and contradicts them by changing what the Law gave as a remedy to "adultery"; by saying what the Law commanded "cometh of evil"; and by forbidding much that the Law expected of us? Can God speak contradicting words out of His mouth? How do we live by that? Jesus is telling the devil that *all* the OT Scriptures came from **God's mouth**.

Mt 22:29 *Jesus answered and said unto them,* **Ye do err, not knowing the scriptures,** *nor the power of God.*

This is the problem with Marcionite/Mennonites. They are sadly ignorant of the OT scriptures. Jesus held the Scriptures up as the Word of an unchanging God just as the prophets said He would do.

Isa 42:21 The LORD is well pleased for his righteousness' sake; he will magnify the law, and make it honourable.

Jn 10:35 ... the scripture cannot be broken;

Isa. 40:6 The voice said, Cry. And he said, What shall I cry? All flesh is grass, and all the goodliness thereof is as the flower of the field:7 The grass withereth, the flower fadeth: because the spirit of the LORD bloweth upon it: surely the people is grass.8 The grass withereth, the flower fadeth: **but the word of our God shall stand for ever.**

Compare this with Peter quoting the above passage from Isaiah:

1Pe 1:25 But the word of the Lord endureth for ever. **And this is the word which by the gospel is preached unto you.**

Many will find this all hard to accept in the light of their indoctrination. *"HOW CAN THIS BE? How can most all our churches be wrong on such important issues? Our parents and grandparents have suffered, lived and died for the Mennonite way; how can we change it?"* Every Roman Catholic, Jew, or person from any other major religion ever converted had these questions; and I had them when I left the Baptist Denomination where my *heritage* was. **Are you willing to love God's Word and believe it over your "way" or "ism"?**

I know you are full of questions. Don't fall for the canned answers you will hear. Some will say, "O, they have a flat Bible", trying to say that we don't place the

New Covenant above the Old, but put it on the same plain; but they fail to realize we **do** have a "flat" God who never changes from one covenant to the other. We have never said we are under the Old Covenant, we are just documenting that we are under **the same God**, with **the same morals**. Unless you wish to be a Marcionite, you must interpret Jesus' teaching as consistent with all God's inspired Word whether OT or NT. You must see Jesus as the one who inspired Moses, and you must see Him as the true interpreter and defender of God's Law.

Here is the Bible Literacy Test again:

1. In our New Testament in many Bibles there are words printed in Black and words printed in Red, which ones did Jesus author?

Answer: Jesus didn't write any of them, but He authored ALL of them.

2. We have an Old Testament and New Testament in our English Bible, which represents the teachings of Jesus?

Answer: It all represents the teachings of Jesus who is the WORD OF GOD from Genesis to Revelation.

If this is not your belief, then you have most likely been a victim of Marcionite Heresy. Do you feel that what Moses and the Apostle's wrote is as important as what Jesus wrote? Now remember: Jesus didn't write anything; but authored all that Moses and the Apostle's wrote. You say, "I will just stick by the red letters that were Jesus' words". If you cannot believe that the Apostles' writings are the Word of God, then how do you know you even have Jesus' Words?? It is the Apostles who have given us Jesus' Words. Marcionism is a dangerous virus that sucks the truth out of unlearned people. Don't allow yourself to be a victim.

Chapter Eleven
What is sin?

I Jn 3:4 Whosoever committeth sin transgresseth also the law: for <u>sin is the transgression of the law</u>. 5 And ye know that he was manifested to take away our sins (transgressions of the Law); and in him is no sin (transgression of the Law).   A.D. 95

Sin is any violation of the moral Law of God and whatever covenant conditions we are under. Rebellion or intentional transgression is called **willful** or **presumptuous** sin.   Unintentional or unknown transgression is called **ignorant** sin (Numbers 15 compare Hebrews 10:26-28)

Jas 4:17 Therefore to him that <u>knoweth to do good,</u> and doeth it not, to <u>him it is sin</u>.

Ro 1:18 For the wrath of God is revealed from heaven against all ungodliness and unrighteousness of men, <u>who hold the truth in unrighteousness;</u>

In **Romans 1:18** we find that God's wrath is revealed from heaven against all **ungodliness** and **unrighteousness** of men who *hold the truth*, but *continue in unrighteousness*.   The word for ungodliness means "improper worship" – Not loving God with all our heart and thus not fulfilling the first and greatest commandment.   The word unrighteousness means "injustice"; and refers to the second commandment being broken – not loving your neighbor as yourself.   God's wrath will be poured out in judgment based on God's

Moral Law being broken by people "who knew better" – they sinned against the light and knowledge of God's moral ways that they had and didn't repent or seek reconciliation as God commanded. Listen to Romans 2:1-16:

Ro 2:1 Therefore thou art inexcusable, O man, whosoever thou art that judgest: for wherein thou judgest another, thou condemnest thyself; for thou that judgest doest the same things.

The Apostle had just concluded in the last chapter that mankind, *"...**knowing the judgment of God**, that they which commit such things are worthy of death, not only do the same, but have pleasure in them that do them."* When men make judgments on other's actions it reveals their understanding of right and wrong; and their *judging* tells God they *understand* something about His moral law. This only condemns them when they are not striving to obey God's moral laws themselves, nor separating from others who don't.

Ro 2:2 But we are sure that the judgment of God is according to truth against them which commit such things. 3 And thinkest thou this, O man, that judgest them which do such things, and doest the same, that thou shalt escape the judgment of God? 4 Or despisest thou the riches of his goodness and forbearance and longsuffering; not knowing that the goodness of God leadeth thee to repentance? 5 But after thy hardness and impenitent heart treasurest up unto thyself wrath against the day of wrath and revelation of the righteous judgment of God; 6 Who will render to every man according to his deeds:7 To them who by patient continuance in well doing seek for glory and honour and immortality, eternal life:

This is the salvation of the believers

2:8 *But unto them that are contentious, and do not obey the truth, but obey unrighteousness...*

This is the unbeliever, and they will get:

*...**indignation and wrath,** 9 **Tribulation and anguish,** upon every soul of man that doeth evil, of the Jew first, and also of the Gentile; 10 But glory, honour, and peace, to every man that worketh good, to the Jew first, and also to the Gentile: 11 For there is no respect of persons with God. 12 For as many as have **sinned without law** shall also perish without law: and as many as have **sinned in the law** shall be judged by the law; 13 (For not the hearers of the law are just before God, but the doers of the law shall be justified. 14 For when the Gentiles, <u>which have not the law, do by nature the things contained in the law, these, having not the law, are a law unto themselves:</u> 15 Which shew the work of the law written in their hearts, their <u>conscience also bearing witness, and their thoughts the mean while accusing or else excusing one another;</u>) 16 In the day when God shall judge the secrets of men by Jesus Christ according to my gospel.*

Every man has a conscience based on God's Moral Law. Even in his fallen state his moral conscience is not totally destroyed, and he will be judged for every violation of knowledge he possessed or <u>could have possessed.</u>

Ro 1:18 *For the wrath of God is revealed from heaven against all ungodliness and unrighteousness of men, who <u>hold the truth in unrighteousness</u>; 19 Because that which <u>may be known of God</u> is manifest in them; for God hath shewed it unto them. 20 For the invisible things of him from the creation of the world are clearly seen, being understood by the things that are made, even his eternal power and Godhead; so that they are without excuse:...*

Vs 28 *And even as <u>they did not like to retain God in their knowledge,</u> God gave them over to a reprobate mind, to do those things which are not convenient;*

Adam Clarke: *They did not like to retain God]* "It would, perhaps, be more literal to translate ouk edokimasan, THEY DID NOT SEARCH to retain God in their knowledge. They did not examine the evidences before them (Ro 1:19,20) of his being and attributes; therefore God gave them over to a REPROBATE mind, eiv adokimon noun, to an UNSEARCHING or undiscerning mind; for it is the <u>same word in both places</u>. They did not reflect on the proofs they had of the Divine nature, and God abandoned them to the operations of a mind incapable of reflection. How men of such powers and learning, as many of the Greek and Roman philosophers and poets really were, could reason so inconsecutively concerning things moral and Divine is truly astonishing. But here we see the hand of a just and avenging God; they abused their powers, and God deprived them of the right use of these powers."

To be "willingly ignorant" (2 Pet.3:5) is no protection against just judgment. If you fail to investigate and justly consider all the evidence, then you are deliberately ignorant, and thus guilty of rejecting truth.

God's Moral Law will be the basis for all judgment on that great Day of Judgment. God's judgment is based on your knowledge, your ability, your opportunities, and your potential, i.e. **what you did with what you had.**

The "work of the law written on their hearts" (Rom. 2:15) is referring to the striving of God's Spirit with man, just like it says He did before Noah's flood (Gen. 6:3); and the remnant of the "image of God" in which man was created. It's not the same as God writing his law in the hearts of New Covenant believers (Heb. 8:10), though it is similar. New Covenant believers have the indwelling Holy Spirit teaching them (John 14:17-26); but other men simply have God's Spirit convicting them from without (John 16:8).

Adam and Eve were created in the image of God; they walked with God; and they were in perfect harmony with God. This means God's Law was in their hearts in the fullest degree. Their very nature was God's Law which is **LOVE**. Adam and Eve knew nothing but LOVE, and this was their very sentiments – The divine nature within them. Adam and Eve were highly intelligent and knew much of GOOD; but they knew nothing of EVIL, for it did not exist in their experience, knowledge, or their world. When they ate the tree of the knowledge of good AND evil, the emphasis was on **AND EVIL.** They now were confronted with the concepts and reality of selfishness and pride which were non-existent in their perfect world of **LOVE**. Though they fell, they didn't completely lose the image of God, but it was marred and confused; and this fallen state was passed to their children who then either cultivated it or degenerated further in varying degrees. Because of this "image of God" which still remains within us in varying degrees, God will judge all men by what they did with what they knew; and this will be perfectly just.

The fall was due to unbelief in the God of LOVE; and now God calls man to reconcile with Him on these terms: Repentance from the ways of selfishness and humble submission to God's Law of Love. This requires man to pursue a course of continued cultivation of the divine nature of love by embracing God's Law of Love and disciplining ourselves to act accordingly. This is "walking in the Light" and "walking by Faith".

Ro 14:23 *...for whatsoever is not of faith is sin.*

Ro 3:31 Do we then make void the law through faith? God forbid: yea, we establish the law.

Faith is doing what you believe pleases God according to His Law of Love. Jesus was God's Word made flesh, and so faith in Christ is not only trusting in His sacrifice and priesthood to cleanse us from sin; but also trusting in His example and teaching to show us God's will and ways. Faith is believing God's Word and God's Son, and properly relating to Him as Lord of the universe. When you knowingly violate this, you are bringing judgment upon yourself. Sin is often spoken of long before Sinai, because sin is the trespass of God's Eternal Moral Law, which pre-dates and post-dates Moses' Law; but is expressed to a large degree in Moses' Law.

1Jn 3:4 Whosoever committeth sin transgresseth also the law: for <u>sin is the transgression of the law</u>. 5 And ye know that he was manifested to take away our sins (transgressions of the Law); and in him is no sin (transgression of the Law).

This verse was written around A.D. 95. Sin has to do with the violation of God's Law from whatever source you have received it – either from Moses, a prophet, John the Baptist, the Lord Jesus, an apostle, or your God given conscience. The Scriptures which manifest God's moral judgments and opinions are to us a law, and to disobey the Scriptural revelation of God's will and way is SIN. We cannot reconcile and live in heaven with God until we are re-trained in God's Law of Love.

Since "iniquity" is from "anomia" "without law" or "lawless", we need to find out what laws we are to obey – because Jesus hates "anomia". See this word in the following verses:

Mt 7:21 Not every one that saith unto me, Lord, Lord, shall enter into the kingdom of heaven; <u>but he that doeth the will of my Father which is in heaven.</u>   22 Many will say to me in that day, Lord, Lord, have we not prophesied in thy name? and in thy name have cast out devils? and in thy name done many wonderful works? 23 And then will I profess unto them, I never knew you: depart from me, ye that work **iniquity (lawlessness)**.

Mt 13:41 The Son of man shall send forth his angels, and they shall gather out of his kingdom all things that offend, and them which do **iniquity** (lawlessness);

Tit 2:14 Who gave himself for us, that he might redeem us from all **iniquity (lawlessness)**, and purify unto himself a peculiar people, zealous of good works.

Heb 1:9 Thou [Jesus] hast loved righteousness, and hated **iniquity (lawlessness)**;

If the doctrine you've been taught, tells you that you don't have to obey the Law of God, and thus leads you to a "law-less" faith, then it is not of Christ. As long as sin is punished by God, the moral laws of God are still obligatory.   Jesus is a King with a Kingdom, and His Kingdom has a Law – it is the eternal Moral Law of God. If you are to live in His Kingdom, you must love and obey God's Law.   The moral laws given through Moses are inspired applications of the eternal Moral Law of God. They are still the "will of the Father" that you must obey, or you will be found "lawless" and cast out.

Chapter Twelve
Moral, Civil, & Ceremonial

There is a definite difference between moral Laws and ceremonial laws. The Bible makes this distinction very plain. The Moral Law is eternal and the Ceremonial Law is temporal and specifically related to the covenant in which it was given. The ceremonies God gave were object lessons about God's plan of salvation. They were merely shadows of eternal principles. They taught that God's relationship with man required more than submission to the moral laws; it also required atonement for man's sins. The Moral Law cannot cease to be obligatory upon moral creatures; but the Ceremonial Law is only obligatory when part of God's covenant arrangement. The Moral Law is God's view of morality for eternity; but the ceremonial laws given to man (including Moses' Law) are types and shadows pointing to the heavenly realities that they illustrate.

Civil Laws are based on moral principles, but deal with social regulations which can change with the times and circumstances. They are the present applications of eternal moral principles to *today's* situation in this culture, climate, etc. Something may not be "morally wrong", but due to the "present circumstances" it is not wise or expedient; therefore a wise ruler will make an ordinance against it. That ordinance may not be relevant or wise in a different country with different circumstances. We will illustrate this later.

Many misunderstand the distinctions between different types of Laws. In Moses' Law we have *Civil Law, Ceremonial Law,* and *Moral law.* All the laws are based on moral principles; but not all the laws are moral in NATURE. Ceremonial Laws are Ceremonial in **nature.** Yes, it is always immoral to disobey God in any command, whether moral or ceremonial; but we are speaking of the **nature** of the Law. Ceremonial Laws have to do with things being holy by **appointment** and not by **nature**. Baptism is a ceremonial law in the New Covenant; but getting wet is not holy by **nature**, but only by **God's appointment.** The Sabbath was just another day until it was made holy by appointment. God can change the sanctity of one day to another day by appointing another day to be holy without changing His **moral** judgment in the slightest. Days are not holy by nature, but only by appointment. God cannot, however, change His mind about adultery, fornication, false witness, murder, covetousness, etc. without changing His MORALS.

Some things are holy because they are made so by "setting them apart" unto a dedicated purpose, like the show bread, priest's garments, temple furniture, etc. The words "hallowed" and "sanctified" refer to **common** things being **made holy** by cleansing and dedication to the service of God – by appointment. Other things are holy because they are **necessary components** of **God's Love**. Ceremonial holiness can change; but God's Love cannot. God can replace the *Temple Service* with the *Church Service*; but He cannot change "thou shalt not commit adultery" into "adultery is now righteous". The lost Gentile didn't know by nature about Jewish sanitation and ceremonial cleanliness; but he had a conscience that murder, rape, adultery, cheating, false witness, and stealing were wrong from the remnants of God's image of love still residing in his heart – Ro 2:14.

The civil laws of God were applications of God's love to social order, conservation, treatment of animals, etc. **De 25:4** *"Thou shalt not muzzle the ox when he treadeth out the corn."* is a civil ordinance – not ceremonial law; but based on a moral principle. Listen to what Paul says about this.

1Co 9:6 Or I only and Barnabas, have not we power to forbear working? 7 Who goeth a warfare any time at his own charges? who planteth a vineyard, and eateth not of the fruit thereof? or who feedeth a flock, and eateth not of the milk of the flock? 8 Say I these things as a man? or saith not the law the same also? 9 For it is written in the law of Moses, Thou shalt not muzzle the mouth of the ox that treadeth out the corn. **Doth God take care for oxen? 10 Or saith he it altogether for our sakes? For our sakes, no doubt, this is written:** *that he that ploweth should plow in hope; and that he that thresheth in hope should be partaker of his hope.*

Here we see that this civil law had a moral principle to teach for mankind, and was not in the same category as *rape, murder,* or *adultery,* which are strictly moral matters which can never be right. When we speak of moral or ceremonial laws, we are speaking of the NATURE of the law, not whether it is immoral to disobey God. Paul says that circumcision was only holy by appointment and was *nothing* apart from that appointment, but as we said earlier, it represented an eternal moral principle of the circumcision of the heart. It was only holy by appointment.

1Co 7:19 Circumcision is nothing, and uncircumcision is nothing, but the keeping of the commandments of God.

This is why it could be changed with the making of a new covenant! It was not a necessary component of God's Love, but only symbolic of a principle as all ceremonial laws are. Ceremonial laws can change with the changing of the covenant; but moral laws can never change because they are necessary aspects of God's Love in either our **relationship with God** or our **relationships with man** – *ungodliness* and *unrighteousness* as used in Romans 1:18.

Ro 1:18 For the wrath of God is revealed from heaven against all ungodliness and unrighteousness of men, who hold the truth in unrighteousness;

Most ceremonial laws of the Old Testament found their fulfillment in the life, death, resurrection, and priestly ministry of Jesus Christ. I say "most" because the fall feasts are typical of Christ's second coming, and have not been fulfilled. The ceremonial sacrifices God gave were man's way of believing in Christ's atonement before Christ even came. The gospel was preached through the animal sacrifices, and as men reverently observed the ceremonial law, they were believing in God's salvation by grace.

It is important to understand that God's relationship with fallen mankind has always been in the form of covenants. These covenants had two basic parts:

1. Man's willingness to live by God's moral standards; and

2. God given rituals or ceremonies to teach about God's conditional salvation through blood atonement.

God could not allow man to think that present submission to God's moral standards was sufficient to maintain a relationship with God, because man had fallen, and could not redeem himself or atone for his own past sin. Sins could not just be forgotten or "brushed under the rug"; but had to lawfully be dealt with. God started teaching man immediately after the fall that two things were necessary for man to have a covenant relationship and thus reconcile with God:

1. Repentance and submission to God's moral laws, and ...
2. A blood atonement.

God taught this principle through what we call ceremonial law or ritual law. This also predates Moses. The Mosaic Covenant was a covenant arrangement with the nation of Israel for a certain time period until Christ came. God had been relating with man on similar principles from the time Adam and Eve were clothed with skins of a slain animal. Moses' Law incorporated and codified these older covenant concepts.

We find that Cain and Abel knew about ritual obligations, and it was Cain's trespass against this arrangement that caused his offering to be rejected. God had taught them to bring an animal sacrifice for blood atonement. This means they also understood what SIN was and knew when God's Ways had been trespassed. God tells Cain that if he had **done well**, he would have **been accepted**, but since he did not do well, a sin offering was at the door, and he could avail himself of it to repent and reconcile with God. Obviously Cain knew what to do.

Ge 4:7 If thou doest well, shalt thou not be accepted? and if thou doest not well, sin **[a sin offering]** *lieth at the door.*

Noah was instructed to take more clean animals on the Ark than unclean animals. This was partly due to animal sacrifices which we find them offering as soon as they were off the Ark. Noah knew the difference between clean and unclean animals, and also about animal sacrifices upon altars.

Ge 8:20 And Noah builded an altar unto the LORD; and took of every clean beast, and of every clean fowl, and offered burnt offerings on the altar.

We find Abraham walking up to Mount Moriah where God told him to offer Isaac on the altar as a type of Christ's atonement. As he walked Isaac asked a very revealing question:

Ge 22:7 And Isaac spake unto Abraham his father, and said, My father: and he said, Here am I, my son. And he said, Behold the fire and the wood: **but where is the lamb for a burnt offering?**

Isaac knew all about this principle long before Moses' Law. Abraham had told his servant that they would go yonder to worship and then return. Isaac knew what that meant. We find in Genesis 26 God declaring to Isaac the reason why Abraham was blessed:

Ge 26:5 Because that Abraham obeyed my voice, and kept my charge, my commandments, my statutes, and my laws.

Hear what God commanded Abraham to do along with these sacrifices which pictures God's plan for atonement in Christ:

Ge 17:1 And when Abram was ninety years old and nine, the LORD appeared to Abram, and said unto him, I am the Almighty God; <u>walk before me, and be thou perfect</u>.

As Abraham obeyed the moral precepts God gave him, followed the "work of the law in his heart" from the "image of God" that still remained; and worshipped through blood sacrifices; his relationship with God was maintained. His faith was seen in his faith-full-ness.

Even the covenant of circumcision was a covenant based on Abraham submitting to God's Moral Law, and having the sign and symbol of circumcision as a ceremony or ritual observance picturing a regenerated heart.

Col 2:11 *In whom also ye are circumcised with the circumcision made without hands, in putting off the body of the sins of the flesh by the circumcision of Christ:*

Circumcision symbolized the faithful obedience of Abraham. It had to do with the principle of crucifying the flesh and walking in the Spirit. Those with the ceremonial letter of the law fulfilled in their flesh; but without the spiritual meaning fulfilled in their heart were missing the point - and their relationship with God.

Ro 2:23 *Thou that makest thy boast of the law, through breaking the law dishonourest thou God? 24 For the name of God is blasphemed among the Gentiles through you, as it is written. 25 For circumcision verily profiteth, if thou keep the law: but if thou be a breaker of the law, thy circumcision is made uncircumcision. 26 Therefore if the **uncircumcision keep the righteousness of the law,** shall not his uncircumcision be counted for circumcision? 27 And shall not uncircumcision which is by nature, **if it fulfil the law**, judge thee, who by the letter and circumcision dost **transgress the law**? 28 For he is not a Jew, which is one **outwardly;** neither is that circumcision, which is outward in the flesh: 29 But he is a Jew, which is one **inwardly**; and circumcision is that of the heart, in the spirit, and not in the letter; whose praise is not of men, but of God.*

These verses prove that there is a definite separation between **moral** and **ceremonial** laws as Paul argues that one who is obeying the moral laws (righteousness of the law); but is an uncircumcised Gentile (not fulfilling the ceremonial laws) is still acceptable to God and has the true essence of being a Jew **within** though not **without**. The Ceremonial Law was to be eventually done away, but the Moral Law (its counterpart) was never done away. The circumcision in the flesh became unnecessary, but the circumcision of the heart would always be necessary.

Ro 4:9 Cometh this blessedness (Salvation by Grace) *then upon the circumcision only, or upon the uncircumcision also? for we say that faith was reckoned to Abraham for righteousness. 10 How was it then reckoned? when he was in circumcision, or in uncircumcision? Not in circumcision, but in uncircumcision. 11 And he received the sign of circumcision, a **seal** of the **righteousness of the faith** which he had yet being uncircumcised: that he might be the father of all them that believe, though they be not circumcised; that righteousness might be imputed unto them also: 12 And the father of circumcision to them who are not of the circumcision only, but who **also** walk in the **steps of that faith** of our father Abraham, which he had being yet uncircumcised. 13 For the promise, that he should be the heir of the world, was not to Abraham, or to his seed, through the law**, (the ceremonial covenant of types and shadows)** but through the righteousness of faith. **(The real entity – obedience to God's moral laws from the heart)**

This whole argument proves the separation between the moral and ceremonial laws and shows that salvation by grace, i.e. God imputing our living obeying faith to us as perfect righteousness by cleansing our record of sin, is a blessing bestowed not only on the "circumcision" (the Jews obeying the ceremonial law by faith in God); but also on the "uncircumcision" (Gentile believers who don't obey the ceremonial law). Paul is explaining why Gentiles could be grafted into God's church and salvation without becoming Jews first as it was before Cornelius. This blessing comes to those who have the faith of Abraham who obeyed God's moral laws as much as he knew them. Whether we are Jews under the obligations of the ceremonial laws or Gentile converts who do not obey the ceremonial laws, we ALL must have the faith that obeys the moral laws of God that we know!

Ro 8:1 *There is therefore now no condemnation to them which are in Christ Jesus,* **who walk not after the flesh, but after the Spirit**. *2 For the law of the Spirit of life in Christ Jesus hath made me free from the law of sin and death. 3 For what the law could not do, in that it was weak through the flesh, God sending his own Son in the likeness of sinful flesh, and for sin, condemned sin in the flesh:* *4* **That the <u>righteousness of the law might be fulfilled in us</u>, who walk not after the flesh, but after the Spirit.** *5 For they that are after the flesh do mind the things of the flesh; but they that are after the Spirit the things of the Spirit. 6 For to be carnally minded is death; but to be spiritually minded is life and peace. 7* **Because the carnal mind is enmity against God: for it is <u>not subject to the law of God,</u> neither indeed can be. 8 So then they that are in the flesh cannot please God.**

If I asked a group of Christians if believers are required to obey God's Moral Laws, they would probably say, NO; but if I asked them if Christians were required to walk in LOVE towards God and man, they would say YES. This is due to the false teaching that has pervaded Christendom. You cannot know and practice God's Love properly unless you know and practice God's Moral Laws, for God's Law teaches us God's view of LOVE.

1Jo 5:2 By this we know *that we love the children of God, when we love God, and keep his commandments. 3 For this is the love* *of God, that we keep his commandments: and his commandments are not grievous.*

Chapter Thirteen
The Old Covenant

What we generally call the Old Covenant is in reality the Mosaic Covenant which established a relationship between God and the nation of Israel. It established the terms for the nation to be **God's People** and to be a vessel of mercy whereby God could demonstrate to the world His Ways as well as His offer of reconciliation to mankind. This was and is the purpose of every covenant God has made with man: To establish a program for reconciliation and salvation proclaimed and demonstrated through the person, family, or nation with whom the covenant was made. Whether with Adam, Seth, Noah, Abraham, Isaac, Jacob, at Sinai, or the New Covenant with Israel; the dictates of God's covenant relationships have been pointing in the same direction. God's covenants were never just to have an inclusive relationship with one family or nation; but a means of calling the whole world to himself. The grand plan of redemption has always been the purpose of God when making a covenant with people. Thus God's covenants were the establishment of the "strait gate and narrow way" for that generation. Every covenant has served to point to Christ and His salvation program. Every covenant preached salvation by grace through faith. Every covenant consistently opened a broader and clearer view of the one and same picture of God's redemption process and plan. Every covenant was based, as we said earlier, on two basic principles:

1. A plumbline showing God's ways. Reconciling with God is not a "meet in the middle" proposition; but man must repent and return to God's will, way, and authority. The moral principles in Moses' Law served as this plumbline to demonstrate God's ways.

2. Ceremonial excercizes as object lessons concerning the truths involved in redemption, atonement, reconciliation, justification, etc. God operates upon set laws and not by whims or arbitrary decrees. God's reconciliation and redemption for man must follow and fulfill the appropriate legal transactions; which is why Jesus had to become man and make atonement for sin.

If you do a study about the Tabernacle and how it pictures Christ and New Covenant realities, you will be amazed at God's design. The earthly rituals, which are only types and shadows, are the parts that teach us and lead us to Christ; and then give way to the reality they foreshadowed – **He is the end** (goal and aim) **of the law for righteousness** (justification) **to every one that believeth (Romans 10:4).** Jesus fulfilled what the blood of bulls and goats could only teach and foreshadow in making a suitable atonement that propitiated God.

The Ceremonial Law, Levitical Priesthood, Tabernacle, etc; were **earthly temporal patterns** of true and eternal realities in heaven. The heavenly realities are **still active** and **necessary** even though the earthly patterns have ceased to operate and be obligatory. When you realize that the spiritual realities of all previous covenants including the Mosaic Covenant are still active and operating in the spirit world so that we can be saved; then you won't be so quick to cast aside the **Old Covenant**.

Heb 8:1 *Now of the things which we have spoken this is the sum: We have such an high priest, who is set on the right hand of the throne of the Majesty in the heavens; 2 **A minister of the sanctuary, and of the true tabernacle, which the Lord pitched, and not man.** 3 For every high priest is ordained to offer gifts and sacrifices: wherefore it is of necessity that this man have somewhat also to offer. 4 For if he were on earth, he should not be a priest, seeing that there are priests that offer gifts according to the law: 5 **Who serve unto the example and shadow of heavenly things,** as Moses was admonished of God when he was about to make the tabernacle: for, **See, saith he, that thou make all things according to the pattern shewed to thee in the mount.***

Heb 9:8 *The Holy Ghost this signifying, that the way into the holiest of all was not yet made manifest, while as the first tabernacle was yet standing: 9 Which was a **figure for the time then present**, in which were offered both gifts and sacrifices, that could not make him that did the service perfect, as pertaining to the conscience;10 Which stood only in meats and drinks, and divers washings, and carnal ordinances, **imposed on them until the time of reformation.** 11 But Christ being come an high priest of good things to come, by **a greater and more perfect tabernacle, not made with hands,** that is to say, not of this building; 12 Neither by the blood of goats and calves, but by his own blood he entered in once into the holy place, having obtained eternal redemption for us....22 And almost all things are by the law purged with blood; and without shedding of blood is no remission. 23 It was therefore necessary that the **patterns of things in the heavens** should be purified with these; but the **heavenly things** themselves with better sacrifices than these. 24 For Christ is not entered into the **holy places made with hands**, which are the **figures of the true**; but into heaven itself, now to appear in the presence of God for us:*

Heb 10:1 *For the **law** having a **shadow of good things to come**, and **not the very image of the things**, can never with those sacrifices which they offered year by year continually make the comers thereunto perfect.*

The Ceremonial Laws were only shadows of spiritual realities that are necessary for our salvation. There is a heavenly tabernacle where Jesus, our High Priest, ministers with His own cleansing blood to maintain our justification and standing with God as we walk in the light of His Word. You still have an obligation to avail yourself of this grace to maintain your justification and relationship with God – Did you know that? You must continually come and confess known sins so they can be cleansed and forgiven – were you taught this? Compare Hebrews 7:24,25 with 1 John 1:7-9. Jewish believers would have naturally known all about this, thanks to the School Master – Moses' Law.

If you are not familiar with the Old Covenant, then you are unavoidably ignorant concerning the mechanics of your own salvation. You cannot fully understand the Gospel if you are not taught in the principles of Moses' Law – both the moral and ceremonial. When Gentile Christians began to interpret the Bible divorced from the roots of Judaism is it any wonder that heresy flourished? This is the very reason Marcion and other heretics could even get a hearing.

It is very clear from these Scriptures that the Ceremonial Law, which included the service of the tabernacle/temple and the priesthood, was only temporary and is done away by Christ's superior priesthood in the New Covenant. It is also very clear from the following verses in the same book of the Bible that some part of the Law of God is carried over and has become the basis of the New Covenant. From the passage it is obvious that it wasn't the Ceremonial Law, but the Moral Law. We know it wasn't animal sacrifices and ceremonial washings that were written on all believer's hearts, but it was the moral precepts of God's own holiness and love which were written on their hearts.

Heb 8:10 For this is the covenant that I will make with the house of Israel after those days, saith the Lord; **I will put my laws into their mind, and write them in their hearts: (preserved)** *and I will be to them a God, and they shall be to me a people: 11 And they shall not teach every man his neighbour, and every man his brother, saying, Know the Lord: for all shall know me, from the least to the greatest. 12 For I will be merciful to their unrighteousness, and their sins and their iniquities will I remember no more. 13* **In that he saith, A new covenant, he hath made the first old. Now that which decayeth and waxeth old is ready to vanish away. (not preserved)**

Heb 10:8 Above when he said, **Sacrifice and offering and burnt offerings and offering for sin thou wouldest not, neither hadst pleasure therein; which are offered by the law;** *9 Then said he, Lo, I come to do thy will, O God.* **He taketh away the first, that he may establish the second***.

Heb 10:16 This is the covenant that I will make with them after those days, saith the Lord, **I will put my laws into their hearts, and in their minds will I write them; (preserved)** *17 And their sins and iniquities will I remember no more. 18 Now where remission of these is,* **there is no more offering for sin***. **(done away)**

We can see that God's eternal moral laws are written in our hearts, but the ceremonial laws of the covenant that pictured Christ's atoning and priestly work have given way to the spiritual realities they foreshadowed. God preserved His moral statutes and judgments: took them out of the Old Covenant setting, and made them the basis of the New Covenant. God's Law in our hearts in a more affective way was the very reason for the New Covenant, according to God's Word. All God's covenants and exhortations from Genesis to Revelation teach us about and lead us to a fuller understanding of God's redemption program through Christ Jesus. There is only ONE GOSPEL MESSAGE unfolded and illustrated through the sixty six books of the Bible. This one message has revealed God's Moral Law: unselfish love; and God's redemption plan: Christ's atonement and priesthood.

Chapter Fourteen
The Priority of Moral over Ceremonial Law

God's separation of the moral precepts from the ceremonial practices shows that without the Moral Law in place, **the Ceremonial is without virtue** – it only has virtue in the context of the Moral Law. When Israel practiced the ceremonial law with cold backslidden hearts, they actually profaned the principles the rituals foreshadowed. Our inside must be right or our outside is of little value. If you read carefully, you will see the distinction between ceremonial laws that only illustrate truth and moral laws that are eternal truth.

The Shadow Vs The Substance

*1Sa 15:22 And Samuel said, Hath the LORD as great delight in burnt offerings and sacrifices, as in obeying the voice of the LORD? Behold, to **obey** is better than **sacrifice**, and to **hearken** than the **fat of rams**.*

*Pro 21:3 To do **justice and judgment** is more acceptable to the LORD than **sacrifice**.*

Is 1:10 Hear the word of the LORD, ye rulers of Sodom; give ear unto the law of our God, ye people of Gomorrah. 11 To what purpose is the multitude of your sacrifices unto me? saith the LORD: I am full of the burnt offerings of rams, and the fat of fed beasts; and I delight not in the blood of bullocks, or of lambs, or of he goats. 12 When ye come to appear before me, who hath required this at your hand, to tread my courts?   13 Bring no more vain oblations; incense is an abomination unto me; the new moons and sabbaths, the calling of assemblies, I cannot away with; it is iniquity, even the solemn meeting.   14 Your new moons and your appointed feasts my soul hateth: they are a trouble unto me; I am weary to bear them. 15 And when ye spread forth your hands, I will hide mine eyes from you: yea, when ye make many prayers, I will not hear: your hands are full of blood.   16 ¶ Wash you, make you clean; put away the evil of your doings from before mine eyes; cease to do evil; 17 Learn to do well; seek judgment, relieve the oppressed, judge the fatherless, plead for the widow.

Hos 6:6 For I desired mercy, and not sacrifice; and the knowledge of God more than burnt offerings.

Jer 7:21 ¶ Thus saith the LORD of hosts, the God of Israel; Put your burnt offerings unto your sacrifices, and eat flesh. 22 For I spake not unto your fathers, nor commanded them in the day that I brought them out of the land of Egypt, concerning burnt offerings or sacrifices: 23 But this thing commanded I them, saying, **Obey my voice,** and I will be your God, and ye shall be my people: and **walk ye in all the ways that I have commanded you**, that it may be well unto you.

Mic 6:6 Wherewith shall I come before the LORD, and bow myself before the high God? shall I come before him with burnt offerings, with calves of a year old?   7 Will the LORD be pleased with thousands of rams, or with ten thousands of rivers of oil? shall I give my firstborn for my transgression, the fruit of my body for the sin of my soul?   8 He hath shewed thee, O man, what is good; and what doth the LORD require of thee, but to do justly, and to love mercy, and to walk humbly with thy God?

Mt 9:12 But when Jesus heard that, he said unto them, They that be whole need not a physician, but they that are sick. 13 But go ye and learn what that meaneth, I will have **mercy**, and **not sacrifice:** for I am not come to call the righteous, but sinners to repentance.

Mt 15:11 *Not that which goeth into the mouth defileth a man; but that which cometh out of the mouth, this defileth a man.*

Mk 12:32 *And the scribe said unto him, Well, Master, thou hast said the truth: for there is one God; and there is none other but he: 33 And to love him with all the heart, and with all the understanding, and with all the soul, and with all the strength, and to love his neighbour as himself, is more than all whole burnt offerings and sacrifices. 34 And when Jesus saw that he answered discreetly, he said unto him, Thou art not far from the kingdom of God.*

Even in the Old Covenant, God taught them that circumcision was only a symbol and that He desired the circumcision of the heart and not just of the flesh.

De 10:16 *Circumcise therefore the foreskin of your heart, and be no more stiffnecked.*

De 30:6 *And the LORD thy God will circumcise thine heart, and the heart of thy seed, to love the LORD thy God with all thine heart, and with all thy soul, that thou mayest live.*

Jer 4:4 *Circumcise yourselves to the LORD, and take away the foreskins of your heart, ye men of Judah and inhabitants of Jerusalem: lest my fury come forth like fire, and burn that none can quench it, because of the evil of your doings.*

Ro 2:25 *For circumcision verily profiteth, if thou keep the law: but if thou be a breaker of the law, thy circumcision is made uncircumcision. 26 Therefore if the uncircumcision keep the **righteousness of the law**, shall not his uncircumcision be counted for circumcision? 27 And shall not uncircumcision which is by nature, if it fulfil the law, judge thee, who by the **letter and circumcision** dost **transgress the law**? 28 For he is not a Jew, which is one outwardly; neither is that circumcision, which is outward in the flesh: 29 But he is a Jew, which is one inwardly; and circumcision is that of the heart, in the spirit, and not in the letter; whose praise is not of men, but of God.*

Jesus' teaching about the "Ox in the ditch on the Sabbath", "healing on the Sabbath", and all the controversy Jesus had concerning the Sabbath, was dealing with the principle that the Moral Law always held precedence over the Ceremonial Law; and that ceremonial laws lost their virtue unless they were in tune with God's eternal moral laws.

Heb 10:11 *And every priest standeth daily ministering and offering oftentimes the same sacrifices, which can never take away **sins:** 12 But this man, after he had offered one sacrifice for **sins** for ever, sat down on the right hand of God;*

Are "Sins" the same in verse 11 as in verse 12? Yes, and that means the Moral Law is still relevant. The apostle John said in AD 95 that sin is the transgression of God's Law and that LOVE was the keeping of His commandments. The only thing that has changed is God's covenant relationship in how we deal with sin now. We have a new priesthood, a sacrifice with eternal merit, a heavenly priest ministering in a heavenly tabernacle in the presence of God, and we access this through the prayer of faith.

Heb 10:16 *This is the covenant that I will make with them after those days, saith the Lord, **I will put my laws into their hearts, and in their minds will I write them;** 17 And their **sins** and **iniquities** will I remember no more. 18 **Now where remission of these is, there is no more offering for sin**.*

Sin is STILL Sin; but now that Jesus has made the atonement, there is <u>no more offering</u> – The OLD Covenant sacrifices are done away! But the moral laws of God are still to be obeyed, or we will not be eligible for Jesus' atonement for us. Jesus' blood will never cleanse sins that are not repented of; nor will He intercede for an unfaithful and rebellious person.

Heb 10:26 *For if* __we__ *[Christians]* **sin wilfully** *after that we have received the* **knowledge of the truth [The Gospel]**, <u>*there remaineth no more sacrifice for sins*</u>,

This means that if a Christian rebels against God's Word, and thereby stops walking in the Light, they forfeit the benefits of Christ's atonement and priesthood on their behalf; and there is no other sacrifice or atonement that will avail for them. Going back to Judaism is worthless because those sacrifices were only shadows of the real one made by Jesus, and can never take away sin. Notice that SIN is still SIN, and God's Moral Law, as the basis of the New Covenant, is still in force.

Heb 10:38 <u>*Now the just shall live by faith*</u>: *but if any man draw back, my soul shall have no pleasure in him.*

Is this only a New Covenant concept? No, Paul is quoting Hab. 2:4 – salvation under the Old Covenant.

Hab 2:4 *Behold, his soul which is lifted up is not upright in him:* <u>*but the just shall live by his faith.*</u>

Adam Clarke: It is contended by some able critics that the words of the original text should be pointed thus: 'o de dikaiov ek pistewv, zhsetai. *The just by faith, shall live*; that is, he alone that is justified by faith shall be saved:

The one God calls "just" is "justified" before God due to his obedient faith, and he shall "live" or "be saved" on this account. This principle is valid from Genesis to Revelation. It is the principle of salvation by grace through faith. Believing and obeying God (faith) is the best we can offer God, and it reverses the unbelief/disobedience of the fall as far as our part of reconciliation is concerned. The principle of faith imputed to us for righteousness (justification) is the only form of salvation offered by God to man. Our living by the obedience of faith (Romans 16:26) is what makes us eligible for the benefits of Christ's atonement and priesthood. Of Course, *living by the terms of the covenant make us eligible for the benefits of the covenant.*

In Heb. 12:18-29 it is clear that sin against the Moral Law has not changed; but the ceremonial arrangement for dealing with sin and rendering service to God has changed.

Heb 7:12 *For the priesthood being changed, there is made of necessity a change also of the law.*

What part of the law changed? The **ceremonial part** that dealt with priesthood, sacrifices, temple service, etc. is what changed. God didn't change His moral compass, His moral opinions, His moral judgments, or His LOVE; but what the ceremonies foreshadowed was now put in place and operating, so the ritual object lessons were no longer needed.

Chapter Fifteen
The Middle Wall of Partition

In Ephesians and Colossians we learn that the ceremonial laws stood as a partition that kept the Jewish people a distinct and separate people until Christ could be born; but now that Christ has come and opened the kingdom doors to also receive non-Jews; that middle wall of partition, the Ceremonial Law that foreshadowed Christ and kept Israel separated, is done away. Compare what Peter said twelve years after Pentecost when God was revealing the new arrangement of accepting believing Gentiles with the following verses:

Ac 10:28 *And he said unto them, Ye know how that it is an unlawful thing for a man that is a Jew to keep company, or come unto one of another nation; but God hath shewed me that I should not call any man common or unclean.*

Eph 2:11 *Wherefore remember, that ye being in time past Gentiles in the flesh, who are called Uncircumcision by that which is called the Circumcision in the flesh made by hands; 12 That at that time ye were without Christ, being aliens from the commonwealth of Israel, and strangers from the covenants of promise, having no hope, and without God in the world: 13 But now in Christ Jesus ye who sometimes were far off are made nigh by the blood of Christ. 14 ¶ For he is our peace, who hath made both one, and hath broken down the middle wall of partition between us; 15 Having abolished in his flesh the enmity, even the law of commandments contained in ordinances; for to make in himself of twain one new man, so* *making peace; 16 And that he might **reconcile both unto God** in one body by the cross, having slain the enmity thereby: 17 And came and preached peace to you which were afar off, and to them that were nigh. 18 For through him we <u>both have access by **one Spirit**</u> unto the Father. 19 Now therefore ye are no more strangers and foreigners, but fellowcitizens with the saints, and of the household of God; 20 And are built upon the foundation of the apostles and prophets, Jesus Christ himself being the chief corner stone; 21 In whom all the building fitly framed together groweth unto an holy temple in the Lord: 22 In whom ye also are builded together for an habitation of God through the Spirit.*

The "Law of commandments contained in ordinances" is speaking of the ceremonial laws in the Old Covenant. It is obviously not speaking of God's holiness revealed in His moral laws. These new Gentiles who did not have to obey the ceremonial laws are now in the **household of God; reconciled to God; walking in the Spirit; washed in the blood; are now saints; and built upon the foundation of the apostles, prophets (includes Moses) and Christ Jesus.** Adultery, lying, coveting, etc. are **still sin**, and Jesus didn't die so we are free to be unholy. God's Moral Law is not the separation or "enmity" between Jew and Gentile that needed to be abolished in order to reconcile both together in one body in Christ. God's Moral Law was the enmity between God and mankind; which is why man must repent and turn around in order to reconcile with God. The fact that these Gentiles were reconciled to God means that they did repent and embrace God's Moral Law. Remember God's Moral Law is LOVE.

Clarke: "Contained in", or rather *concerning, ordinances*; which law was made merely for the purpose of keeping the Jews a distinct people, and pointing out the Son of God till he should come. When, therefore, the end of its institution was answered, it was no longer necessary; and Christ by his death abolished it.

Instead of this separation, Jesus has made one NEW man from the two separate entities: believing Jew and believing Gentile. The New man is bound by the moral laws of God, as he is now in the household of God, and God hasn't changed. We are now fellowcitizens with the what? The saints – holy people.

What determines holy? Has God's holiness changed? Pay attention to where these verses are found that say, "Be ye holy for I am holy":

Le 11:44 For I am the LORD your God: ye shall therefore sanctify yourselves, and ye shall be holy; for I am holy:

Le 11:45 For I am the LORD that bringeth you up out of the land of Egypt, to be your God: ye shall therefore be holy, for I am holy.

Le 19:2 Speak unto all the congregation of the children of Israel, and say unto them, Ye shall be holy: for I the LORD your God am holy.

Le 20:7 Sanctify yourselves therefore, and be ye holy: for I am the LORD your God.

Le 20:26 And ye shall be holy unto me: for I the LORD am holy, and have severed you from other people, that ye should be mine.

*1Pe 1:14 As obedient children, not fashioning yourselves according to the former lusts in your ignorance: 15 But as he which hath called you is holy, so be ye holy in all manner of conversation; **16 Because it is written, Be ye holy; for I am holy.** 17 And if ye call on the Father, who without respect of persons judgeth according to every man's work, pass the time of your sojourning here in fear:*

Is God's holiness the same? Holiness means "set apart to God", and we must still be set apart to the same God, though under a different Covenant. If God says He doesn't change; the Apostles tell us He doesn't change; and they tell us Jesus is the same in the past, in the present, and in the future; WHY do Marcionites work so hard to make God a liar?

Isa 51:6 *Lift up your eyes to the heavens, and look upon the earth beneath: for the heavens shall vanish away like smoke, and the earth shall wax old like a garment, and they that dwell therein shall die in like manner: but my salvation shall be for ever, **and my righteousness shall not be abolished.***

The God of holiness has not changed. God's idea of holiness has not changed in regard to moral precepts. Yes, disobedience to ceremonial law would have been sinful and unholy while it was still in force; but we have shown that these ceremonial laws were only for a certain time and purpose under a specific covenant that was meant to foreshadow Christ's atonement and present priesthood. Paul says plainly that circumcision was in and of itself "nothing", and only had moral relevance when it was "keeping the commandment of God".

1Co 7:19 *Circumcision is nothing, and uncircumcision is nothing, but the keeping of the commandments of God.*

The Law of Love never loses relevance like this. Bearing false witness, dishonoring parents, etc. are not just sins because God has forbidden them under this covenant; but are sins by their very **nature**. Circumcision is not this way.

Issues like Circumcision and Sabbath observance are ceremonial in nature, which means they are only "holy" or "unholy" by God's appointment, not by their nature. If

God had not commanded it, there would be no scruple about it – no moral obligation at all. Moral issues are different; and are such by nature. Murder, adultery, lying, stealing, cheating, etc. are immoral by nature, not just by the appointment of God. If God had given no direct command concerning them, they would still be wrong by their very nature.

The "Law" as a *system* or *covenant* between man and God was abolished through the Cross of Christ; but the moral judgments of God contained in the Law are still God's eternal view on that particular issue. This abolishing did not take affect for Jews until God destroyed the temple and made it impossible for them to practice the rituals of the Law. God's ways as revealed in the Old Testament are still God's ways; and as such the moral aspects of the Law are still valid.

Jesus came to enforce and vindicate God's ways. He cleared the misconceptions about God's moral precepts given through Moses. The moral precepts themselves can never be changed. Only the ceremonial covenant rituals can be changed with the making of a new covenant by the same eternal unchanging God.

*Col 2:13 And you, being dead in your sins and the uncircumcision of your flesh, hath he quickened together with him, having forgiven you all trespasses; 14 Blotting out the handwriting of ordinances that was against us, which was contrary to us, and took it out of the way, nailing it to his cross;15 And having spoiled principalities and powers, he made a shew of them openly, triumphing over them in it. 16 Let no man therefore judge you in **meat**, or in **drink,** or in **respect of an holyday**, or of the **new moon**, or of the **sabbath days**: 17 Which are a **shadow** of things to come; but the body is of Christ.*

Ephesians and Colossians were written around the same time, and are "sister" epistles with much of the same content. Here we are speaking of the same thing as what we previously read in Ephesians. It is clear that what is done away is not God's holiness and moral statutes; but **meat, drink, respect of holy days, new moon, circumcision, and Sabbath day observances** – all ceremonial laws – conditions of a covenant relationship. Paul tells us these things are simply a **"shadow",** but the body is of Christ – **He is the reality** – the fulfillment of the types.

*Ga 5:6 For in Jesus Christ neither circumcision availeth any thing, nor uncircumcision; but **faith which worketh by love.***

Faith is only virtuous as it establishes the Moral Law of God (law of love) in the life of the believer; and produces a new creature fulfilling the righteousness of His eternal laws. "Circumcision" in this context is a term used to refer to the whole Ceremonial Law/Judaism.

*Ga 6:15 For in Christ Jesus neither circumcision availeth any thing, nor uncircumcision, but a **new creature.***

This "new creature" is supposed to have the mind of Christ, which is the Moral Law of God written on the heart. **Galatians 5:24** and **25** tell us about this new creature:

*Ga 5:24 And they that are Christ's have crucified the flesh with the affections and lusts. 25 If we live in the Spirit, let us also **walk in the Spirit.***

*Ro 8:4 That the **righteousness of the law might be fulfilled in us,** who walk not after the flesh, but after the Spirit.*

*Ro 3:31 Do we then make void the law through faith? God forbid: yea, **we establish the law.***

How does faith establish the Law? Faith obeys God, repents, and walks in the SAME Spirit that gave the Law. The Ceremonial Law taught us about Christ's atonement, and when we believe in Him, we are establishing the truth of what the Law foreshadowed. God's eternal Moral Law is established by those who believe in him and take his prescription for living – holiness – the law of love. Salvation by faith also establishes the righteousness of the Law by confessing our guilt and just condemnation for not keeping the Law perfectly; by confessing we need a Savior to redeem us; and thereby confessing, "God was right, we were wrong, and our humble submission now is reasonable service."

Ro 8:3 *For what the law could not do, in that it was weak through the flesh, God sending his own Son in the likeness of sinful flesh, and for sin, condemned sin in the flesh: 4 That the* **righteousness of the law might be fulfilled in us,** *who walk not after the flesh, but after the Spirit. 5 For they that are after the flesh do mind the things of the flesh; but they that are after the Spirit the things of the Spirit. 6 For to be carnally minded is death; but to be spiritually minded is life and peace. 7 Because the* <u>carnal mind is enmity against God</u>: **for it is not** <u>**subject to**</u> <u>**the law of God**</u>*, neither indeed can be. 8 So then they that are in the flesh* <u>cannot please God.</u> *9 But ye are not in the flesh, but in the Spirit, if so be that the Spirit of God dwell in you. Now if any man have not the Spirit of Christ, he is none of his.*

Being Christ's and walking in His Spirit brings us in line with God's holiness and we then **fulfill** the moral laws of God. If you are not subject to the Law of God, then you are not walking in the Spirit, and you are not Christ's! Did you ever notice what mind frame was necessary to be on the Narrow Road?

Mt 7:12 *Therefore all things whatsoever ye would that men should do to you, do ye even so to them:* **for this is the law** *and the prophets*. *13 Enter ye in at the strait gate: for wide is the gate, and broad is the way, that leadeth to destruction, and many there be which go in thereat: 14 Because strait is the gate, and narrow is the way, which leadeth unto life, and few there be that find it.*

The Narrow Way that leadeth to life *is the Law and the prophets.*

Chapter Sixteen
What did the Schoolmaster Teach?

The confusion concerning our God ordained Schoolmaster is astounding. In Galatians three the Apostle Paul is using the term *Law* to refer to the "Mosaic Covenant" as a **whole system** and not any of the components by themselves. The point being made is that the *Law* or *Mosaic Covenant* was never meant to justify; but as earthly patterns of the heavenly realities, it was only meant to teach us about Christ's sacrifice and priesthood so we could properly appreciate it and know how to be saved by it. Paul had just emphatically declared that looking for justification from the Mosaic covenant sacrifices or ceremonies, was actually saying that Christ's death was not necessary for our salvation.

Ga 2:21 I do not frustrate the grace of God: for if **[justification]** *come by the law, then Christ is dead in vain.*

This is the context for the rest of the epistle; and this is the issue being discussed. I am going to walk you through Galatians chapter three with injected helping words, so you understand what is being said; and then we will discuss how these precious truths affect our salvation.

Ga 3:1 O foolish Galatians, who hath bewitched you, that ye should not obey the truth, before whose eyes Jesus Christ hath been evidently set forth, crucified among you **(As the Lamb/atonement of God)**? *2 This only would I learn of you, Received ye the Spirit by the works of the law* **(justified by the** law), *or by the hearing of faith* **(believing the gospel as Abraham did)***? 3 Are ye so foolish? having begun in the Spirit, are ye now made perfect by the flesh* **(justified by the law)***? 4 Have ye suffered so many things in vain? if it be yet in vain. 5 He therefore that ministereth to you the Spirit, and worketh miracles among you, doeth he it by the works of the law* **(justified by the law)**, *or by the hearing of faith* **(Justified by Faith)***? 6* ___Even as Abraham believed God, and it was accounted to him for righteousness.___ *7 Know ye therefore that they which are* **(justified)** *of faith, the same are the children of Abraham. 8 And the scripture, foreseeing that God would* **justify** *the heathen* **through faith**, *preached before the* **gospel unto Abraham,** *saying, In thee shall all nations be blessed. 9 So then they which be* **(justified)** *of faith are blessed with faithful Abraham. 10 For as many as are* **(justified)** *of the works of the law are under the curse: for it is written, Cursed is every one that continueth not in all things which are written in the book of the law to do them* **(forensic justification)**. *11 But that no man is* **justified** *by the law in the sight of God, it is evident: for, "The just* **(justified)** *shall live* **(be saved)** *by faith"* **(Hab 2:4)** *And the law* **(law's justification)** *is not of faith: but, The man that doeth them shall live in them* **(forensic justification)**. *13 Christ hath redeemed us from the curse of the law, being made a curse for us: for it is written, Cursed is every one that hangeth on a tree: 14 That the blessing of Abraham might come on the Gentiles through Jesus Christ; that we might receive the promise of the Spirit through* **(the justification of)** *faith. 15 Brethren, I speak after the manner of men; Though it be but a man's covenant* **(even men's covenants)**, *yet if it be confirmed, no man disannulleth, or addeth thereto* **(covenants that are ratified are binding)**. *16 Now to Abraham and his seed were the promises made. He saith not, And to seeds, as of many; but as of one, And to thy seed, which is Christ. 17 And this I say, that the covenant* **(with Abraham)**, *that was confirmed before of God in Christ, the law, which was four hundred and thirty years after, cannot disannul,* ___that it should make the promise ___**___(of justification through faith)___** ___of none effect___ **(by producing** another means of justification). *18 For if the inheritance be* **(through justification)** *of the law, it is no more of promise* **(of justification through faith)**: *but God gave it to Abraham by promise. 19 Wherefore then serveth the law* **(and its sacrifices)?** *It was added because of transgressions* **(to preserve and teach Israel about the principles of justification)**, *till the seed* **(Christ)** *should come to whom the promise was made; and it* **(law/Old Covenant)** *was ordained by angels in the hand of a mediator* **(Moses)**. *20 Now a mediator is not a mediator of one* **(but two parties)**, *but God* **(who made the promise)** *is one. 21 Is the law then against* **(in conflict with)** *the promises of God? God forbid: for if there had been a law given which could have given life* **(make atonement)**, *verily righteousness* **(justification)** *should have been by the law. 22 But the scripture hath concluded all under sin, that the promise* **(of justification)** *by faith of Jesus Christ might be given to them that believe* **(like Abraham)**. *23 But before* **(the)** *faith* **(of Christ)** *came, we were kept under the law, shut up unto the faith which should afterwards be revealed. 24 Wherefore the* **_law was our schoolmaster_** *to bring us unto Christ,* **_that we might be justified by faith_**. *25 But after that* **(the)** *faith is come, we are no longer under a schoolmaster* **(ceremonial system)**. *26 For ye are all the children of God by faith in Christ Jesus.*

As we stated earlier, now that the spiritual realities are in place and operating, the object lessons and introductory instructions are not obligatory i.e. we don't have to practice the ceremonial laws; but we still need them to properly learn about the heavenly realities they are patterned after.

"Faith" refers to "**The Faith**" as in "The faith once delivered to the saints". Paul has told us that personal faith in God has always been the means of justification and salvation (Heb 11). But "The Faith of Christ" or "Doctrine of Christ", which is the spiritual meaning of all the types and shadows, is now come to supersede the Old

Covenant relationship between God and man. So...what did the Law of Moses teach us that brings us to a productive relationship with Christ in the New Covenant?

Some contend that this "schoolmaster" (Greek *paidagogos* – origin of "pedagogue") was simply a servant who took the children to school; but this servant actually raised the children and was as a parent to them in the absence of their parents. See I Cor 4:15 where the same word is translated "instructors". The Law of Moses raised us up and instructed us to have a proper view, appreciation, and relationship with Christ. Don't new converts still need this teaching? Doesn't every generation need to understand how the heavenly realities work for our salvation by studying the earthly patterns? Yes indeed.

1. The law as a system was not in conflict with God's promise to Abraham because the purpose of the Law was not to justify and make atonement; but simply to teach the principles and prepare the people to understand salvation through Christ.

2. The principles of justification, which Christ would fulfill, were demonstrated with earthly figures, which were patterns of the heavenly realities

*Heb 8:1 Now of the things which we have spoken this is the sum: We have such an high priest, who is set on the right hand of the throne of the Majesty in the heavens; 2 A minister of the sanctuary, and of the **true tabernacle, which the Lord pitched, and not man**. 3 For every high priest is ordained to offer gifts and sacrifices: wherefore it is of necessity that this man have somewhat also to offer. 4 For if he were on earth, he should not be a priest, seeing that there are priests that offer gifts according to the law: 5 **Who serve unto the example and shadow of heavenly things,** as Moses was admonished of God*

when he was about to make the tabernacle: for, **See, saith he,**
that thou make all things according to the pattern shewed to
thee in the mount.

Heb 9:11 *But Christ being come an high priest of good*
things to come, by a **greater and more perfect tabernacle**, **not**
made with hands, *that is to say, not of this building*
(construction); *12 Neither by the blood of goats and calves, but*
by his own blood he entered in once into the holy place, having
obtained eternal redemption for us....22 And almost all things
are by the law purged with blood; and without shedding of
blood is no remission. 23 **It was therefore necessary that the**
patterns of things in the heavens should be purified with
these; but the heavenly things themselves with better
sacrifices than these. *24 For Christ is not entered into the holy*
places made with hands, **which are the figures of the true;** *but*
into heaven itself, now to appear in the presence of God for us:

3. The fact that they were patterns means that the
heavenly realities operate in a very similar manner.

4. The fact that they were patterns to *lead us to Christ*,
means that *Christ's justification operates after very*
similar principles.

5. The heavenly realities cannot be seen; but the earthly
types and patterns can be seen, studied, and thus we
can learn the principles of heavenly operations.

6. The fact that the ceremonies were patterns of real
heavenly operations means that those very operations
in the heavens **are NOW operating** after the same
principles and **are NECESSARY for our justification in**
Christ

Heb 7:22 *By so much was Jesus made a surety of a better*
testament. 23 And they truly were many priests, because they
were not suffered to continue by reason of death: 24 But this
man, **because he continueth ever, hath an unchangeable**

priesthood. 25 Wherefore he is able also to **save them to the uttermost** that **come unto God by him,** seeing **he ever liveth to make intercession for them**.

1Jn 1:6 If we say that we have fellowship with him, and walk in darkness, we lie, and do not the truth: 7 But **if we walk in the light**, as he is in the light, we have fellowship one with another, and the blood of Jesus Christ his Son cleanseth us from all sin. 8 If we say that we have no sin, we deceive ourselves, and the truth is not in us. 9 **If we confess our sins,** he is faithful and just to **forgive us our sins**, and to **cleanse us from all unrighteousness.**

7. This all means that **each generation** and **each convert** still needs the schoolmaster to **teach** them the principles so they understand justification through Christ or they will be ignorant of the heavenly operations, and not know what to do to be justified by Christ – which is exactly the problem with Christianity Today!!!

What our God ordained *instructor* has taught:

1. The Law/Covenant of Moses was in two parts: The moral plumb line that shows man is crooked and in need of atonement; and then the tabernacle, which taught them about God's salvation through blood atonement, a proper sacrifice, the application of the atonement, the necessity of the priesthood, being eligible for the benefits of the priest's labors, etc.

2. The Law taught us that God will not have a relationship with fallen man outside of God's conditional covenant arrangements. If we would reconcile with God, we must come under such a covenant that God has devised.

3. The Law taught that "without the shedding of blood there is no remission of sin". We cannot hope to have a forensic justification based on our perfect record, but must obtain a pardon by God's grace through repentance, obedience, and our High Priest with His blood sacrifice to cover transgression.

4. The Law taught us about the necessity of priesthood; and how to relate to God through a priest. We need to "come unto God by him" (Heb. 7:25), and keep our record clean before God. Jesus is now our acting High Priest to apply His own atonement to our case every time we sin and confess (1Jn 1:7-9)

5. The Law taught us about the "Lamb of God" that takes away the sins of the world. It taught that this lamb must be pure and without blemish: A picture of Christ, who never transgressed God's Law so He could vicariously die for those who did transgress God's Law.

6. The Law taught that atonement required the goat which died as a sin offering and the goat which was let go into the wilderness and bear the sins away (Le 16). This pictures Christ's vicarious death and also His resurrected Lordship, Priesthood, and Shepherding work to "save us to the uttermost".

7. The Law taught us about the difference between **clean** and **unclean**, **holy** and **unholy**; and the need to keep ourselves clean and "set apart to God" in order to have a relationship with God. It also taught the due reverence for holy things and the consequences when this is violated.

8. The Law taught us that without submission and obedience to the moral laws of God, you are not

even eligible for the forgiveness and cleansing of the blood atonement that God has provided. A Jew who was put out of the assembly or "cut off" from his people through trespass and apostasy gained no benefit from the Day of Atonement, and had no access to God through the priest.

*Heb 10:26 For if we **sin wilfully** after that we have received the knowledge of the truth, there remaineth **no more sacrifice for sins**, 27 But a certain fearful looking for of judgment and fiery indignation, which shall devour the adversaries. 28 He that **despised Moses' law died without mercy** under two or three witnesses:*

9. In the Law we are taught the difference between "ignorant or unintentional sin" and "presumptuous or intentional sin". The willful sin spoken of in Hebrews 10:26 is referring directly to Numbers 15, and what is taught there.

*Nu 15:22 And if ye have erred, and not observed all these commandments, **which the LORD hath spoken unto Moses**, 23 Even all that **the LORD hath commanded you by the hand of Moses**, from the day that the **LORD commanded Moses**, and **henceforward among your generations**; 24 Then it shall be, if ought be committed by **ignorance without the knowledge of the congregation**, that all the congregation shall offer one young bullock for a burnt offering, for a sweet savour unto the LORD, with his meat offering, and his drink offering, according to the manner, and one kid of the goats for a sin offering. 25 And the priest shall make an atonement for all the congregation of the children of Israel, and it shall be **forgiven them**; for **it is ignorance**: and they shall bring their offering, a sacrifice made by fire unto the LORD, and their sin offering before the LORD, for **their ignorance**: 26 And it shall be forgiven all the congregation of the children of Israel, and the stranger that sojourneth among them; seeing all the people were in **ignorance**. 27 And if any **soul** sin through **ignorance**,* *then **he** shall bring a she goat of the first year for a sin offering. 28 And the priest shall make an atonement for the soul that sinneth ignorantly, when **he sinneth by ignorance** before the LORD, to make an **atonement for him**; and it shall be forgiven him. 29 Ye shall have one law for him that **sinneth through ignorance**, both for him that is born among the children of Israel, and for the stranger that sojourneth among them. 30 ¶ But the soul that doeth ought **presumptuously**, whether he be born in the land, or a stranger, the same reproacheth the LORD; and that soul shall be cut off from among his people. 31 Because he hath **despised the word of the LORD**, and hath broken **his commandment**, that soul shall utterly be cut off; his iniquity shall be upon him.*

10. **Every example the Apostles use** in the New Covenant Scriptures about salvation's program is from an Old Covenant person or situation. Without the Old Covenant Scriptures we cannot fully understand or appreciate the New Covenant teachings!

11. The Law taught us about "due order" and that God loves orderliness. The Tabernacle, Temple, and synagogues were God ordained formats for worship and instruction. The Apostles set up the Christian churches after the order and form of the Jewish synagogue worship, because that is what the school master taught them. Many today think a lack of form and order is the *spiritual* way to worship; but they are not listening to the school master. God is not the author of confusion and disorder; *but another spirit is.*

In the New Covenant, we have Christ as our High Priest in the Tabernacle of Heaven offering His own blood for our sins. We must still follow the principles taught in the Old Covenant so we can properly relate to our High

Priest, and appreciate what He is doing for us. Most people don't understand the mechanics of salvation (how it works); and this causes much confusion to Satan's delight. If they would study to understand the Old Covenant mechanics of salvation, it would teach them the New Covenant mechanics of salvation.

I Jn 1:5 This then is the message which we have heard of him, and declare unto you, that God is light, and in him is no darkness at all. 6 If we say that we have fellowship with him, and walk in darkness, we lie, and do not the truth: 7 But if we walk in the light, as he is in the light, we have fellowship one with another, and the blood of Jesus Christ his Son cleanseth us from all sin. 8 If we say that we have no sin, we deceive ourselves, and the truth is not in us. 9 If we confess our sins, he is faithful and just to forgive us our sins, and to cleanse us from all unrighteousness.

This is just what the school master taught us: We must walk in the light God gives or we have no fellowship and are not eligible for the benefits of the atonement. If we walk in the light of God's holy moral laws, then we can have a relationship with God, and we are then eligible for the benefits of Christ as our High Priest. While we walk in the light, doing what we know to be right in God's sight; our High Priest keeps our record clean. If we know we have sinned, we must come to our High Priest (Jesus) and confess our sins for cleansing and forgiveness.

Don't be confused when the Bible says Jesus offered one offering *for ever*. Jesus **offering** His one sacrifice, and Him **applying the benefits** to my case are TWO very different things. This is why two goats had to be used in the OT to picture Christ's Atonement – One pictured Christ's death; and the other pictures His Priestly work in heaven (Le 16). His once for all offering was for the sins of the whole world, but that doesn't automatically save

202

them. The offering of one sacrifice of **eternal merit** doesn't void the necessity of each person of each generation having to repent, believe, walk in the light, continue in the faith, and continually confess their sins for forgiveness and cleansing. By one offering, Jesus has made *provision* for our eternal justification and salvation to them which are **"sanctified"** or **"set apart unto God"** or **"in covenant with God"**; but the process is still a daily "coming" to our High Priest; confessing our trespasses; and asking Him to intercede for us. This process is necessary to maintain our clean record on high, which is our justification and necessary for our salvation. Compare the following verses in the same chapter and see that Christians are not unconditionally secure; but must strive to obey and not sin.

Heb 10:14 *For by one offering he hath perfected for ever* **them that are sanctified...**

...26 **For if we sin wilfully after that we have received the knowledge of the truth, there remaineth no more sacrifice for sins, 27 But a certain fearful looking for of judgment and fiery indignation, which shall devour the adversaries.** *28 He that despised Moses' law died without mercy under two or three witnesses: 29 Of* **how much sorer punishment**, *suppose ye, shall he be thought worthy, who hath trodden under foot the Son of God, and hath counted the blood of the covenant,* **wherewith he was sanctified**, *an unholy thing, and hath done despite unto the Spirit of grace?*

Perpetual justification is dependent upon perpetual walking in the light by faith in Christ. We are justified by faith, which means as long as faith keeps us walking in the light, we continue to be justified through Christ's Priestly Ministry. A "faith" that stops walking in the light is no longer *faith*, but *unbelief*; and when this happens, our justification stops, because Christ stops cleansing our record until we repent and start walking in the light again. Walking in the light is synonymous with "walking in the Spirit", "having the obedience of faith", "walking on the narrow way", or, "living by faith" – they all mean the same thing.

While we are walking in the light, we will have two types of sins: **known trespass** and **unknown trespass**. The known trespasses must be confessed and repented of, or they become willful rebellion and we have *"no more sacrifice for sin, but a certain looking for of judgment and fiery indignation" (Heb. 10:26).* If we confess our sins, Jesus, our High Priest will cleanse us and our record in heaven. The *ignorant sins* or *unknown trespasses* are automatically covered while we are walking faithfully in the light we have and willing to receive and obey more.

Heb 7:22 *By so much was Jesus made a surety of a better Covenant. 23 And they truly were many priests, because they were not suffered to continue by reason of death: 24 But this man, because he continueth ever, hath an unchangeable priesthood. 25 Wherefore he is able also to save them to the uttermost that **come** unto God by him, **seeing he ever liveth to make intercession for them.***

Here we see that Jesus is a much greater High Priest; but we must continually come and make use of His services so we can be saved all the way to the end. The word "come" in verse 25 is "present participle" in the Greek and means to **"keep coming"**. If we don't keep coming to our High Priest and making confession, He will not keep interceding and "keeping us saved" to the uttermost – to the end. The schoolmaster has taught us all these principles; and we must follow them in order to be saved by the Faith/Doctrine of Christ.

Chapter Seventeen
"Moses Said" – How Important Is that?

The Law of Moses was the **Law of God** to *all* mankind for their reconciliation with God. God's Law leads men to repentance and shows them their need for Atonement. God's Law shows us what sin is (Ro 3:20), and what we need to repent of (Ro 7:7). It was not just for Israel, but a manifestation of God's ways to *all* mankind. How do I know? Because any man from any nation who wanted to reconcile with God once Moses' Law was given had to convert to Moses' Law and the prescribed atonements. Sin is still today the transgression of God's Law; it is the Law Jesus lived to fulfill and shed His blood to satisfy; and if you want to get right with God, you must get right with His Law!

In Matthew 22:36 Jesus was asked which commandment in the Law was the greatest. The man most likely had the Ten Commandments in view as these are the ones written with the finger of God on the tables of stone; but Jesus didn't mention one of them. Jesus, **instead**, quoted an exhortation which Moses later gave the people as the **greatest commandment in the Law**.

De 6:5 *And thou shalt love the LORD thy God with all thine heart, and with all thy soul, and with all thy might.*

Those defending Marcion's premise while denying they are Marcionites usually try to claim that "Yes, Jesus' Father is the God of the OT; and there is only one true

God". They think this delivers them from being Marcionites; but as long as they are trying to make Jesus' teaching contrary to Moses' Law they are still fighting for Marcion's heresy with a different approach. They think they avoid implicating God as having changed by blaming and thus demeaning what "Moses said". They dream that Moses gave compromising commands because, "*them old Israelites had hard hearts*"; but they are too Biblically illiterate to realize what Jesus was saying about the "hard hearts". **All** sin and carnality today is still due to hard hearts. All fallen men have hard hearts until God's Law is written in their hearts by the Holy Ghost. **Show me ONE divorce that isn't due to a hard heart in one of the two!**

Jesus's own disciples had hard hearts at times and Paul warns the Jewish Christians to beware of having hard hearts like Israel in Hebrews chapter 3. It wasn't just the Jews who had hard hearts! We have to crucify our flesh and circumcise our hearts just like all fallen men who wish to have a relationship with God. The heathen Gentile idolaters were certainly more hard hearted than God's covenant people when Moses gave the Law.

People who have divorce and remarriage in their past and come to the Mennonites/Amish as they are growing in grace and seeking a more conservative church, are then told they are living in adultery and must separate. These Mennonites/Amish claim that Moses' teaching was *just for hard hearts*; but don't even think about these people having come from the world as lost sinners and are *only now* seeking God! What lost sinner doesn't have a hard heart? What divorce is not due to a hard heart? I am convinced this false Marcion based doctrine is really because the *Mennonites/Amish have hard hearts...and heads.* They really don't want to nurture and disciple these hard cases; so they like their Marcionite escape.

All God's commandments in Scripture are given as remedial directives to a fallen, hard hearted race of people. Jesus was reminding the Jews of this fact, which is why He immediately compared their present state and present needs with how it was in the Garden of Eden. Jesus didn't say that Moses wrote the commandment for "those ancient Jews with hard hearts"; but He clearly said, "For the hardness of **your** heart he wrote **you** this precept." Jesus was speaking to the same type of people that Moses was speaking to. God's Law included the first five books of the Bible with the history and the precepts from Sinai. ALL of it was the Law, so you were to interpret it as a WHOLE. Thus, you have the ORIGINAL INTENT OF MARRIAGE given in the Garden before man sinned; then you have MAN'S FALL; and then you have THE LAWS given as God's directives for "What to do now with a fallen society". Jesus was reminding the Jews of this fact, so they would rightly interpret Moses' Law in light of its INTENT. All God's Laws were intended to be used by sincere, godly people in order to FIX problems and maintain holiness in society – NOT to *make* problems and *cause* injustice. It is the abuse of Moses' Law that Jesus is correcting, not the proper usage!

In Numbers 12 we find two other people trying to demean Moses – *Big Sister Miriam* and *Big Brother Aaron*. They learned a hard lesson that Marcionites will someday learn the hard way if they do not repent of trying to demean Moses.

***Nu 12:1** And Miriam and Aaron spake against Moses because of the Ethiopian woman whom he had married: for he had married an Ethiopian woman. 2 And they said, Hath the*

LORD indeed spoken only by Moses? hath he not spoken also by us? And the LORD heard it. 3 **(Now the man Moses was very meek, above all the men which were upon the face of the earth.)** *4 And the LORD spake suddenly unto Moses, and unto Aaron, and unto Miriam, Come out ye three unto the tabernacle of the congregation. And they three came out. 5 And the LORD came down in the pillar of the cloud, and stood in the door of the tabernacle, and called Aaron and Miriam: and they both came forth. 6 And he said,* **Hear now my words: If there be a prophet among you, I the LORD will make myself known unto him in a vision, and will speak unto him in a dream. 7 My servant Moses is not so, who is faithful in all mine house. 8 With him will I speak mouth to mouth, even apparently, and not in dark speeches; and the similitude of the LORD shall he behold: wherefore then were ye not afraid to speak against my servant Moses?**

So often I find that heresy and error come from a lack of discernment between two different principles which are mistakenly lumped together as one. An example of this is with those who say, "Don't you believe Jesus was greater than Moses?" Why, OF COURSE I do! But that is not the issue! *Were Jesus' words greater than Moses' inspired writings?* **This is the issue**. We are not comparing Jesus with Moses as a man; but Jesus' teaching with Moses' teaching. **If Jesus, THE WORD, inspired ALL SCRIPTURE, then Moses' words WERE JESUS' WORDS**. Moses was just a messenger; but God's Word is clear that Moses was a **FAITHFUL** messenger.

Heb 3:1 *Wherefore, holy brethren, partakers of the heavenly calling, consider the Apostle and High Priest of our profession, Christ Jesus; 2* **Who was faithful to him that appointed him, as also Moses was faithful in all his house. 3 For this man was counted worthy of more glory than Moses, inasmuch as he who hath builded the house hath more honour than the house.** *4 For every house is builded by some man; but* *he that built all things is God. 5 And **Moses verily was faithful in all his house, as a servant, for a testimony of those things which were to be spoken after;** 6 But **Christ as a son over his own house**; whose house are we, if we hold fast the confidence and the rejoicing of the hope firm unto the end.*

Jesus as a man was much more eminent than Moses; but the Word of God through Moses, was still the Word of God.

Some try to build on the situation with the appearance of Moses and Elijah with Jesus on the Mount of Transfiguration where God says, "This is my beloved Son: hear Him"; and try to say that this means "Hear Jesus in correction of Moses and Elijah". However, this is not what the Apostles received from that experience by Peter's own words to the contrary.

2Pe 1:16 *For we have not followed cunningly devised fables, when we made known unto you the power and coming of our Lord Jesus Christ, but were eyewitnesses of his majesty. 17 For he received from God the Father honour and glory, when there came such a voice to him from the excellent glory, This is my beloved Son, in whom I am well pleased. 18 And this voice which came from heaven we heard, when we were with him in the holy mount. 19 **We have also a more sure word of prophecy;** whereunto ye do well that ye take heed, as unto a light that shineth in a dark place, until the day dawn, and the day star arise in your hearts: 20 **Knowing this first, that no prophecy of the scripture is of any private interpretation. 21 For the prophecy came not in old time by the will of man: but holy men of God spake as they were moved by the Holy Ghost.***

Obviously Peter knew the difference between the preeminence of Jesus as the Son of God and the consistent purity and inspiration of the Scriptures regardless of the channel used.

Did Jesus believe it was right to make God's moral judgments given by Moses of **none affect** by **new teaching?** Listen to Jesus, and His esteem for what "Moses said". Do you think Jesus would come and do the same that He is rebuking these men for doing?

*Mk 7:5 Then the Pharisees and scribes asked him, Why walk not thy disciples according to the tradition of the elders, but eat bread with unwashen hands? 6 He answered and said unto them, Well hath Esaias prophesied of you hypocrites, as it is written, This people honoureth me with their lips, but their heart is far from me. 7 Howbeit in vain do they worship me, teaching for doctrines the **commandments of men**. 8 For laying aside the **commandment of God,** ye hold the **tradition of men,** as the washing of pots and cups: and many other such like things ye do. 9 And he said unto them, Full well ye reject the **commandment of God,** that ye may keep your own tradition. 10 For **Moses said,** Honour thy father and thy mother; and, Whoso curseth father or mother, let him die the death: 11 But ye say, If a man shall say to his father or mother, It is Corban, that is to say, a gift, by whatsoever thou mightest be profited by me; he shall be free. 12 And ye suffer him no more to do ought for his father or his mother; 13 Making the **word of God** of none effect through your tradition, which ye have delivered: and many such like things do ye.*

Notice how Jesus makes what "Moses said" synonymous with "commandment of God" and "Word of God" and also contrasts it with the "tradition of men". These religious leaders were making a moral obligation void by the introduction of new teaching, i.e. teaching introduced since the Law was given by Moses. Jesus makes it clear that no new teaching is valid or correct if it makes the Scriptures void or "of none affect". We can be sure that Jesus never did such a thing as present new teaching which makes one of God's moral judgments **of none affect.**

Who actually said "Honor thy Father and Mother"?

Mt 15:4 For <u>God commanded</u>, saying, Honour thy father and mother: and, He that curseth father or mother, let him die the death.

Mark's Gospel has "Moses said" while Matthew has "God commanded" – which is true? Obviously what Moses said was inspired by God, and **everywhere** you read of Moses saying something in the New Testament, you can insert **"God"** in the passage without doing any injustice to the meaning! Try this with Matt. 19:7-8 and you'll get the right idea.

Mt 19:6 Wherefore they are no more twain, but one flesh. What therefore God hath joined together, let not man put asunder. 7 They say unto him, Why did **GOD** then command to give a writing of divorcement, and to put her away? 8 He saith unto them, **GOD** because of the hardness of your hearts suffered you to put away your wives: but from the beginning it was not so.

Marcionite pride causes men to demean Moses' writings as less than God's Holy and Eternal Word to mankind. People with the same pride also demean the Apostles and "Only follow the RED LETTERS" that Jesus spoke. They don't realize that it was the Apostles who wrote those RED LETTERS. The only thing Jesus ever wrote as far as we know is when He knelt down and wrote in the sand with His finger. Jesus is the *author* of the RED LETTERS AS WELL AS THE BLACK LETTERS IN THE OLD TESTAMENT AS WELL AS THE NEW TESTAMENT; but He *wrote* NONE of them.

When people don't like part of God's Law given through Moses, they want to say that, "Well, in this place Moses is compromising or in error"; but this means that not all Moses' Law is God's Law or inspired. How are we then to know what is *the inspired Word of God* and what is not? If you believe God's Apostles then you know what Moses wrote *was* **THE WORD OF GOD**, not the word of Moses – **see 2Pe 1:21; 2Ti 3:16; He 3:2-5.**

Could not the Pharisees have justly condemned Jesus with hypocrisy had he been making the commandments of God of none effect by his own tradition? What would these Jews think if they heard Jesus correcting Moses' Law and then telling of the rich man and Lazarus? The rich man cries for someone to go back to his brothers on earth and warn them to repent – and what does Jesus say to them by way of Abraham speaking to the rich man? "They have **Moses and the prophets**; **let them hear them**." This was Jesus' salvation message to the people via the story in Luke 16:19-31.

The Sabbath

But, someone will say, "Jesus broke the Sabbath" (Jn 5). **Did He?** Before making such accusations, you might want to find out who you are agreeing with.

*Jn 5:17 But Jesus answered them, My Father worketh hitherto, and I work. 18 Therefore the Jews sought the more to kill him, because he not only had **broken the sabbath,** but said also that God was his Father, making himself equal with God.*

The Jews claimed that Jesus broke the Sabbath by healing a man and having him go home carrying his bed. **Was this really breaking the Sabbath? Of course not! Listen to Jesus' defense and explanation.**

Jn 7:22 Moses therefore gave unto you circumcision; (not because it is of Moses, but of the fathers;) and ye on the sabbath day circumcise a man. 23 If a man on the sabbath day receive circumcision, that the law of Moses should not be broken; are ye angry at me, because I have made a man every whit whole on the sabbath day? 24 **Judge not according to the appearance, but judge righteous judgment.**

Mt. 12:1 *At that time Jesus went on the sabbath day through the corn; and his disciples were an hungred, and began to pluck the ears of corn, and to eat. 2 But when the Pharisees saw it, they said unto him, Behold, thy disciples do that which is not lawful to do upon the sabbath day. 3 But he said unto them,* **Have ye not read what David did,** *when he was an hungred, and they that were with him; 4 How he entered into the house of God, and did eat the shewbread, which was not lawful for him to eat, neither for them which were with him, but only for the priests? 5 Or* **have ye not read in the law**, *how that on the sabbath days the priests in the temple profane the sabbath,* **and are blameless?** *6 But I say unto you, That in this place is one greater than the temple. 7 But if ye had known what this meaneth, I will have mercy, and not sacrifice,* **ye would not have condemned the guiltless.** *8 For the Son of man is Lord even of the sabbath day. 9 And when he was departed thence, he went into their synagogue: 10 And, behold, there was a man which had his hand withered. And they asked him, saying, Is it lawful to heal on the sabbath days? that they might accuse him. 11 And he said unto them, What man shall there be among you, that shall have one sheep, and if it fall into a pit on the sabbath day, will he not lay hold on it, and lift it out? 12 How much then is a man better than a sheep?* **Wherefore it is <u>lawful</u> to do well on the sabbath days.**

Jesus was doing God's work just like the priests in the temple who do not get to rest on the Sabbath day, but are blameless. Not only that, but Jesus explains to them that **it is indeed lawful to "do well" i.e. works of charity or mercy on the Sabbath day.** The word Sabbath means "rest". God wanted them to rest from normal labor and focus on spiritual matters on the Sabbath day. The Sabbath was meant to be a blessing, not a curse. They understood the necessity for taking care of their animals on the Sabbath day; but refused to acknowledge Jesus' higher claim to healing the sick; which they never dealt with before and could not emulate. They were jealous fault finders, rather than sincere truth seekers. The Sabbath is not broken by child birth, circumcision, temple service, or **any other necessity of life**. Jesus, as Lord and author of the Sabbath, said the Sabbath was made for man, not man for the Sabbath. He as The WORD made flesh gave the proper interpretation of the Law concerning the Sabbath. The Jew's own writings about David eating the showbread acknowledge, *"There is nothing which may hinder taking care of life, beside idolatry, adultery, and murder."* According to the Jews, one should do any thing but these in order to preserve life; even if on the Sabbath Day. (See Clarke on Mt. 12:3) The Moral Law superceded the Ceremonial obligations. We all understand this principle unless we are trying to find fault as these men were.

Though the Sabbath Day was part of the ceremonial law, Jesus did not violate it. In fact, Jesus perfectly obeyed both the moral and ceremonial Law so He could be SINLESS as the spotless Lamb of God to take away the sins of the world. To violate God's Law was SIN, and Jesus committed NO SIN.

The Woman Caught In Adultery

Others will say that Jesus violated God's Law when He did not condemn the woman taken in adultery (Jn 8). Is this true? Absolutely not! They are just showing they do not have an understanding of the Scriptures. One minute the "in denial" Marcionites say that Jesus "raised the bar" in not allowing divorce and remarriage; and in the next breath they say Jesus did away with the death penalty for adultery. Can you see the inconsistency in this? What principle would He be operating on to raise the demand upon people and then lower the penalty? Their reasoning is confused and we know God is not the author of confusion.

*Mk 7:9 And he said unto them, Full well **ye reject the commandment of God, that ye may keep your own tradition**. 10 For Moses said, Honour thy father and thy mother; and, **Whoso curseth father or mother, <u>let him die the death:</u>** 11 But ye say..."*

Jesus defended the death penalty for dishonoring parents, and reproved the Pharisees for violating God's Word, so why would He change it for the adulterer? He didn't! Jesus agreed 100% with Moses, because HE INSPIRED MOSES. The facts of the case are as follows.

*De 17:6 At the mouth of two witnesses, or three witnesses, shall he that is worthy of death be put to death; **but at the mouth of one witness he shall not be put to death. (Nu 35:30; De 19:15)***

How many witnesses did Jesus have to condemn her? **None - they all left.** The witnesses were to be the ones who cast the first stones, which is what He told them to do; but they were not righteous in what they were doing, and so they felt convicted and left. They were simply trying to get Jesus in trouble with the authorities; because the Romans had taken away the Jews right to put people to death by their own law.

*Joh 18:31 Then said Pilate unto them, Take ye him, and judge him according to your law. The Jews therefore said unto him, **It is not lawful for us to put any man to death:***

Jesus knew they were not righteous witnesses, because they said they caught her **in the very act**, but, "**Where was the man**?" Where was the angry husband? Jesus knew what they were up to:

Lu 20:20 *And they watched him, and sent forth spies, which should feign themselves just men, that they might take hold of his words, **that so they might deliver him unto the power and authority of the governor.***

When Jesus stooped down and wrote, we all wonder what He wrote in that sand – maybe, "*Thou shalt not bear false witness*"? Jesus knew the law better than they did, and put it back in their lap. Jesus said that, **if they were just and not sinful in what they were doing, then let the true and just witnesses cast the first stones** as the Law commanded. This is what Jesus meant by "He that is without sin" i.e. "He that is a just witness", and therefore not sinning in this situation; **not** "He that is sinless in all of life". Jesus knew that nobody is sinless!! I've had people argue with me that this is what Jesus meant. So, can they spank their child when they themselves are not sinless? Can the police or magistrate ever arrest or punish criminals without being themselves SINLESS? Is this what they think Jesus was teaching? So, now we know where the world gets their faulty "judge not" mentality when you try to lead them to repentance – *from these faulty Bible scholars*. It is terrible to take Jesus' clear words and make them into nonsense and heresy like many have done.

De 17:7 *The **hands of the witnesses shall be first upon him to put him to death,** and afterward the hands of all the people. So thou shalt put the evil away from among you.*

The witnesses were to cast the first stones.

De 19:18 *And the judges shall make diligent inquisition: and, behold, if the witness be a false witness, and hath testified falsely against his brother; 19 Then shall ye do unto him, as he had thought to have done unto his brother: so shalt thou put the evil away from among you.*

All legal proceedings under God's Laws were a part of a complete legal program with judges overseeing and investigating the situation. People could not just gather two witnesses and stone somebody apart from the proper oversight and authority of leaders being present. These men were purposely avoiding God's order in trying to trick Jesus into breaking the law so they could accuse Him. **Why?? Because they knew that Jesus was FAITHFUL to Moses' Law and defended its original intent! They knew that Jesus would obey the Scriptures, so they thought they could trap Him this way. This speaks volumes against Marcion to anyone who is listening.** This is not the only time they tried to take advantage of Jesus' faithful commitment to the Scriptures to try and get Him in trouble. Satan even used this tactic because He knew Jesus would not violate the Scriptures – And what did Jesus tell that old devil?

Mt 4:4 *But he answered and said, It is written, Man shall not live by bread alone, but by **every word** that proceedeth out of the mouth of God.*

After the unjust witnesses all left, Jesus said to the woman, "hath no man condemned thee?" i.e. "are there not any witnesses?" Jesus then also did not condemn her to death, as that would be contrary to God's Law. Jesus could not condemn her to death without any witnesses. Jesus was not "two witnesses" or even a magistrate. YES, Jesus condemned her sin; but that is not what the context is speaking of. The context is "condemning her to death".

This Jesus could not lawfully or righteously do under Moses' Law. Jesus fully did what was lawful and right in this situation, and in so doing He called their bluff, as they simply wanted to entangle Him with the Roman authorities who had taken the power of life and death away from the Jews. He **did** condemn her as a sinner, for He told her to **go and sin no more**; but He didn't condemn her to death, as there were no reliable witnesses.

God says He would write His laws – **not new and different laws** - in our hearts as the foundation of the New Covenant. Obviously our adversaries are confused. How sad they will not accept the obvious truth of God's Word. God told Moses what every true prophet would be like; and this very description includes Jesus the Christ and ultimate prophet.

*De 18:17 And the LORD said unto me, They have well spoken that which they have spoken. 18 I will raise them up a Prophet from among their brethren, **like unto thee**, and will put **my words in his mouth**; and he shall speak unto them all that I shall command him. 19 And it shall come to pass, that whosoever will not hearken unto **my words** which **he shall speak in my name**, I will require it of him.*

This applied to every prophet and ultimately pointed to the Lord Jesus Christ. Notice God is telling Moses that all the prophets, including the Messiah, would **only** be speaking **God's Words** (like Faithful Moses: He 3:5). Would they or could they contradict or change God's moral judgments or speak contradictory messages? Never! Moses spoke **God's Word**, the prophets spoke **God's Word**, and Jesus spoke **God's Word** (**He WAS God's Word**) – wouldn't they be the same in judgment? Wouldn't they give the same prescription? All the prophets after Moses were actually discerned to be true or false according to how they lined up with Moses' writings.

Remember our Bible Literacy Test:

1. In our New Testament in many Bibles there are words printed in **Black** and words printed in Red, which ones did Jesus author?

Answer: Jesus didn't write any of them, but He authored ALL of them.

2. We have an Old Testament and New Testament in our English Bible, which represents the teachings of Jesus?

Answer: It all represents the teachings of Jesus who is the WORD OF GOD from Genesis to Revelation.

Chapter Eighteen
We Establish The Law

Ro 3:25 *Whom God hath **set forth** to be a propitiation through faith in his blood, to declare his* **[justification]** *for the remission of sins that are past* **(Genesis to Christ),** *through the forbearance of God; 26 To declare, I say, at this time his* **[justification]***: that he (God) might be **just**, and the **justifier** of him which believeth in Jesus...31 Do we then make void the law through faith? God forbid: yea, **we establish the law.***

The Crucifixion of Jesus Christ was a public display of God's attitude toward man's sin as well as a legal substitute for the execution of all sinners. Without such an awful display and substitute, God could never forgive one sinner, lest he be thought to sympathize with sin or sinners - Lest his hatred for sin, and love for holiness come into question - Lest some should think he didn't fully agree with His Law, or thought it was too harsh, etc. I first learned to appreciate the following principles from reading over Charles Finney's Systematic Theology.

In Establishing Government and upholding law and order, the governor is pledged to duly administer laws in support of public order, in support of public morals, and to reward the innocent and punish those who violate the law. Every time someone violates the law, the innocent, law abiding citizens are damaged, thus, the governor is committed to upholding the law for the sake of society as a whole. God's Law is LOVE and therefore seeks the highest good for all creation.

There is an important difference between retributive justice, and public justice. Retributive justice demands punishment without exception upon the individual criminal to uphold the honor and obedience due to the law for the protection of the public interests; whereas public justice may allow for mercy on the individual if a higher good for society may be procured. Public justice allows mercy or pardon upon the individual on the condition that **something else be done** that upholds and supports law and order for all society as effectively as the execution of the law would do with an added benefit which makes it preferable and even considered.

The design of legal penalties is to secure respect and obedience to the law. The same is also the reason for executing penalties when the law is violated. The penalties are to be regarded as an expression of the views of the lawgiver, in respect to the importance of his law.

His execution of the penalties reveals his sincerity, commitment, and determination to abide by the principles of his government. The execution of the penalties reveals his abhorrence for all crime, and his love for his faithful law abiding subjects. The execution of the penalties shows his unalterable determination to carry out, support and establish the authority and righteousness of his laws. The execution of the penalties proves his perfect satisfaction and agreement with His Law – He does not think it is too hard or asking too much. He believes His Law is reasonable and His subjects have the ability to keep it.

It is a fact well established by experience of all ages and nations, that the exercise of mercy, in setting aside the execution of penalties, is a matter of extreme delicacy and danger. The influence of law, as might be expected, is found very much to depend upon the certainty felt by the subjects that it will be duly executed. The exercise of mercy has always been found to weaken government by begetting and fostering a hope of exemption, second chance, or escape from the penalties of the law in the minds of those who are tempted to violate the law. I say, it always weakens law and order *unless* a **sufficient substitute** is set forth instead of the execution of the penalties of the law on the offender - a substitutionary action which not only vindicates the Law; but also excites new motives for obeying the law over the previous fear of execution and thus seeks a higher end.

WHAT IS a sufficient substitute? Since the head of government is pledged to protect and promote the public interests by a due administration of righteous laws, if in any instance where the law is violated, he would set aside the execution of the penalties, public justice and LOVE requires that a substitute for the execution of the law is provided, or that something is done that **will as effectually** secure the influence of law, as the execution of the penalty would have done. He cannot make exceptions to the spirit of the law (LOVE) – Either the soul that sinneth must surely die, according to the letter of the law and retributive justice; or a substitute must be provided in accordance with the spirit of the law and public justice. The letter and the spirit of the Law have the same ultimate goal, and the letter demanding execution may be set aside as long as this goal is still reached or reached in a better way. A higher good, one that is more advantageous to society on the whole, must be in view for a substitute to be considered by the lawgiver.

When these conditions are fulfilled, the lawgiver's regard for his law is upheld; His determination to support it is manifested; His abhorrence for sin is expressed; the danger to violators is as clearly displayed; and **new motives** for obedience instituted so that violaters genuinely repent, make restitution, change their heart to agree with the lawgiver, and return to obedience; then and only then is it safe to pardon and extend mercy, because by this substitutionary action, public justice and the spirit of the law have been upheld with a higher good being procured.

When you add together the life, teachings, example, sacrifice, sanctification, rehabilitation program, heavenly priesthood, and overall administration of Jesus Christ, the Son of God, and how it can transform and save fallen man; you have God's infinite wisdom in not just executing all sinners; but choosing to pardon those who are redeemed and rehabilitated in Jesus Christ.

If you notice, the *Day of Atonement* in the Law of Moses incorporated both the goat for the Sin Offering and also the Scapegoat. Why did God's picture of atonement need two goats?

Le 16:7 And he shall take the two goats, and present them before the LORD at the door of the tabernacle of the congregation. 8 And Aaron shall cast lots upon the two goats; one lot for the LORD, and the other lot for the scapegoat. 9 And Aaron shall bring the goat upon which the LORD'S lot fell, and offer him for a sin offering. 10 But the goat, on which the lot fell to be the scapegoat, shall be presented alive before the LORD, to make an atonement with him, and to let him go for a scapegoat into the wilderness.

Atonement in God's eyes is more than just the blood sacrifice; but also includes the resurrected Savior and His continued work as our High Priest to apply His blood and intercede. The goat that *bear the sins away* into another land pictured Christ's Priestly work in the heavens. They could not have a goat die and then rise again to picture Christ's full work of atonement; so God used two goats. The scapegoat never came back; but listen to Hebrews in referring to Christ as our sin-bearer:

Heb 9:28 *So Christ was* **once offered to bear the sins of many**; *and* **unto them that look for him shall he appear the second time** *without sin unto salvation.*

The sinless and perfect sacrifice of the Son of God fully paid the price for sin satisfying the Law and propitiating the Lawgiver – God; but no man would be saved without Christ's continued work as our Priest and Shepherd. Christ's offering himself without spot as a sin offering; then rising to administrate His rehabilitation program and Priesthood so fully displays God's love for his law, his hatred of sin, His determination to uphold law and order, and his unwillingness to compromise with sin, that it opens the door for God to safely pardon repentant sinners in Jesus' name, love them, and ultimately save them if they continued under Christ's rehabilitation and sanctification program.

Pardoning the repentant sinner and satisfying the Law with Christ's atonement, rather than the execution of the penalty, seeks a greater good; which is why it is even considered and acceptable. Consider the Apostle Paul: Had God executed the penalty of the Law; Paul's damnation would have served to uphold the Law through retributive justice. Wasn't it a much grander goal to convert, pardon, and enlist him in the service of the Lord

225

to "preach the faith which he once destroyed"? Of course! And BECAUSE Paul repented, surrendered, suffered, and served with all his might, **God's choice** to pardon, rather than execute the law **was justified**; and **Jesus' atonement** in his behalf **was also justified**. However, if Paul had proven to be a Simon, Judas, Demas, etc; it would have undermined God's integrity and credibility to **save him anyway**, *which is why He doesn't*. God's investment of love and mercy in Paul was fully justified because of his faithfulness to demonstrate and cooperate with God's higher loving purpose.

Consider reading Hebrews 11 if all the men were lazy, faithless, wretches who just prayed a "sinner's prayer" and lived in selfishness and pride. **What would this say about God's holiness and administration as *Judge of all the earth*?** What would it say about Christ's wisdom in dying and saving them from the due reward of their deeds? What message would it send to God's loyal subjects who love and revere His Law? (Ez. 13:22) It certainly would not make Him JUST *and* the JUSTIFIER of those that believe in Jesus. You must live in such a way that you actually **justify your justification** and vindicate God's salvation plan; or you betray your Savior and bring reproach upon the Gospel. This is why the righteousness of the law must be fulfilled in all believers. This is how we establish the Law by our faith.

*Ro 8:1 There is therefore now no condemnation to them which are in Christ Jesus, **who walk not after the flesh, but after the Spirit**. 2 For the law of the Spirit of life in Christ Jesus hath made me free from the law of sin and death. 3 For what the law could not do, in that it was weak through the flesh, God sending his own Son in the likeness of sinful flesh, and for sin, condemned sin in the flesh: 4 **That the righteousness of the*** *law might be fulfilled in us, who walk not after the flesh, but after the Spirit.*

He 11:16 *But now they desire a better country, that is, an heavenly:* **wherefore God is not ashamed to be called their God:** *for he hath prepared for them a city.*

Mt 7:21 *Not every one that saith unto me, Lord, Lord, shall enter into the kingdom of heaven;* **but he that doeth the will** *of my Father which is in heaven.*

By demanding that we become disciples of Jesus Christ, and suffer for his cause (*Ph. 1:29*), as a true test of our repentance and sincere conversion, God has thoroughly protected against any idea that He sympathizes with sin.

Php 1:29 *For unto you it is given in the behalf of Christ,* **not only** *to* **believe on him,** *but also* **to suffer for his sake;**

Jesus perfectly qualified before God as the administrator of salvation because He "loved righteousness and hated iniquity" (Heb. 1:8,9). God so trusts Jesus to uphold the honor of God's government and Law that He has decreed that *only* those who **obey** and **please** Jesus will be saved (Heb. 5:9). See: Mark 8:34-38; 2 Cor. 6:17-7:1, etc. **Do you see then how Marcionite ideas are straight from hell? Marcionism slanders Jesus with changing God's Law and thus condemning God's wisdom and direction in the past.**

Satan, by his false antinomian Gospel with no demand of repentance, obedience, and faithfulness is also trying to misrepresent God, and thereby destroy the influence of God's Law and government! Satan hopes to defeat the effects of Christ's atonement and administration, so as to slander God's LOVE and WISDOM:

- By insinuating that God sympathizes with sinners

- By reducing or diluting the manifestation of God's hatred for sin
- By implying that sinners are victims, rather than deserving of God's wrath
- By implying that God actually created some to be sinners
- By implying that God doesn't expect us to obey his law – that he never intended us to do so, or that we can't, etc.
- By inventing a false program where sinners do not become saints and God's justification is not thereby justified.

Satan, in all this, is striving to slander the holiness and righteousness of God's Law and government – WHY? To cover his own rebellion; and make him appear as a victim, rather than the villain. When anyone believes Satan, and follows his false gospel they are sure to be damned because they are helping Satan slander God rather than cooperating with and thus justifying God's salvation program.

The Antinomian gospel of "easy believe-ism" and "once saved – always saved" is destroying law and order in America as it did in Israel; because the proper respect and fear of God's Law and government is eroding fast! Jesus had to display a perfect hatred for iniquity (lawlessness), and love for righteousness (lawfulness) to even qualify as the Lamb to be slain:

Heb 1:8 *But unto the Son he saith, Thy throne, O God, is for ever and ever: a sceptre of righteousness is the sceptre of thy kingdom. 9 **Thou hast loved righteousness, and hated iniquity; therefore God, even thy God, hath anointed thee with the oil of gladness above thy fellows.***

The false teachings today concerning *grace, love, faith, God's Law*, and *Christ's rehabilitation program in the local church*, are all designed by the grand deceiver to erode the justifying of God's justification and bring dishonor upon the **Just One**. God's justice is slandered by all heretical teaching; but the true Gospel vindicates God's Law and justice. When sinners repent, turn to God, and do works **meet for repentance**, they are justifying God's wonderful mercy and grace toward mankind.

Jesus had to be extremely important, innocent and pure; and then die, suffering sufficient agony, shame, and reproach to display God's hatred of our sin, His determination to uphold the righteousness of His Law, and His unwillingness to compromise or sympathize with sin or sinners. Jesus had to willingly sacrifice Himself for our sins; then rise to minister in the tabernacle of heaven as our High Priest; and serve as our Chief Shepherd administrating His rehabilitation and sanctification program in His faithful churches. **All of this so my pardon would not compromise God and dishonor His government?! God did all this to protect the honor of His Law? Yes, and that is why Marcionism is so offensive to God. To insinuate that God's Law was a concession to sin which Jesus obviously didn't approve of and therefore changed is the doctrine of devils.**

Ro 3:31 *Do we then make void the law through faith? God forbid: yea, **we establish the law.***

Chapter Nineteen
No Law, No Grace

There can be no GRACE where this is no LAW. You cannot have a *grace period*, unless you first have a *deadline* or *due date*. There can be no pardon where there is no indictment. There can be no repentance, justification, pardon, or reconciliation, if there is no Law that is trespassed. When you are "under Law" it means you are under the Law *without grace*; but when you are "under grace", you are still under the law; but now you face the law **with** God's grace, and not without it. Jesus would not need to minister as our High Priest with His own blood and intercede for us to God if there were no laws trespassed and no obligation to obey God's Laws. God still commands, "be ye holy, for I am holy". The "grace period" never nullifies the debt owed; it only gives you another chance to pay without penalty. Similarly Jesus' blood and priesthood gives you another opportunity to do right and be victorious over temptation by cleansing the past failure. The Law is a vital part of the Gospel, and it is the Law of God's Kingdom. Jesus is the Lamb of the Law to make atonement for man's trespasses against God's Law. He had to fulfill the requirements of God's Law to qualify as God's Lamb.

The Gospel is God's plan to pardon and redeem us since we broke His Law and brought upon ourselves the sentence of death. Before we can appreciate this, we must know the Law we broke and understand the sentence of death upon us. Our repentance is our re-commitment to God's Moral Law, and our agreement with this Law against our sin. There is no way to reconcile with God unless we reconcile with His Law. Once we are pardoned, we are to live under God's moral law and strive to obey it – this is holiness.

You say, but how can I fulfill the righteousness of the Law? We are not speaking of a forensic justification; but Gospel justification, which is described in this chapter. **God's decision to operate upon Gospel justification, rather than demand forensic justification IS His GRACE.** 2 Cor. 8:12 gives us the very principle upon which our salvation rests.

*2Co 8:12 For if there be **first a willing mind,** it is **accepted according to that a man hath,** and **not according to that he hath not.***

Paul is speaking in the context of us pleasing God with monetary offerings, but it is the **same principle** for us pleasing God in any area. Pleasing God means "finding grace or favor in the sight of the Lord" like Noah did.

Ge 6:8 But Noah found grace in the eyes of the LORD.

Noah was saved by God's grace just like we are; and he became eligible for this grace by:

- **First**, having a willing mind and heart to please God;
- **Second**, giving God all that was in his power to give.

God accepted this by grace, which opened the door for God to pardon Noah and wash him in the blood of Jesus.

232

Heb 11:7 *By faith Noah, being warned of God of things not seen as yet,* ***moved with fear,*** ***prepared an ark*** *to the* ***saving of his house****; by the which he condemned the world, and* ***became heir of the righteousness (justification) which is by faith****.*

The word "righteousness" in the New Testament often means "justification", i.e. obtaining a righteous record or standing before God. God's gracious justification through the cleansing of Christ's blood, which gives us a righteous record and standing before God, is only given to those who <u>walk</u> by faith, and thus are faithful (Heb. 5:9; 11:6).

Abraham's faith is seen in giving to God what he could give with a willing mind/heart. In this he became the father of the faithful (Gal. 3:9).

Ge 26:5 *...Abraham obeyed my voice, and kept my charge, my commandments, my statutes, and my laws.*

God had commanded him, "Walk before me and be thou perfect" (Gen. 17:1). Was God asking something that Abraham could not give? Jesus commands the same thing of us:

Mt 5:48 *Be ye therefore* ***perfect****, even as your Father which is in heaven is perfect.*

Is Jesus commanding more than we can perform? No, He is not. He is not commanding us to offer perfect performance or a perfect record of obedience; because He knows this is impossible. He is commanding us to have a sincere heart desire and whole hearted effort to please God with the light and ability we have.

Some try to say God gave His Law just to show we could not obey it; but this is foolishness. Which of the Ten Commandments can you not do? Consider what the

233

Bible says about Zacharias and Elisabeth as being righteous before God.

Lu 1:5 *There was in the days of Herod, the king of Judaea, a certain priest named Zacharias, of the course of Abia: and his wife was of the daughters of Aaron, and her name was Elisabeth.* *6 **And they were both righteous before God, walking in all the commandments and ordinances of the Lord blameless.***

Does this mean they didn't need a Savior? Did they need the Gospel? *Yes they did*; and these principles are important for you to understand. **Blameless** doesn't mean **sinless,** but that they were doing their best, and could not justly be blamed. It is the same principle as:

Mt 22:37 *"Thou shalt love the Lord thy God with **all thy** heart, and with **all thy** soul, and with **all thy** mind."*

I'm not asked to love God with all **your** heart; all **Paul's** heart; or all **Jesus'** heart; but with all **MY** heart. This I can give if I truly surrender and strive to do so – this is what the Bible says is having a "perfect" heart before God. This is not "sinless perfectionism" or "salvation by works", as neither of those positions require Christ's atonement for salvation. Being "perfect" in the Bible sense is what God requires before He will pardon us and wash us with Christ's atoning blood. It means **genuineness** in my repentance and faith. Sometimes it also means "mature" or "complete" depending on the context. Do a word study on the word "perfect" in the Bible.

We can take the principle of 2 Cor. 8:12 and state it in many different, yet synonymous ways:

1. For if there be first a willing mind, it is accepted according to that a man hath, and not according to that he hath not.

2. If there first be the obedience of faith, which we can offer, it is accepted in the place of perfect obedience, which we cannot offer.

3. God's grace is seen in accepting what we can give – the obedience of faith/willing mind; and not requiring what we cannot give – a perfect record of obedience. His acceptance makes us eligible for the atonement and priesthood of Christ to cleanse us and keep us clean.

In **2 Co 8:12** the word translated "willing mind" is *prothumia,* (proth-oo-mee'-ah), *predisposition*, *i.e. alacrity*; which means *cheerful readiness* or *cheerful willingness.* You can see this in the following verses:

Ac 17:11 *These were more noble than those in Thessalonica, in that they received the word with all readiness of mind, and searched the scriptures daily, whether those things were so.*

2Co 8:11 *Now therefore perform the doing of it; that as there was a readiness to will, so there may be a performance also out of that which ye have.12 For if there be first a willing mind, it is accepted according to that a man hath, and not according to that he hath not.*

This is the same principle which we see in the next two verses:

2Co 9:7 *Every man according as he purposeth in his heart, so let him give; not grudgingly, or of necessity: **for God loveth a cheerful giver.***

Ac 11:29 *Then the disciples,* **every man according to his ability, determined** *to send relief unto the brethren which dwelt in Judaea:*

God sees this as righteous — "they cheerfully determined to do their best!" This is the Spirit of Psalms 119:

Ps 119:1 *Blessed are the undefiled in the way, who walk in the law of the LORD. 2 Blessed are they that keep his testimonies, and* **that seek him with the whole heart.** *3 They also do no iniquity: they walk in his ways. 4 Thou hast commanded us to keep thy precepts diligently. 5* **O that my ways were directed to keep thy statutes!** *6 Then shall I not be ashamed, when I have respect unto all thy commandments. 7 I will praise thee with uprightness of heart, when I shall have learned thy righteous judgments....32* **I will run the way of thy commandments**, *when thou shalt enlarge my heart.*

This is what God is looking for, so He can righteously pour out His grace and mercy. This is all He requires from man, because He knows we have fallen and cannot atone for our own sins.

Mic 6:6 *Wherewith shall I come before the LORD, and bow myself before the high God? shall I come before him with burnt offerings, with calves of a year old? 7 Will the LORD be pleased with thousands of rams, or with ten thousands of rivers of oil? shall I give my firstborn for my transgression, the fruit of my body for the sin of my soul?*

This man sees the futility of trying to atone for his own sins. What is the answer?

Mic 6:8 *He hath shewed thee, O man, what is good; and* **what doth the LORD require of thee, but to do justly, and to love mercy, and to walk humbly with thy God?**

We cannot save ourselves; but we can offer a cheerful submission and obedience to the best of our ability. God accepts this living obeying faith – *according to what we have to offer,* and not, *according to what we do not have to offer!* And **God knows** when we are doing our best.

De 5:29 *O that there were **such an heart in them**, that they would **fear me**, and **keep all my commandments always**, that it might be well with them, and with their children for ever!*

He 8:10 *For this is the covenant that I will make with the house of Israel after those days, saith the Lord; **I will put my laws into their mind, and write them in their hearts:** and I will be to them a God, and **they shall be to me a people**:*

Giving ourselves to God cheerfully is our reasonable service:

Ro 12:1 *I beseech you therefore, brethren, by the mercies of God, that ye present your bodies a living sacrifice, holy, acceptable unto God, **which is your reasonable service**.*

Tit 2:11 *For the **grace of God that bringeth salvation** hath appeared to all men, 12 **Teaching us that, denying ungodliness and worldly lusts, we should live soberly, righteously, and godly, in this present world;** 13 Looking for that blessed hope, and the glorious appearing of the great God and our Saviour Jesus Christ; 14 Who gave himself for us**, that he might redeem us from all iniquity, and purify unto himself a peculiar people, zealous of good works.***

From Genesis to Revelation God's plan of salvation by grace has been the same in principle; and those who knew God understood what He expected if they would find grace in His sight. Romans 4 says David understood, and listen what he tells his son.

1Ch 28:9 *And thou, Solomon my son, know thou the God of thy father, and **serve** him with a **perfect heart** and with a **willing mind:** for the LORD searcheth all hearts, and understandeth all the imaginations of the thoughts: if thou **seek***

him, **he will be found of thee;** but if thou forsake him, he will cast thee off for ever.

The willing mind is not accepted alone, but is accepted along with us doing what we can do, and giving what we can give. This is the only righteous way God can accept us and wash us in the blood of Jesus, and make us His children.

2Co 6:17 Wherefore come out from among them, and be ye separate, saith the Lord, and touch not the unclean thing; **and I will receive you,** 18 And **will be a Father unto you,** and **ye shall be my sons and daughters,** saith the Lord Almighty

I could fill volumes with illustrations of this principle from Scripture; but I'm trying not to over burden you. Bear with me now as I explain a very important chapter dealing with this very subject. Please pay close attention.

Ro 10:1 Brethren, my heart's desire and prayer to God for Israel is, that they might be saved. 2 For I bear them record that they have a zeal of God, but not according to knowledge. 3 For they being ignorant of God's **[justification],** and going about to establish their own **[justification]**, have not submitted themselves unto the **[justification]** of God **(God's way of justifying men).** 4 For Christ is the end **(goal and aim)** of the law for **[justification]** to every one that believeth. 5 For Moses describeth the **[justification]** which is of the law **(alone without grace)**, That the man which doeth those things shall live by them. **(perfect obedience = life)** 6 But the **[justification]** which is of faith speaketh on this wise, Say not in thine heart, Who shall ascend into heaven? (that is, to bring Christ down from above:) 7 Or, Who shall descend into the deep? (that is, to bring up Christ again from the dead.)

Paul is adapting a passage from the OT to illustrate the difference between **justification by God's plumb-line alone**, which demands perfect obedience; and **justification by grace,** which demands us believing God and doing what we can do – and that being accepted by grace. The passage Paul is adapting is Deut. 30:10-16

De 30:10 *If thou shalt hearken unto the voice of the LORD thy God, to keep his commandments and his statutes which are written in this book of the law, and* ***if thou turn unto the LORD thy God with all thine heart, and with all thy soul.*** *11 ¶ For this commandment which I command thee this day, it is not hidden from thee, neither is it far off. 12 It is not in heaven, that thou shouldest say, Who shall go up for us to heaven, and bring it unto us, that we may hear it, and do it? 13 Neither is it beyond the sea, that thou shouldest say, Who shall go over the sea for us, and bring it unto us, that we may hear it, and do it? 14 But the word is very nigh unto thee, in thy mouth, and in thy heart, that thou mayest do it. 15 ¶ See, I have set before thee this day life and good, and death and evil; 16 In that I command thee this day to love the LORD thy God, to walk in his ways, and to keep his commandments and his statutes and his judgments, that thou mayest live and multiply: and the LORD thy God shall bless thee in the land whither thou goest to possess it.*

What is the point? This passage in Deut. is dealing with God's people getting right **after** they have been carried away into captivity due to sin. What if they want to turn their hearts back to God and obey all his Laws, but they don't have a complete copy, and can't obtain it?

"Who shall go over the sea for us, and bring it unto us, that we may hear it, and do it?"

Are they lost without hope? NO! Praise the Lord! God never expected perfect obedience, but a **perfect heart** – a sincere desire and effort to obey what they **did have**. This was "nigh" them, and they could do it anywhere. Paul uses this to illustrate the difference between justification before God through the principle of Law alone without grace – *forensic justification*; and then justification through God's gracious acceptance of me doing that which I can and know to do – *Gospel jusification*.   In Romans he adapts the passage to someone in the New Covenant thinking they must be perfect and understand all Christ's will as though obeying Christ for a forensic type justification:

Ro 10:6 *But the righteousness* **(justification)** *which is of faith speaketh on this wise, Say not in thine heart, Who shall ascend into heaven? (that is, to bring Christ down from above:) 7 Or, Who shall descend into the deep? (that is, to bring up Christ again from the dead.) 8 But what saith it? The word is nigh thee, even in thy mouth, and in thy heart: that is, the word of faith, which we preach; 9* **That if thou shalt confess with thy mouth the Lord Jesus, and shalt believe in thine heart that God hath raised him from the dead, thou shalt be saved***.*

Since Christ is the culmination and climax of the Law concerning our justification; Paul replaces Moses' Law in the passage with Christ's will and teaching – it is the same principle (Jesus is the Word). If you confess Jesus as your Lord and sincerely believe with your heart, you don't have to perfectly "know" it all, or perfectly "do" it all. Paul is showing that the principle of justification through a living, striving faith is taught in the OT; and is God's only means of saving sinners in the NT and the OT. The Jews went about to establish self atonement/justification through keeping Moses' Law as in a forensic type justification, and then thought God owed them justification (declaration of righteousness) as a debt.   They vainly assumed the blood of bulls and goats could take away sins apart from Christ's sacrifice and the grace of God.   Paul continues:

Ro 10:10 *For with the heart man believeth unto righteousness; and with the mouth confession is made unto salvation. 11 For* **the scripture saith,** *"Whosoever believeth on him shall not be ashamed." 12 For there is no difference between the Jew and the Greek: for the same Lord over all is*

rich unto all that call upon him. *13 For "whosoever shall call upon the name of the Lord shall be saved."*

Notice Paul is quoting the OT in order to establish his doctrine. "Believing unto justification" and "confessing unto salvation" are the same as "calling upon the name of the Lord". This term refers to the sincere worship and service of the true God in the OT and NT – look it up. This speaks of a living obeying faith unto the end of ones' life (I Pet. 1:9; Rom. 16:26). Paul assumes that one who confesses Jesus as Lord will then live in obedience to his professed Lord. Salvation by grace is God's gracious acceptance of what we can give; which makes it right for Him then to apply the atonement to us and wash us clean. As long as we abide in this faith – walk in the Light – we are safe and will be saved when we finish our course.

Maybe this principle can be understood better if we put it into the realm of the home. If a child has done their best, but has nevertheless failed; and the parent is cross and merciless; we charge them with not being gracious. If the child did their best and failed; and the parent draws them close in loving forgiving acceptance; then we say the parent is gracious and merciful. If the child is rebellious, deceitful, self-justifying, lazy, and sneaky; yet the parent draws them close in loving forgiving acceptance; we don't call the parent "gracious" but foolish and guilty of producing a monster! The grace becomes lasciviousness when the child is not striving to please. Grace is only virtuous and noble when given to one who has repented, confessed, made restitution where possible, and is now striving to be righteous.

Here is the principle again in the Parable of the Talents:

Mt 25:15 *And unto one he gave five talents, to another two, and to another one; to every man **according to his several ability**; and straightway took his journey.*

What happened to the man who did not do what he could do?

Mt 25:30 *And cast ye the unprofitable servant into outer darkness: there shall be weeping and gnashing of teeth.*

The true grace of God is consistent with demanding obedience to God's Holy Law. Offering grace without demanding us to obey according to our ability is "turning the grace of God into lasciviousness" – turning grace into lawlessness or "looseness" on God's part.

Jude 3 *Beloved, when I gave all diligence to write unto you of the common salvation, it was needful for me to write unto you, and exhort you that ye **should earnestly contend for the faith which was once delivered unto the saints.** 4 For there are certain men crept in unawares, who were before of old ordained to this condemnation, ungodly men, **turning the grace of our God into lasciviousness**, and denying the only Lord God, and our Lord Jesus Christ.*

"Denying the Lord" means denying his "lordship" or denying that you have to obey him!   This makes God's grace simply capitulation to sin; the destruction of His Law; and rank confusion concerning what salvation is all about -- but this is what is being preached in our day! It is amazing that the attack on God's Grace began while the Apostles were still alive! All the Apostles had to combat Satan's presentations of "false grace". Read Peter's first epistle and you will find him presenting **"the true grace of God"**.

1Pe 1:9 *Receiving the **end of your faith**, even the salvation of your souls... 13 Wherefore gird up the loins of your mind, be sober, and **hope to the end** for the grace that is to be brought* unto you at the revelation of Jesus Christ;   14 **As obedient children**, not fashioning yourselves according to the former lusts in your ignorance: 15 But as he which hath called you is holy, **so be ye holy in all manner of conversation;** 16 Because it is written (OT), Be ye holy; for I am holy. 17 And if ye **call on the Father...**

Remember this term? - **Ro 10:13** "whosoever shall call..."

...who without respect of persons judgeth according to every man's work, **pass the time of your sojourning here in fear:** 18 Forasmuch as ye know that ye were not redeemed with corruptible things, as silver and gold, from your vain conversation received by tradition from your fathers; 19 But with the precious blood of Christ, as of a lamb without blemish and without spot:..

1Pe 4:17 For the time is come that judgment must begin at the house of God: and if it first begin at us, what shall the end be of them that obey not the gospel of God? 18 And if the **righteous scarcely be saved**, where shall the ungodly and the sinner appear? 19 Wherefore let them that suffer according to the will of God **commit the keeping of their souls to him in well doing,** as unto a faithful Creator...

1Pe 5:12 ...I have written briefly, exhorting, and testifying that this is **the true grace of God wherein ye stand.**

Chapter Twenty
Same Gospel – Same Law

*Re 14:6 And I saw another angel fly in the midst of heaven, having the **everlasting gospel** to preach unto them that dwell on the earth, and to **every nation, and kindred, and tongue, and people,***

Just how many Gospels are there? Some teach that there are different Gospels for different people and for different dispensations. **The careful student of Scripture will find there is but one Gospel for all time, and for all people.** Being that the Bible is a progressive revelation, man's ability to understand the mechanics of the Gospel has expanded with added revelation; but **the mechanics have never changed**. Because man fell, God devised means so that his banished would not have to be eternally expelled from Him (2Sa 14:14). When man fell, God had a choice: He could execute the full penalty of the Law and destroy man; or He could graciously devise a plan to satisfy the Law, and provide a path of pardon and reconciliation. God chose to provide a just and righteous program whereby man could be offered salvation – **a narrow way that leads to eternal life - reconciled to God's favor – restored to God's family. This good news is the Gospel**...the **one and only Gospel**! (See our book *Salvation Strait and Narrow*)

The SAME Gospel requires the SAME Law. Before someone can appreciate the Gospel, they must feel the condemnation of the Law. Before they can see the gloriousness of God's salvation; they must see the penalty of death upon their sin. The Gospel is not good news to the un-convicted sinner; but when the spotlight of the Law condemns them to hell (Romans 7), they then can appreciate the Gospel's offer of salvation through Christ (Romans 8).

No person has been saved by any other Gospel. This good news was first preached to Adam and Eve in Gen. 3:15 and demonstrated in Gen. 3:21. The seed of the woman was promised to bruise the serpent's head, and in order to cover the nakedness brought on by sin, God killed an innocent animal, and made coats for them. This was a type of Christ's **atonement**, a word which simply means "to cover" (*kippur*-OT) with the idea of making expiation or reconciliation (*katallage* –NT).

We have seen already that Cain and Abel understood the need for blood sacrifices in order to maintain a relationship with God and cover transgressions. From the very beginning those who sought God did so with a blood sacrifice to atone (in type) for their sins. God pardoning repentant sinners on the basis of Christ's atonement has always been the Gospel, and always will be. Offering animals as sin offerings was God's method for man to show his faith in God's promised salvation through Christ's atonement before they even understood all about it.

Did Adam and Eve or Cain and Abel understand how Jesus would die on the cross and rise again, etc. etc.? Of course they didn't; but they could still have faith in God's gracious offer of pardon. They could still repent and seek God with hope and assurance of complete future reconciliation. This very point is what Paul is communicating in Hebrews 11 – that salvation by grace through faith, and not due to our own perfect record (*forensic justification*), has been the **only way**; and there has been **no other Gospel**. Why do you think every illustration of salvation used by the writers of the New Testament is from Old Testament saints? When the Apostle Paul wanted to illustrate saving faith to NT believers, he did so with people who were both under the Law of Moses and before the Law of Moses (Heb 11; Ro 4). When He wanted to illustrate "faith imputed for righteousness" to NT believers he wrote about Abraham's faith being imputed to him for righteousness (*before the Old Covenant*), and David's rejoicing in the same principle (*under the Old Covenant*) in Romans chapter four. Did you know the New Testament declares that THE Gospel was preached to Abraham?

*Ga 3:8 And the scripture, foreseeing that God would justify the heathen through faith, preached before the **gospel** unto Abraham, saying, In thee shall all nations be blessed.*

Did you know the Gospel was preached to the Children of Israel in the wilderness? And that it was essentially the same Gospel preached to first century saints?

*He 4:2 For unto **us** was **the gospel** preached, as well as unto **them**: but the word preached did not profit them, not being mixed with faith in them that heard it.*

Did you know the gospel was preached to the people who died in the flood of Noah's day? These two passages are speaking of the same people.

1 Pe 3:18 For Christ also hath once suffered for sins, the just for the unjust, that he might bring us to God, being put to death in the flesh, but quickened by the Spirit: 19 By which also he *(previously)* *went and* ***preached*** *unto the spirits* **(now)** *in prison; 20 Which sometime were disobedient, when once the longsuffering of God waited in the days of Noah, while the ark was a preparing, wherein few, that is, eight souls were saved by water.*

1Pe 4:6 *For for this cause was the* ***gospel*** **(previously)** *preached also to them that are* **(now)** *dead, that they might be judged according to men in the flesh, but live according to God in the spirit.*

The Spirit of Christ was preaching through Noah (2 Pet. 2:5) as it had through Enoch (Jude 14). These men, as with all the OT saints, were preaching the same message that Paul preached.

Ac 26:20 *But shewed first unto them of Damascus, and at Jerusalem, and throughout all the coasts of Judaea, and then to the Gentiles, that they should* ***repent and turn to God, and do works meet for repentance.***

Why should they repent and turn to God, and do works meet for repentance? So they could be eligible for God's gracious pardon based on Christ's atonement. This is the same message Isaiah preached:

Isa 55:7 *Let the wicked forsake his way, and the unrighteous man his thoughts: and let him return unto the LORD, and he will have mercy upon him; and to our God, for he will abundantly pardon. See also (Isaiah 1:16-20)*

Every time you see or hear of God's gracious offer of **pardon** and **reconciliation** to the **repentant sinner** you are hearing the everlasting glad tidings or good news (Gospel) that we are not hopelessly condemned; but have hope in a merciful God's amazing plan of redemption. This message is offered to all mankind.

Col 1:23 *If ye continue in the faith grounded and settled, and be not moved away from the* **hope of the gospel,** *which ye have heard, and* **which was preached to every creature which is under heaven;** *whereof I Paul am made a minister;*

Adam Clarke: *To every creature which is under heaven]* A Hebraism for the whole human race, and particularly referring to the two grand divisions of mankind, the Jews and Gentiles; to both of these the Gospel had been preached, and to each, salvation by Christ had been equally offered. And as none had been excluded from the offers of mercy, and Jesus Christ had tasted death for every man, and the Jews and Gentiles, in their great corporate capacity, had all been invited to believe the Gospel; therefore, the apostle concludes that the Gospel was preached to every creature under heaven, as being offered without restrictions or limitations to these two grand divisions of mankind, including the whole human race.

Tit 2:11 *For the* **grace of God that bringeth salvation hath appeared to all men,** *12 Teaching us that, denying ungodliness and worldly lusts, we should live soberly, righteously, and godly, in this present world; 13 Looking for that blessed hope, and the glorious appearing of the great God and our Saviour Jesus Christ;*

Ro 10:15 *And how shall they preach* **(the Gospel),** *except they be sent? as it is written* **(Isa 52:7),** *How beautiful are the feet of them that preach the* **gospel** *of peace, and bring glad tidings of good things! 16 But they have not all obeyed the* **gospel.** *For* **Isaiah** *saith, Lord, who hath believed our report* **(the Gospel)?** *17 So then faith cometh by hearing* **(the Gospel),** *and hearing by the word of God* **(the Gospel).** *18 But I say, Have they not heard* **(the Gospel)?** *Yes verily, their sound* **(the Gospel) went into all the earth,** *and their* **words unto the ends of the world.**

The apostle is referring to Ps. 19

Ps 19:1 *The heavens declare the glory of God; and the firmament sheweth his handywork. 2 Day unto day uttereth speech, and night unto night sheweth knowledge.* **3 There is no speech nor language, where their voice is not heard. 4 Their line is gone out through all the earth, and their words to the end of the world.**

These two passages of Scripture **prove** that Paul considered the Gospel as being the message of God's salvation to all men from the beginning to the end. Just because you've figured out another aspect of this amazing Gospel; or just because you've lived in a time where more of the program was manifest; the great plan of God to offer salvation to mankind has not changed from the original.

You say, well the Jews had to obey the ceremonies, etc. Yes, because they lived during that part of God's great unfolding plan; but the plan didn't change. They had to obey God to find grace in His sight just as Abel, Enoch, Noah, Abraham **...and you!** They had a different test for their faith just as you have a unique race of faith to run (Heb.12); but were still saved by grace as they exercised their faith. Those who try to say Paul preached a different Gospel than Peter and Jesus are confused. Paul and Peter both preached the **Gospel of Christ** to *"the Jew first, and also to the Gentile".*

Ro 1:16 *For I am not ashamed of the* **gospel of Christ***: for* **it is the power of God unto salvation** *to* **every one** *that believeth; to the* **Jew first***, and* **also to the Greek***.*

1Pe 1:25 *But the* **word of the Lord endureth for ever***. And* **this is the word** *which by the* **gospel** *is preached unto* **you***.*

The people - the "you" - that Peter is writing to are both Jews and Gentiles to whom Paul had also written. They preached the same salvation through the longsuffering (grace) of God.

*2Pe 3:15 And account that the longsuffering of our Lord is salvation; **even as our beloved brother Paul** also according to the wisdom given unto him hath written unto **you**;*

The everlasting Gospel is the good news that God isn't just sending us all hopelessly to Hell; but has offered us a way to find mercy and pardon. The way is simple on our end – **"repent and turn to God, and do works meet for repentance."** On God's end, the way is complex and multi-faceted. Jesus made it all legal through His atoning death, and makes it applicable to us through His present Priesthood. Everyone who has repented and put faith in God's offered salvation has put faith in the Gospel of Jesus Christ. Those who have not repented and gratefully made use of God's provision have not obeyed the Gospel of Jesus Christ.

*2Th 1:7 And to you who are troubled rest with us, when the Lord Jesus shall be revealed from heaven with his mighty angels, 8 In flaming fire taking vengeance on them that know not God, and that **obey not the gospel of our Lord Jesus Christ**:*

*1Pe 4:17 For the time is come that judgment must begin at the house of God: and if it first begin at us, what shall the end be of them that **obey not the gospel of God?***

Mt 7:13 Enter ye in at the strait gate: for wide is the gate, and broad is the way, that leadeth to destruction, and many there be which go in thereat: 14 Because strait is the gate, and narrow is the way, which leadeth unto life, and few there be that find it.

There is a **strait gate** to enter; and there is a **narrow way** to walk. You must walk all the way to the end to find life. Most don't want or appreciate it – BUT IT IS WONDERFUL NEWS! There is a way! It is possible to be reconciled to God and saved from sin! Don't believe the false gospels which offer unrealistic unconditional security without any striving or sacrifice of your own. Don't complain that the true gate is strait; but thank God you are not hopelessly headed for Hell. Don't complain that the path is narrow; but thank God that there *is* a narrow path that leads to eternal life! **Take it!**

Chapter Twenty One

Does *[Your]* Love Fulfill The Law?

The woman's voice coming through the phone was emphatic and passionate, **"To obey God is simply to "love"; for when you love, you have obeyed all his commands. Love fulfills the law!"**

Have you ever heard this before? This is the war cry of every liberal, feminist, and humanist who claims to be a Christian. Is it true? They wish to make a Pharisee out of every person who disagrees with them. It is astounding how much bold irreverence and disobedience to Scripture is applauded as long as it is from a "loving" person, or done for the "cause of charity". Since Satan's first tactic to deceive mankind was to masquerade as having a "loving" concern for their best interests; while he at the same time slandered God's love and intentions; we need to examine this issue in the light of Scripture, lest we be found no wiser than Eve. Well, why don't we put all emotion aside and look at what the Scripture says with a humble, teachable heart.

Mt 22:36 Master, which is the great commandment in the law? Jesus said unto him, Thou shalt love the Lord thy God with all thy heart, and with all thy soul, and with all thy mind. This is the first and great commandment. And the second is like unto it, Thou shalt love thy neighbor as thyself. <u>On these two commandments hang all the law and the prophets.</u>

Now, Jesus said one of two things:

#1 Either He was saying that God's law was based on (or hung from) Loving God first and our neighbor as ourselves; and therefore the individual commandments were meant to show us how to love properly in each situation; which would mean that the purpose of the law was simply to teach us **how** to love, and our sincere obedience to God's Law would be a demonstration of God's definition of love...Or...

#2 He was saying that the Jews really only had to be **"loving"** and God would have been pleased, whether or not they obeyed the specific commands. As long as they were "loving" or "nice" in their attitude toward others, they would have pleased God, even if they didn't obey the law.

In deciding this question we first need to remember that when Jesus said, **"On these two commandments hang all the law and the prophets"**; he was saying, **"It has always been this way"**, not just, **"From now on it will be this way"**. The "law and the prophets" is a term that applies to the whole Old Testament; and therefore what Jesus is teaching also applied to the Old Testament saints and Scriptures. Jesus also said this of the "Golden Rule", which many believe *replaced* the Law of God.

Mt 7:12 *Therefore all things whatsoever ye would that men should do to you, do ye even so to them: <u>for this is the law and the prophets.</u>*

Notice that the "Golden Rule" so far from replacing the Law is actually said to **be** the Law – God's Law and the prophets all taught this very rule; and Jesus is simply giving us the proper view of HIS Law. Yes, Jesus is the one who inspired Moses: and Jesus was the WORD made flesh. Jesus was the Law in the flesh. If you have any other concept of God's Law, then you need to trade in the foundation stones of your doctrine. From this it is clear what God meant when the Bible says that Love fulfills the Law – it is the Law!

Since **#2 concept** is so popular i.e. *the idea that Jesus meant people only needed to be nice and loving, and this took the place of obeying the Law;* let us suppose it to be the case in the Old Testament. What if a man got the idea that he did not have to keep the Sabbath as long as he was nice to people, loved God, and was loving toward others. He understood that "love" fulfilled the Law, so he decided as long as he praised God, prayed and sang, and didn't hurt anyone that he didn't have to keep the Sabbath, which wasn't hurting anyone – right? Well, fortunately for us, there was such a case in the Old Testament in Numbers 15. A man who was caught picking up sticks on the Sabbath was set aside to see what God would say. God's verdict was that anyone who knowingly disobeys one of God's commandments, however small it may be (picking up sticks is pretty small); was, in fact, despising the Word of the Lord, and therefore should be stoned to death. This man was not said to be guilty of any other violations, but evidently was otherwise a good Israelite. So, no matter how much this man thought he loved God, God saw his deliberate disobedience to Scripture as the opposite of love. Rather than God seeing him as a nice guy, God saw him and his ideas as so dangerous to the congregation as a whole that God commanded them to stone him.

Another case may even be more pertinent to our subject. In 2 Samuel 6 we find King David and all Israel bringing the Ark of the Covenant to Jerusalem with great joy, dancing, and singing out of *love* to the Lord. God had clearly instructed them to carry the Ark with staves through golden rings on the sides of the Ark, and not to touch it, lest they die (Numbers 4:15). On this occasion, however, due to carelessness and possibly assuming **"love fulfills the Law";** they moved the Ark on an ox cart, like the heathen had done. They were full of *love* and **good intentions**, but they were not careful to obey the WORD of God. At one point the oxen stumbled, and out of *love* for the Ark, Uzzah, a Levite, put forth his hand and took hold of the Ark to protect it from falling. God, rather than seeing their love as fulfilling the Law, struck the man dead on the spot, as the Law warned in Numbers 4:15. If they really *loved,* as they should have, they would have carefully read God's instructions, and not presumed upon God's grace. Their carelessness manifested laziness and love for convenience - not love for God. Their actions, though "nice", "loving", "positive", etc. were seen as so dangerous that God made an example of Uzzah so others would not follow his error.

Isn't "being loving" also the way that Balaam instructed Balak to overcome Israel? "Just be loving to them, invite them to your love festivals, etc. etc." This nearly caused the destruction of Israel by God's wrath. Read Numbers 25 and see what God thought of all their "love".

Therefore, we need to rephrase our question. Instead of, *"Does love fulfill the Law?"* we need to ask, *"Does your concept of love fulfill the Law?" "Does your definition of love fulfill the Law?" "Do your actions of love fulfill the Law?" "Does YOUR love fulfill the Law?"* In

256

God's mind, the love that fulfills the Law is the love that **obeys** the Law in the fear of God with the "spirit" or attitude expected by the Law-giver - benevolence. **Obedience is doing what you're told, when you're told, with the right attitude.** This is exactly what Jesus did in His walk on earth. Jesus never broke the least of the Law's commandments. This was necessary for Him to be a spotless lamb for His atoning sacrifice. Jesus lived in perfect harmony with God's Law and never taught or acted contrary to God's Holy Word. Jesus even taught that any preacher who told people they could disregard any of God's commandments would himself be disregarded in the Kingdom of God.

Mt 5:19 Whosoever therefore shall break one of these least commandments, and shall teach men so, he shall be called the least in the kingdom of heaven: but whosoever shall do and teach them, the same shall be called great in the kingdom of heaven.

Well, what about in the New Testament? Is it different in the New Testament? What if someone got the idea that, as long as they were showing love, they didn't have to be honest. As long as they were nice, had good intentions, weren't hurting anyone; but actually helping others, did they have to obey God's Law? Well, fortunately we have just that case in Acts 5. Again, the verdict of the Lord was that love that didn't obey, wasn't really love; therefore, Ananias and his wife were actually given the death penalty for lying to God's Spirit. Everybody knows that their actions *appeared* loving on the *outside*, and surely would help the needy; but, no matter how loving they appeared, God saw double motives and dishonesty. Much "love" today is of the same character; Just as "Jezebel" at the church in Thyatira was "all about love" – the sensual, emotional kind which led to fornication – God said the whole church was going to be judged if they didn't get rid of her.

God saw their "nice" and "loving" actions as dangerous when they were undermining the moral law of God. He saw this precedent as so subtle and damaging to His kingdom that He had to make an example of them in a very harsh way. Satan's most subtle deception and most powerful weapon is to use Scriptural principles in the **wrong context.** In this example the previous verse (Mt 5:19) was literally fulfilled.

Charity In Context

All the virtues spoken of in the Scriptures lose their virtue and become vile when placed in any context other than within the realms of God's moral law and His kingdom. Charity or love is no exception. People often bring up the "fruit of the Spirit" as stated in Galatians:

Ga 5:22 But the fruit of the Spirit is love, joy, peace, longsuffering, gentleness, goodness, faith, 23 Meekness, temperance

Every one of these can be perverted when placed in any context other than that which Paul was speaking of. Paul is speaking of these in the context of God's **Holy** Spirit, and God's own holiness and attributes. If you take love, joy, peace, longsuffering, gentleness, goodness, faith, meekness and temperance and place them in the world view of the homosexual, lesbian, pedophile, thief, rapist, drunkard, Satanist, Buddhist, Muslim, Communist, Athiest etc. they become perverted and often vile. If you rebuke the homosexual in the name of the Lord, and warn him of impending judgment; he may respond that, '*You lack grace and the fruit of the Spirit because you are not showing love, joy, peace, gentleness,"* etc. Does he have a valid point? Of course not; the fruit of the Spirit is only virtuous and valid in the context of God's Law. Violators of God's Law are under judgment; and warning them of such is the only love they are eligible for. Those who are under God's Law, within the boundaries of God's ways, and full of God's Holy Spirit are the only ones who can exhibit the fruits of God's Spirit in a right way. When God's prophets, the Lord Jesus, and the Apostles, rebuked sin, called men to repentance, and warned of judgment, they were exhibiting **God's** love, patience, and goodness toward sinful men. Joy, peace, and faith can **only** be right when in a right relationship with God and His holy law; otherwise they all become presumptuous and deceitful. Only those who love God's Law can understand the character, relations, and applications of the fruit of the Spirit.

If there is a real nice and sweet lady in the church who is always positive and smiling and friendly; but dresses immodest and insists on showing herself in a provocative manner; how do we categorize her? Is she righteous because she is "nice", "sweet", "helpful", "friendly" and "positive"? If she is full of "faith", "joy", "love", "gentleness", "patience" etc; but dresses ungodly; is she full of the fruit of the Spirit? No. She has the heart of a wicked ungodly harlot that is showing through in her dress; and she is an enemy of God's Kingdom and government. She is "nice" because this is part of her snare – part of her appeal – part of her evil power over those whom she wants to impress and seduce. "Nice" does not equal "righteous". The one who reproves her according to the Scripture and thus "hurts her feelings" is not the unrighteous one or "weaker brother"; but is actually the one showing forth the fruit of the Holy Spirit of God. When this is done, you will probably see another side of her as well. Most who love to quote Galatians 5:22, 23 have not noticed Ephesians 5:8-11

Eph 5:8 *For ye were sometimes darkness, but now are ye light in the Lord: walk as children of light: 9* **(For the fruit of the Spirit is in all goodness and righteousness and truth;)** *10 Proving what is acceptable unto the Lord. 11 And have no fellowship with the unfruitful works of darkness,* **but rather reprove them.**

Love in any context outside God's holiness is ungodly. "Hate" in the proper context is actually consistent with "Love":

Ps 139:17 *How precious also are thy thoughts unto me, O God! how great is the sum of them! 18 If I should count them, they are more in number than the sand: when I awake, I am still with thee. 19 Surely thou wilt slay the wicked, O God: depart from me therefore, ye bloody men. 20 For they speak against thee wickedly, and thine enemies take thy name in vain. 21 Do not I hate them, O LORD, that hate thee? and am not I grieved with those that rise up against thee? 22 I hate them with perfect hatred: I count them mine enemies. 23 Search me, O God, and know my heart: try me, and know my thoughts: 24 And see if there be any wicked way in me, and lead me in the way everlasting.*

You cannot *Love* God without *hating* what opposes God. God is LOVE, yet He hates sin – your worst enemy. The virtue of "love" is determined by **what is *loved*** – the object of the affection. The Bible clearly says:

I Jo 2:15 **Love** *not the world, neither the things that are in the world. If any man* **love** *the world, the* **love** *of the Father is not in him.16 For all that is in the world, the lust of the flesh,* *and the lust of the eyes, and the pride of life, is not of the Father, but is of the world.*

In every instance in this verse the Greek word for love is the same. The object of love is what determines its virtue. The same goes for "Joy" – why are you joyful? Do you find joy in something God calls sin? Why do you feel "Peace"? Have you made peace with the Devil or your flesh? Is the peace from ungodly compromise? Are you being "Longsuffering" toward that which is forbidden of God? This simply makes you an enabler to rebellion against God. Are you being "Gentle" to please man contrary to God's commands? Are you defining "Goodness" from God's Word? Are you having "Faith" in man's idea or in God's holy commandments? Is your "Meekness" actually compromise with evil? Is your "Temperance" according to your definition or God's? Are you being "temperate" in your use of drugs and alcohol by just having a few beers and cigs every day? You just smoke a little dope, and so you are temperate?

Can you see that all these virtues must be defined by God through His Holy Word, and not by man's limited perception? Do you realize that everything Jesus did or said was a manifestation of the fruit of God's Spirit? Do you realize that everything taught and commanded in Scripture is a revelation of the fruit of God's Holy Spirit? Do you understand that the best you can do in exhibiting the fruit of the Spirit is to diligently obey everything taught to you in the Bible? When Jesus was rebuking harshly He was showing forth the fruit of God's Spirit in its proper context and definition. When Jesus was cleansing the temple He was showing the fruit of God's Spirit – He was loving God first and His neighbor as himself; He was finding His joy in God's righteousness, He was maintaining

261

His peace with God by executing God's wrath in the realm of His God given jurisdiction; He was being longsuffering by just driving them out and not sending them straight to hellfire; He was being gentle by becoming a man and trying to teach them before judgment came; His goodness was seeking to bring them to repentance and save them from hell; He was showing forth faith in God's Word and Ways; His meekness was seen in submission to His Father's will; His temperance was seen in the withholding of God's wrath and just giving them a good rebuke for the time being. If you want to truly show forth the fruit of the Spirit, then follow and emulate Jesus and his chosen apostles.

I Co. 11:1 *Be ye followers of me, even as I also am of Christ.*

Why did Paul say this? Because he had just finished demonstrating to them how their supposed "knowledge" was completely contrary to God's will and way. Paul understood God much better than they, and so in order for them to be led of God's Spirit, they are instructed to follow the example of one who knew God's Spirit better. This applies to us today! You will not improve on Jesus or the apostles; but will be doing really good if you simply follow and obey what they taught and exemplified.

In the realm of the unrighteous and ungodly rebel, God's Spirit is angry – not loving. It was God's Spirit who struck down Ananias and Sapphira in Acts 5. Ungodliness is a wrong relationship with God, and unrighteousness is a wrong relationship with your fellow man. Listen to how God feels about this:

Ro 1:18 *For the wrath of God is revealed from heaven against all ungodliness and unrighteousness of men, who hold the truth in unrighteousness;*

We can only experience God's love, joy, peace, longsuffering, gentleness, goodness, meekness, faith, temperance, etc. when we are in submission to His will – when we are living in His favor.

Jas 4:6 *God resisteth the proud, but giveth grace unto the humble. 7 Submit yourselves therefore to God.*

1Pe 5:5 *God resisteth the proud, and giveth grace to the humble. 6 Humble yourselves therefore under the mighty hand of God,*

You are only eligible for God's grace when you humble yourself before Him, and seek to do your best in obeying His Word. The love of God to those outside His will and favor is that of calling them to repentance and warning them of impending doom if they don't. Our relationship with mankind must be the same if we are to exhibit God's love. We can only show love, joy, peace, to those who are seeking God with a humble heart. To all others our love is to call them to repentance and warn them of hell if they don't.

God's love is a matter of attaching proper value to objects, and then relating to that object according to the attached value in the light of what is best for that object in relation to the good of the universe as a whole. God loves man more than the animals and plants He created. This means He has attached a greater value to man than animals and plants, and He acts toward them according to what is best for them in relation to the good of the universe as a whole. The good of the universe as a whole is dependent on truth and righteousness being upheld and enforced. Though God values man highly, He has placed a higher value on holiness and righteousness. If man violates holiness and righteousness God brings judgment and punishment; because man is not more valuable than holiness and righteousness. If man wants to maintain his value in the eyes of God, he must support holiness and righteousness, otherwise he is devaluing himself and God will ultimately cast him away forever unless he falls in line with what is good for God's universe as a whole. If I had a cow that was supporting the good of the farm as a whole, she would be a valuable cow; but if she was continually trying to harm me or my children, she would be sold or eaten. A cow has intrinsic value, but they destroy that when they are rebellious against their lord and master. The same is true of mankind in God's kingdom. God wants to show you love, joy, peace, etc.; but He cannot and will not when you militate against things higher and more valuable than you are. Man is not the most valuable thing to God, and he needs to figure that out fast.

Charity or Carnality?

God's love is much different than what most men call love. Carnal men base their love on their value system. Their value system says that the happiness of man is the highest "good". Therefore to "love" is to do whatever makes people **happy**. They believe that they have the right to pursue their own happiness as the highest good; and must not interfere with others doing the same. However, man's happiness is not the highest good in God's eyes, and he has sacrificed man's happiness many times for a much higher cause. It is a shock and offense to most people to find out that they are not the biggest thing going, and that the world doesn't revolve around them. This is manifested in how they treat God when things go wrong. Look at this verse and tell me who the "loving" person is:

Pro 28:4 *They that forsake the Law, praise the wicked, but such as keep the Law, contend with them*

Who is the **"negative"** person? Who is the **"compassionate"** and **"loving"** person? Well, it depends on whose value system you use. The wicked will claim the person who has forsaken the Law as the loving person; but the righteous will say that the one contending is the one who loves God and man with a true love. The wicked see the contentious person as "interfering" with another's right to pursue their own happiness, and do that which seems right in their own eyes.

God's love is a love that sees what is best for his entire universe, not what is pleasant to one at the expense of another. God's Law is a "win, win" situation that causes everyone to win; but man's ways are a "win, lose" situation where someone gains at another's expense. Any compromise or violation of God's Law causes someone to suffer loss, and thus is not a loving move. What was it that the Father saw in the Son that pleased him most? Listen to God's proclamation as he crowns the Son:

Heb 1:8-9 *Thy throne, O God, is for ever and ever: a scepter of righteousness is the scepter of thy kingdom. Thou hast loved righteousness and hated iniquity; therefore God, even thy God, hath anointed thee with the oil of gladness above thy fellows*

"God is love" was still true when God destroyed the earth with a flood and burned up Sodom. His love is not based on man's happiness being the highest good; but on the love of righteousness and hatred of iniquity. The word iniquity comes from the Greek, anomia, which means "Lawlessness". So, the love that fulfills the Law, really fulfills God's Law of righteousness. That is why

Romans 8:4 says the righteousness of the Law is fulfilled in the life of a believer who walks not according to carnal appetites, but according to the leading of the Holy Spirit within him. This is true love; and this is the real fruit of the Spirit. Obeying the specifics of God's Law was meant to expand your perspective of love to fit God's. The New Covenant is God's moral Law written on our hearts – appropriate, mature, and divine love.

1Jo 5:2-3 By this we <u>know</u> that we love the children of God, <u>when we love God and keep his commandments</u>. For this is the love of God, that we keep his commandments.

2Jo 6 And this is love, that we walk after his commandments.

1Jo 2:15 <u>Love not the world</u>, neither the things that are in the world. If any man love the world, the love of the Father is not in him.

In contrast to this:

Joh 15:19 If ye were of the world, <u>the world would love his own</u>: but because ye are not of the world, but I have chosen you out of the world, therefore the world hateth you.

...so, the world loves the worldlings -- are they fulfilling God's Law by their love? No.

...so, we are commanded to <u>not</u> love the world; are we in this violating the Law of God? No.

Charity or *Conspiracy?*

It is amazing how "loving" Absalom was when trying to win the hearts of Israel away from his father, David. He was the picture of "love", but it was only love of revenge and his own ambitions that drove him to act that way. **The motive of love is all important.**

The false prophet will usually appear more "loving" to the carnal man than the true prophet will – just ask old Ahab (II Chron. 18). The liberal compromiser is not grieved at your sin, pride, vanity, or worldliness; so naturally he will appear more "loving" – he is a good politician, and that's all. Concern about the leaven in your life, and its potential effect on his own family and church, as well as on your soul, is absent; because it doesn't affect his agenda. He is like the quack who gives you a clean bill of health, while ignoring your highly contagious disease; because he doesn't want to hurt the relationship – His "love" is fatal. Satan could afford to be really nice to Eve, but she couldn't afford to be nice to him.

You see, the approach of the false prophet is to "allure through the desires of the flesh"; to "promise liberty"; and he "speaks great swelling words" (II Peter 2) to flatter and draw you into his error. This all sounds **"loving and kind";** and that is why carnal men, who choose not to endure sound doctrine, will run to these false teachers with their humanistic "love" gospel (II Tim 4:3-4). The false prophet always sympathizes with the rebel, the worldly, the independent individualist, the feminist, etc. The true preacher expects men to repent and align themselves with truth and righteousness – but this is love, because this is what is best for them and brings glory to God. However, no matter how nice one says it; and no matter how much sacrifice one puts into helping men do it; "repent and turn to God and do works meet for repentance" does not have the "taste of love" that carnal men are looking for. They will say in their hearts, **"I want someone to love me, not try to change me".** Therefore we see why "come as you are", "we will accept you as you are", and "God's love is unconditional" are such popular concepts today. They want God to be pleased, but they don't want to please God – Cain's type of love. Cain brought to God what Cain wanted, and was angry when God was not pleased. He wanted God to be pleased, but he didn't want to do what it took to please Him.

No Christian was ever persecuted for being "loving" in the eyes of carnal men; but for truly loving in speaking the truth in love and calling men to repentance. The Bible doesn't say, "Love God and Love man"; rather it says, "love God first with all your heart, soul, mind, and strength; and then love your neighbor as yourself - not "as God". Therefore, if I expect myself to love and obey God; and I love you as I love myself; it is only consistent to expect you to love and obey God also. Did Jesus expect men to love and obey God above all? Did the apostles expect men to love and obey God above all else? Of course they did. They loved their neighbor as themselves. By the way, have you ever looked at the Scripture Jesus was quoting?

Lev 19:17 Thou shalt not hate thy brother in thine heart: thou shalt in any wise rebuke thy neighbour, and not suffer sin upon him. 18 Thou shalt not avenge, nor bear any grudge against the children of thy people, but thou shalt love thy neighbour as thyself: I am the LORD.

Charity without Chastity!

"Charity" is the pseudo-spiritual cloak behind which the fleshly man hides while watering down the Faith once delivered to the saints. May God help all true saints to cry out loud and clear; **"When charity has lost chastity it ceases to be a virtue!"** Charity without chastity is **seduction**. To be chaste is to be "pure from sensual

268

appetites, modest, simple in style, refined, immaculate, holy and pure". The idea is that the carnal appetites are crucified by the believer to produce a life separate from the lust of the eyes, the lust of the flesh, and the pride of life. It is a life stemming from a heart that loves righteousness and hates Lawlessness. When "charity" has lost this quality, it is simply humanistic love that opposes the love of God. This explains why men often call good evil and evil good – their value system is the opposite of God's.

1Jo 5:2,3 *By this we <u>know</u> that we love the children of God, <u>when we love</u> <u>God and keep his commandments</u>. For this is the love of God, that we keep his commandments.*

Is it any wonder that John gave this criterion for determining whether we are really loving our brethren; ***"By this we know we love the brethren, when we love God and keep his commandments"***. John knew all about "Jezebel" and her "love" in the New Testament church at Thyatira. He had encountered Diotrephes' good intentions. He knew all about the Gnostics who touted "love" as the justification for their disobedience to the teachings of Christ- even unto fornication. It was this John who said in I Jn. 2:4, "He that saith, I know Him, and keepeth not His commandments, is a liar, and the truth is not in him." We are seeing Jezebels on every hand – pastor's wives who are immodest, painted, fixed in the latest fashion with gold, pearls and costly array all around us. They act "sweet" and "kind"; but are also impudent and assertive. They are a continual show to be sure. It wasn't that long ago that their "fashion" would have been called the "attire of an harlot" even in this nation. Their bold, unchaste conduct better fits the description of the harlot in Proverbs 7, than that of a meek, modest, quiet, chaste, shamefaced, sober-minded, submissive, spiritual Christian lady called for to be the pastor's wives in the New Testament.

These libertine Christians misinterpret Romans 14 so that the god-fearing man becomes the "weaker brother", and the licentious is the "stronger brother"; and so that everyone can do as they please and nobody can *judge* them. They ignore the historic context of Jew and Gentile relations along with what the Apostle commands at the end of the previous chapter, which totally destroys their false interpretation.

Ro 13:14 But **put ye on the Lord Jesus Christ**, and **make not provision for the flesh, to fulfil the lusts thereof.**

These same people misinterpret I John 4:18 to say that the "stronger" believers with "perfect" love don't fear God; but only those "weaker" brothers do. This is such a wresting of St. John's meaning that only Satan could invent such. The word in John means "dread", not the proper and wise "fear of the Lord", which is the "beginning of wisdom" Pr 9:10.

1Jo 4:18 *There is no fear in love; but perfect love casteth out fear: because fear hath torment. He that feareth is not made perfect in love.*

When you are living HOLY, which means your LOVE is COMPLETE by walking in the Spirit and fulfilling the righteousness of the law; then you don't DREAD meeting God; but long for it.

Charity or Quackery?

Paul, in describing the actions of the false teachers in Corinth, suggests in II Cor. 11:20 that if a man "exalts himself", he is committing the same basic sin against his neighbor as if he "brought him into bondage, devoured him, took of him, or smote him on the face"- **He is gaining at their expense**. If you have ever been in the presence of one who is boasting and exalting himself above you, you have surely felt the smack in the face, the robbery, the devouring, and the bondage to vain competition that it brings. The people of Corinth were allowing themselves to suffer in this way; because, due to their immature minds, they were impressed with this vain show and carnal boasting. The carnal man feels secure with an arrogant, dogmatic, worldly wise man for a leader.

Pr 14:16 *A wise man feareth, and departeth from evil: but the fool rageth, and is confident.*

They were happier to introduce their worldly friends to this slick false apostle, than to the true apostle, who did not value the vanities of this world. Paul came not to them with "excellency of speech" or "enticing words of man's wisdom". People who are spiritually immature will gravitate to the boaster and the one excelling in carnal pursuits who sets himself as a spiritual leader, though they suffer bondage by it. Yet, they will flee from the true spiritual leader who is teaching them to observe apostolic faith and practice, since their false teacher calls *that* bondage. Just read Corinthians. Paul had abased himself among them to walk the road of humility; but his opponents labeled this a weakness. "Charity vaunteth not itself, Is not puffed up, doth not behave itself unseemly, seeketh not her own..." The point is that the Corinthians couldn't figure out who loved them – Paul or the false teacher. Because they were too immature to recognize true love, we find Paul saying, "The more abundantly I love you, the less I be loved"

271

If I live a chaste, humble life, then I love you by setting a proper example for you and convicting you to also live this way. I am not provoking you to excel in worldly pursuits, but only in spiritual graces by my example and teaching. I love you by honoring you and protecting your dignity in that I am holding myself in check and not exalting myself over you in the areas where I may be more fortunate. Everyone has strong points and weak points. If I keep my strong points veiled in your presence, then you will not feel the need to flaunt your strong points, and we can just love one another without competing to protect our dignity. In fact, we are free to praise each other's strong points.

Pr 27:2 *Let another man praise thee, and not thine own mouth;*

However, if I dress up in costly array, brag on my accomplishments, boast of my riches and abilities or (in the woman's case) paint, polish, and perm in the latest fashion, I am not loving my neighbor for a number of reasons:

1. I am being a bad example, and example is the strongest moral influence.

2. I am leading you into the bondage of a carnal, self-glory, race and competition.

3. I may be attracting the eye of your mate to desire me or defrauding and offending their thought life by my immodest dress or conduct.

4. I may be causing your wife to be discontent with the money you make when I flaunt or boast of my vacations, possessions, fun, etc.

5. I may be building dangerous appetites in your children to dress up, live it up, gratify unholy desires,

pursue pleasure or vanity, etc. I am leading others into my bondage to the flesh.

6. I am ultimately gaining at another's expense and loss. I am insulting your dignity by exalting my strong points.

7. I am promising liberty, and promoting a prosperity gospel, when in fact I am enslaved by my own pride. I am promoting the fruits of pride and worldly values.

...And all the time I am smiling, speaking sweet words – yea, swelling words of vanity (*2Pe 2:18*). All the time I am being so "sweet" and "friendly", and telling how much I "love". This Charity is quackery. The worst part of it all is that this is done by those who attempt to represent Christ to a lost and dying world. God hates it.

Any time I exalt myself, I smack you in the face. This is not love. The world sees these pleasure and glory seeking "Christians" and the convicting work of the Holy Spirit is thwarted because sinners justify their broad-road pursuits by the "Christian's" example. It is obvious to them that you live by the same values they do – though you claim to add Christ to it. And indeed much doctrine today simply teaches that all they have to do is add Christ to their present way, and they are sure for heaven without changing from the broad road to the narrow road.

1Jo 3:18 My little children, let us not love in word, neither in tongue; but in deed and in truth.

Charity or Charm?

If you read the Scripture, you will find it was the false prophets whom "all men spoke well of", because they spoke "smooth" things that sympathized with the

273

people's sinful attitudes. They made them "feel" loved by God, by their "ear tickling fables", though they had not fully submitted and obeyed God's Word. This has always been one of Satan's best tactics – **the false libertine prophet** (2 Peter 2; 2 Timothy 4; 1 John; Jude, etc.).

2Pe 2:19 *While they promise them liberty, they themselves are the servants of corruption*

If I speak good things, yet live wrong; I am simply leading you to believe good things while you live wrong. This is the most subtle form of deception – To convince you that your performance does not affect your position with God – **"Ye shall not surely die."**

This applies to many Christian books on the market. Much of the contents may be profitable, but the context is poison – I mean the connection to the author's doctrine and lifestyle on the whole.

Ro 16:18 *For they that are such serve not our Lord Jesus Christ, but their own belly; and by good words and fair speeches deceive the hearts of the simple.*

The good words in the book endear you to the author so you will swallow his entire package – rat poison is 99% good food. Love is that which provokes me to urge you onward to reach your potential, not by my boasting of myself, but by washing you with the Word of God, and teaching you true doctrine. Yes, true doctrine will spur you on to perfection, whereas Antinomian heresy (Unconditional eternal security) only dulls you down and makes you feel secure, thereby putting you into greater danger than you were already in. True doctrine sets you to overcoming, enduring, holding fast, humbling down, running with patience, and laying hold on eternal life by a living faith in the conditional love and grace of God.

Joh 15:10 If ye keep my commandments, ye shall abide in my love; even as I have kept my Father's commandments, and abide in his love.

Maybe this section should be called "Charity or Charmin" (as in, "Don't squeeze the Charmin"). Many people are proud to be "softies"; but that is not "true Christian love", only miss-placed priorities and jelly spine syndrome. Read how Nehemiah loved his nation so much that he dealt severely with transgressors who hindered God's blessings on the nation. Read how much Jesus loved God's house when he drove out the moneychangers. When Jesus returns to rule with a rod of iron, it will be in the purest love.

Carnal minded people often live for the acceptance and safety of their "camp", and don't look at truth objectively. They cannot decide right from wrong objectively, because they can't get around the real question in their heart: **"What about me?"** The big question of **"how will this affect my wellbeing?"** is so intrinsically connected to their perspective of right and wrong, that it becomes their acid test for life's issues. The very beam in their eye that blinds them to matters of right and wrong is the beam called "self-preservation". They are so concerned about "feelings", and so prone to "feel" their way through issues, rather than "thinking" through them, that they interpret doctrine and actions according to what they deem "best"; rather than what God says is "right". You need to love from the heart; but only if at the same time, you are thinking with your head according to Bible principles with "self" dethroned and Christ enthroned in your heart and mind. The Word of God must be the acid test for life's issues, not your feelings or the feelings of others. "If any man come to me, and hate not his father, and mother, and wife, and children, and brethren, and sisters, yea, and his own life also, he cannot be my disciple. And whosoever doth not bear his cross, and come after me, cannot be my disciple." (Lu 14:26, 27) Jesus knew that only those who live and love by eternal principles, rather than feelings, will make it in the Christian life.

Charity or $\bigcirc$ensuality**?**

We know that the Spirit of God, who labors to write God's Law in our hearts, and thereby sheds abroad God's Love in our hearts, is not the same as the sensual spirit of many churches. The Apostles warned of this difference numerous times in various ways.

Jude 1:19 *These be they who* **separate** *themselves,* **sensual,** *having* **not** *the* **Spirit.**

Many today want "pastorless" churches where there is no leadership, order, structure, or form; but all is "spontaneous", "led of the spirit", and left to each individual's feeling and impulse. They think this is spiritual and that this is what the Holy Spirit desires; but God's Word shows that when God organized worship and spiritual instruction, it was very orderly and strict with properly ordained leaders. God's Law was full of order with attention to detail, and whenever there was revival among God's people, it was always in the form of getting BACK to the "due order" of God's Law and following the instructions more carefully. The *feely squeely* movement ignores Paul's command that all things be done "*decently and in order*". The early church was set up in the order of the Jewish synagogue, and in that God ordained order you would not find the casualness, rash, impulsive, spontaneous, sensual, pastor-less, and humanistic worship that many are sporting today as "true spirituality". They have separated themselves from God's Spirit of orderliness and are following their appetites, thinking that this is the Spirit of God talking to them; and they glory in their disorderliness, lack of structure, lack of leadership, and lack of submission to order.

Php 3:19 *Whose **end is destruction**, **whose God is their belly**, and whose **glory is in their shame**, **who mind earthly things***.

Charity with **Character.**

1Jo 2:3-5 *And hereby we do know that we know him, **if we keep his commandments.** 4 He that saith, I know him, and keepeth not his commandments, is a liar, and the truth is not in him. 5 But whoso keepeth his word, in him verily is the love of God perfected: hereby know we that we are in him.*

Ro 8:4 *That the righteousness of the Law might be fulfilled in us, who walk not after the flesh, but after the Spirit*

Ro 13:10 *Love worketh no ill to his neighbor: therefore love is the fulfilling of the Law.*

Yes! Love fulfills the Law, because true love indeed fulfills the Law by making us **"doers of the righteousness of the Law"** – we are speaking of God's eternal moral Law presented to the Jews in the Old Testament and written on Christian's hearts in the New Testament. We New Testament believers are called to prepare for Christ's Kingdom and live under the "Law of Christ" (Ga 6:2) – fulfilling the spirit and intent of God's Law through Moses. We are now the true worshippers who worship God in spirit and in truth seeking for spiritual and eternal riches; not just physical worship in carnal ordinances for temporal blessings. We are called to live by a higher standard of action and attitude. Attitude never takes the place of action – you must have both.

Yes! Biblical Love works no ill to his neighbor; but *your concept* of love may be doing exceeding ill to your neighbor – *Spiritually and eternally!* Jesus told His disciples to teach, baptize, and teach the converts to observe **ALL** things whatsoever he commanded – **not just go love everybody**. Why? Because every ordinance and principle taught in the Word of God teaches you **HOW TO LOVE PROPERLY**. You don't know how to love until you are doing it God's way! Until you are obeying every command and precept in God's Word, your "love" is lacking important ingredients that keep it from fulfilling God's Law.

1Jo 2:5 But whoso keepeth his word, in him verily is the love of God perfected (completed)

The seven churches of revelation had different ideas about love. We need to observe well, and not emulate what Christ rebuked. Notice that those who were *not* rebuked, were suffering persecution for their love. Many today who think they love Christ are really in love with their denomination, ism, dogma, or lifestyle – all which they wish to defend with sanctified sophistry. Those who truly love Christ, also love all truth, and hunger and thirst after righteousness. They are willing to leave the leeks and garlics of old Egypt and "tough-it" for the sake of following truth. The world's reaction to this move out of the "camp" or "herd" is usually some form of persecution.

Heb 13:13 Let us go forth therefore unto him without the camp, bearing his reproach. For here we have no continuing city, but we seek one to come

Have you ever seen the parents who just "loved" their children so much they never told them "no" or disciplined them? The Bible calls this "hate", not love (Pr 13:24). The Bible says this will send your child to Hell, not lead them to Heaven (Pr. 23:13,14). Now, if the Bible says that love works no ill to his neighbor, then is the Scriptural use of the rod of correction working ill? I suppose that depends on what your value system says – ask the rebellious child who hasn't received his needed share. The rebel will say spanking is working ill; but God says the neglect of spanking is working ill. Do you see how love can easily be turned around to the opposite of what God intended, and how carnal minded men will immediately latch on to the fallacious meaning? The person who spanks is the loving one in God's estimation – if, of course, they are practicing **both** the "letter" and the "spirit" of the Law.

"As many as I love, I rebuke and chasten: be zealous therefore, and repent" –Jesus

Love has priorities. Jesus said to love our enemies; but not more than we love our Lord, children, wife, neighbor, friends, faith, etc. Love in proper priority will help you to understand the relationship between God ordained discipline (on family, church and state levels) and God's love and mercy. **"God resisteth the proud, but giveth grace to the humble."** Love without proper priorities will end up supporting all sorts of foolishness: From protecting animals to the detriment of people, to protecting criminals while aborting babies. All this stupidity is excused in the name of "love".

Obeying every principle and command in "The Faith once delivered to the saints" is the only definition of "love" that can be used in the Bible verses that speak of love. If this love is not your love, then your love is not what God commands, nor are you in a position to judge others as "unloving" based on your perspective. Your judgment is not mature yet.

Some have said that "agape" love is what we need; however, this is a myth. "Agape" is a Greek noun; and "Agapao" is the verb form of the same word. Observe these two words in the following verse:

1Jo 2:15 *"Love **<agapao>** not the world, neither the things that are in the world . If any man love **<agapao>** the world, the love **<agape>** of the Father is not in him."*

It is clear that what gives love virtue is the object of that love, not the presence of affection. Love is virtue or vice depending on its object. If your "agape" is set on sin and evil, then your "agape" is sinful and evil.

Col 3:2 *Set your affection on things above, not on things on the earth*

Of Charity and Church

Most people judge the love of a church group by how much acceptance they received from the people; but this is not right thinking. We should judge the love of a church group by:

1. How much they are trying to please God, and...

2. How much they are sincerely trying to help us be pleasing to God.

1Co 13:6 *Charity...rejoiceth not in iniquity, but rejoiceth in the truth*

Usually, when I have heard people complain that a group is unloving, I have later learned two things:

1. The person complaining was a "taker" and not a "giver" – they didn't do much loving, but expected to receive plenty; and

2. The person needed to change some things that they were unwilling to change. So they concluded this church lacked love because they didn't feel unconditional acceptance. The people wanted to help them with a need in their life; however, this offended them, because they didn't want to acknowledge a need in their life – and if they did, "they could take care of it themselves just fine, thank you".

If we, as professing Christians, love Christ first, then our church will diligently seek to please Christ and preserve his Faith and Practice. Our drive will then be to make man pleasing to God. But, if our love is to please and "win" people; then our church will be geared to attract people, entertain them, and make them feel comfortable and accepted - and "Christ" will be "seasoned" to be more palatable and pleasing to man.

I'll tell you who the <u>unloving</u> church is:

• It is the church that draws you into a fashion race by exalting themselves in this way.

• It is the church where your husband has to be careful where his eyes go because of the immodesty.

• It is the church where your wife is encouraged to fix and flaunt at your expense.

• It is the church where there is not a standard of holiness upheld for all members equally.

• It is the church where the leaders don't meet Bible qualifications.

• It is the church which labels the God fearing conscientious believer as "the weaker brother"; and justifies the liberal who sports his "Christian liberty" to live ungodly.

- It is the church where "worldly gain" is trumpeted as God's blessing to the faithful.
- It is the church where the youth group tears down the chastity you teach your young person at home.
- It is the church where people who carefully obey all the teachings of God's Word are called "Pharisees".
- It is the church that is in love with "pleasing people" more than pleasing Christ.
- It is the church who labels as "unloving" those parents who back away from fellowship in this environment because it tears away at the godly fabric of their faith and home order.

May we not become uncharitable towards those who malign us for teaching the truth.

"Charity suffereth long and is kind"

Ro 3:31 Do we then make void the law through faith? God forbid: yea, **we establish the law.**

Chapter Twenty Two
Misunderstood Scriptures and Concepts

Because men are so out of touch with the Jewish roots of Christianity and the historic setting of the New Testament Scriptures, they often miss the point of the passage. When they read something concerning the "law" they don't usually know whether the apostle is speaking of the *Old Covenant*; the *Ceremonial Law*; or the *Moral Law.* The term LAW is used in all these senses; and the context must be analyzed to determine what we are referring to. Some antinomians think the term Law refers to all laws, rules, standards or boundaries whatsoever! It is vital to understand the context in which the Apostles are writing before assuming one knows what is being said in a passage. If we give God's writers proper credit as inspired by the Holy Ghost and thus perfectly consistent with all the Holy Ghost said, we will see a beautiful harmonious message emerge which is consistent from Genesis to Revelation.

When uninformed people read Galatians, they think it tells them that they have no obligation to God's moral laws; but Galatians is for a completely different purpose. Judaizers were trying to convince the Gentile believers in Galatia that they had to be circumcised and come under Judaism to be saved. Paul is refuting this false concept, which also is why the council in Acts 15 was held in

Jerusalem. Paul is teaching that the law as a system or covenant arrangement was not able to **justify**; and was never intended for that purpose. The blood of bulls and goats could not take away sin. He, in his use of the word "law", is speaking of all five books of Moses – moral and ceremonial as a covenant which was not meant to take the place of Christ, but to teach us about Christ. Gentiles are not under the *law* or *Old Covenant arrangement* **for justification**; but what does Galatians also plainly state?

Ga 5:6 *For in Jesus Christ neither circumcision availeth any thing, nor uncircumcision;* **but faith which worketh by <u>love.</u>**

Ga 6:15 *For in Christ Jesus neither circumcision availeth any thing, nor uncircumcision,* **but a new creature.**

What is LOVE? What makes a new creature? Paul tells us in Romans that those who walk in the Spirit have the righteousness of the Law fulfilled in them – which is LOVE and that makes them a new creature. In Galatians Paul says we must walk in the Spirit and sow to the Spirit – the same concept as in Romans 8; which means we live out the righteousness of God's Law. It is the Spirit of God that writes God's **Law** in our hearts and thus sheds abroad His **Love** in our hearts.

Ro 3:31 *Do we then make void the law through faith? God forbid: yea,* **we establish the law.**

When people read Hebrews they often have the same misunderstandings. They confuse the *Old Covenant* waxing old with *God's Law* waxing old. They read verse thirteen, but somehow miss verse ten just before it!

Heb 8:13 *In that he saith, A* **new covenant,** *he hath made the first old. Now that which decayeth and waxeth old is ready to vanish away.*

Heb 8:10 *For this is the* **covenant** *that I will make with the house of Israel after those days, saith the Lord;* **I will put my laws into their mind, and write them in their hearts:**

God's eternal moral laws are written in our hearts in a new and living way, which makes the old arrangement *old* and outdated and unneeded. It is not God's Law that decays, but the old arrangement – Old Covenant – that is done away in the making of a New Covenant. God's moral laws written in our hearts by the indwelling Holy Ghost makes God's Laws more glorious and important, not less. The New Covenant is all about us obeying God's Law **better**, not **worse**.

What Does 1 Timothy 1:4-11 Say?

1Ti 1:4 *Neither give heed to fables and endless genealogies, which minister questions, rather than godly edifying which is in faith: so do. 5* **Now the end of the commandment is charity out of a pure heart, and of a good conscience, and of faith unfeigned:**

This is plain enough, and is exactly what Jesus taught about God's Law through Moses in Mt 7:12 & 22:36-40: The goal/end of the Law was proper love to God and our fellow man. The Apostles all taught the same when they declare that love in its proper context fulfills the Law (Ro 13:10). John tells us in his epistles that sin is the transgression of God's Law; while loving God and man is keeping God's commandments (1Joh 5:2-3; 2Joh 1:6). God is LOVE and the goal of all His commandments is the appropriate application of His love to that situation. This is clear.

1Ti 1:6 *From which some having swerved have turned aside unto vain jangling; 7 Desiring to be teachers of the law; understanding neither what they say, nor whereof they affirm.*

If anyone teaches the Law in any other context or with any other goal, they are just making empty noise, not knowing what they are talking about. This is clear as well.

__1Ti 1:8__ But we know that the law is good, if a man use it lawfully; 9 Knowing this, that the law is not made for a righteous man, but for the lawless and disobedient, for the ungodly and for sinners, for unholy and profane, for murderers of fathers and murderers of mothers, for manslayers, 10 For whoremongers, for them that defile themselves with mankind, for menstealers, for liars, for perjured persons, and if there be any other thing that is contrary to sound doctrine; 11 According to the glorious gospel of the blessed God, which was committed to my trust.

This passage has confused some partly because of the way it is translated. We know the Law was made for God's people; it was our schoolmaster to teach us about heavenly realities with earthly patterns (Heb); it is spiritual (Ro 7:14); its righteousness is fulfilled in believers who walk in the Spirit (Ro 8:4); and when we walk by faith we establish the Law (Ro 3:31). So what is Paul saying in this passage? He is stating the same principle which Romans 7 & 8 teach: *That the law is for convicting the sinner and showing him his certain damnation so he will repent and reconcile with God.* The Law is not meant to condemn the man who is walking in the Light with God's Love shed abroad in his heart; but meant to convict the lawless. He is also stating the same truth which he spoke in Galatians:

__Ga 3:19__ Wherefore then serveth the law? It was added __because of transgressions__, till the seed should come to whom the promise was made; and it was ordained by angels in the hand of a mediator.

Ga 5:14 For all the law is fulfilled in one word, even in this; Thou shalt love thy neighbour as thyself. 15 But if ye bite and devour one another, take heed that ye be not consumed one of another. 16 This I say then, Walk in the Spirit, and ye shall not fulfil the lust of the flesh. 17 For the flesh lusteth against the Spirit, and the Spirit against the flesh: and these are contrary the one to the other: so that ye cannot do the things that ye would. 18 But if ye be led of the Spirit, ye are not under the law. 19 Now the works of the flesh are manifest, which are these; Adultery, fornication, uncleanness, lasciviousness, 20 Idolatry, witchcraft, hatred, variance, emulations, wrath, strife, seditions, heresies, 21 Envyings, murders, drunkenness, revellings, and such like: of the which I tell you before, as I have also told you in time past, that they which do such things shall not inherit the kingdom of God. 22 But the fruit of the Spirit is love, joy, peace, longsuffering, gentleness, goodness, faith, 23 Meekness, temperance: **against** *such there is no law. 24 And they that are Christ's* **have crucified the flesh with the affections and lusts.** *25 If we live in the Spirit, let us also walk in the Spirit.*

Those who are breaking God's Law by not loving with God's Love are the one's the Law is **against** in the sense that it condemns them, restrains them, and declares their punishments. If Missouri passes laws against fornication, adultery, abortion, etc. those laws are not **against** me, because I don't participate in the crimes they stand against. Christians who belong to Christ and live according to His Love do not have to worry about the condemnation of the Law; because they are fulfilling it. The Law is the love of God to bring men to repentance so they see their danger and appreciate the Gospel.

Listen to Adam Clarke who was an expert in Bible languages.

Adam Clarke on Verse 9: The law is not made for a righteous man] There is a moral law as well as a ceremonial law: as the object of the latter is to lead us to Christ; the object of the former is to restrain crimes, and inflict punishment on those that commit them. It was, therefore, not made for the righteous as a restrainer of crimes, and an inflicter of punishments; for the righteous avoid sin, and by living to the glory of God expose not themselves to its censures. **This seems to be the mind of the apostle; he does not say that the law was not MADE for a righteous man, but ou keitai, it does not LIE against a righteous man; because he does not transgress it: but it lies against the wicked; for such as the apostle mentions have broken it, and grievously too, and are condemned by it.** The word keitai, lies, refers to the custom of writing laws on boards, and hanging them up in public places within reach of every man, that they might be read by all; thus all would see against whom the law lay.

No man ever appreciated the Gospel as "Good News" until by the Law of God he came to feel and say, "O wretched man that I am". Once we repent and reconcile with God and are again under subjection to His Law (Ro 8:4-8), we LOVE God's Law and it is our delight – Ps 119 – because we have the same end or goal as the law has – LOVE; and thus the law no longer *lies against* us but lights our path. See it applied to a righteous man 1 Tim 5:17-18. We see it as expressions of God's eternal love and wisdom.

Ps 1:1 Blessed is the man that walketh not in the counsel of the ungodly, nor standeth in the way of sinners, nor sitteth in the seat of the scornful. 2 But his delight is in the law of the LORD; and in his law doth he meditate day and night. 3 And he shall be like a tree planted by the rivers of water, that bringeth forth his fruit in his season; his leaf also shall not wither; and whatsoever he doeth shall prosper. 4 The ungodly are not so: but are like the chaff which the wind driveth away. 5 Therefore the ungodly shall not stand in the judgment, nor sinners in the congregation of the righteous. 6 For the LORD knoweth the way of the righteous: but the way of the ungodly shall perish.

What about 2 Corinthians 3:6-16?

Some interpret this passage to mean that the Old Covenant was death, while the New Covenant is life; but that is not the point. The contrast is between "the letter, that *by itself* killeth" with the "spiritual meaning, which *if followed* gives life". Many Jews rested in the letter of the law without the spiritual understanding; and this only condemned them as it could not save them. The New Covenant IS the spiritual meaning and fulfillment of the Old Covenant. Jesus taught the spirit of the Law and spiritually fulfilled the law by making a true atonement. Let's read the passage with some helps.

2Co 3:6 *Who also hath made us able ministers of the [**New Covenant**]; not of the letter, but of the spirit: for the letter killeth, but the spirit giveth life.*

Notice, the Old Covenant is not even mentioned yet; but we are contrasting the letter and spirit of what? The New Covenant. What was the letter of the New Covenant? **The SAME as the Old Covenant at this time in history; for the New Covenant, remember, was the LAW written on men's hearts**. When Paul says here, "new covenant" he is not saying, "New Testament Scriptures". The new covenant was not just *new Scriptures*, but a new understanding and arrangement built upon the existing Scriptures. On the day of Pentecost, which everyone knows was a *New Covenant experience*, there were NO "New Testament" Scriptures – only OT Scriptures. Our Bibles would do better to call the OT Scriptures "Scriptures before Christ came" and the NT Scriptures, "Scriptures after Christ came". We could probably call the

NT Scriptures, "Explanation of the New Covenant". The word covenant is an agreement or arrangement of relationship conditions between man and God. The word **testament** really doesn't even belong in our Bibles anywhere as **diatheke** should have always consistently been translated **covenant** like it was the majority of the time. We are in covenant with God; we are not the recipients of His "Last Will and Testament", as He is not dead, and the legalities are totally different.

The Day of Pentecost was actually the commemoration day of the Jews meeting with God on Sinai some 50 days after the Passover in Egypt. On Sinai 3000 offenders died so the nation could continue in covenant with God. At Pentecost 3000 were added to a remnant in covenant with God, and the nation that rejected Christ was cast out of a covenant relationship with God. God is now working with a remnant who obey Him, and has rejected the nation who would not obey Him – But it is the same God with the same character and morals.

Before we go on, let's look at the context of this passage.

2 Co 3:1 *Do we begin again to commend ourselves? or need we, as some others, epistles of commendation to you, or letters of commendation from you? 2 Ye are our epistle written in our hearts, known and read of all men: 3 Forasmuch as ye are manifestly declared to be the **epistle of Christ ministered by us, written not with ink, but with the Spirit of the living God; not in tables of stone, but in fleshy tables of the heart.***

What is new in this covenant is **not** God or His ways, morals, or judgments. What is new is the **arrangement** for our relationship with Him. The primary difference is **HOW** the Law of God is ministered to His people – **not**

written with ink or on stone; but with the Spirit of God writing God's Law on our hearts.

Jer 31:31 *Behold, the days come, saith the LORD, that I will make a* <u>new covenant with the house of Israel, and with the house of Judah</u>*: 32 Not according to the covenant that I made with their fathers in the day that I took them by the hand to bring them out of the land of Egypt; which my covenant they brake, although I was an husband unto them, saith the LORD: 33 But this shall be the covenant that I will make with the house of Israel; After those days, saith the LORD,* ***I will put my law in their inward parts, and write it in their hearts; and will be their God, and they shall be my people.***

Since God's Law is LOVE, then the following verse is speaking of the same work.

Ro 5:5 *...the **love of God is shed abroad in our hearts** by the Holy Ghost which is given unto us.*

Jesus came and made the real and final atonement so we have a *new* High Priest, a *new* sacrifice with eternal merit, a *heavenly* tabernacle, and therefore relate to God through the spiritual realities of which the Old Covenant ceremonies were only types. The New Covenant is the completion and fulfillment of the purpose of the Old Covenant. The Old Covenant was full of types and shadows to introduce us to Christ, so we could understand the New Covenant arrangement.

2 Co 3:6 *Who also hath made us able ministers of the **new Covenant**; not of the letter, but of the spirit: for the letter killeth, but the spirit giveth life. 7 But if the ministration of death* **(the giving of the "letter" that condemned sin)***, written and engraven in stones, was glorious, so that the children of Israel could not stedfastly behold the face of Moses for the glory of his countenance; which glory was to be done away: 8 How shall not the ministration of the spirit be rather glorious?* **(The Holy Spirit to write God's Laws in our hearts and help us obey)** *9 For* *if the ministration of condemnation **(the plumb-line which showed us crooked)** be glory, much more doth the ministration of righteousness **(God's plan of justification)** exceed in glory.*

If the giving of the letter on Sinai, which condemned to death all transgressions, was glorious; how much more God's plan of justification through Christ Jesus and giving of the Holy Ghost exceed in glory. If God's holy plumb-line which shows us as a fallen sinful people was glorious, how much more glorious is God's means of saving us from this condemnation. Here again is the word *righteousness, dikaiosunhv*, which would be better understood if translated *justification;* because that is what we are speaking of.

The Old Covenant arrangement was a condemning plumb-line (God's Law) plus blood sacrifices to appease God's wrath on sin. The spiritual fulfillment is our justification and regeneration through the sacrifice and priesthood of Christ. Life is not in the mere observance of the ceremonial letter, but in the understanding of the spiritual meaning and walking by faith in it. God was actually propitiated through the sacrifice of Jesus Christ; the Law was satisfied; and the door was open for the Holy Ghost to indwell believers - writing God's Law of love on our hearts – What could be more glorious?

The "Ministration of death" was that plumb-line and continual animal sacrifices – lots of blood and condemnation. God was showing the price of sin – the "sinfulness of sin" to prepare a people for the Messiah. God wanted people to appreciate Jesus when He came and understand what He had accomplished. The Law was our schoolmaster to teach us about Jesus, so we could find life in Him. **Before someone can appreciate the Gospel, they must feel the condemnation of the Law.**

Before they can see the gloriousness of God's salvation; they must see the penalty of death upon their sin. The Gospel is not good news to the un-convicted sinner; but when the spotlight of the Law condemns them to hell (Romans 7), they then can appreciate the Gospel's offer of salvation through Christ (Romans 8).

There can be no GRACE where this is no LAW. You cannot have a *grace period*, unless you first have a *deadline* or *due date*. There can be no pardon where there is no indictment and conviction. There can be no repentance, justification, pardon, or reconciliation, if there is no Law that is trespassed. The Gospel is God's plan to pardon and redeem us since we broke His Law and brought upon ourselves the sentence of death. Before we can appreciate this, we must know the Law we broke and understand the sentence of death upon us. Our repentance is our re-commitment to God's Law, and our agreement with this Law against our sin. Once we are pardoned, we are to live under God's moral law and strive to obey it – this is holiness.

2 Co 3:10 For even that which was made glorious (the ministration of the letter) had no glory in this respect, by reason of the glory that excelleth (the ministration of justification). 11 For if that which is done away (the old typical arrangement) *was glorious, much more that which remaineth* (the new spiritual arrangement) *is glorious. 12 Seeing then that we have such hope, we use great plainness of speech: 13 And not as Moses, which put a vail over his face, that the children of Israel could not stedfastly look to the end of that which is abolished: 14 But their minds were blinded: for until this day remaineth the same vail untaken away in the reading of the old Covenant; which vail is done away in Christ. 15 But even unto this day, when Moses is read, the vail is upon their heart. 16 Nevertheless when it shall turn to the Lord, the vail shall be taken away.* *17 Now the Lord is that Spirit: and where the Spirit of the Lord is, there is liberty.*

Vss. 12-17 show us that we are talking about reading Moses' Law *without the spiritual understanding*, which will come when the heart turns to God and recognizes Christ for what He is. When they recognized Christ for who He was, then reading Moses' Law came alive (Acts 21)! The spiritual meaning of the types and shadows; the loving purpose of the Law; the Son of God dying to redeem us; and the priesthood of Jesus to justify us ALL speak of LIFE and HOPE for those who have trespassed God's Law. The unbelieving Jews had no spiritual life because of hard and blind hearts, rejecting Jesus, and walking in dead ceremonialism.

Don't miss this: The Christian Jews were still under Moses' Law while in the New Covenant (Acts 15, 21); and the righteousness of Moses' Law was still to be fulfilled in every Christian Gentile under the New Covenant (Rom. 8:4). Being in the New Covenant did not mean the complete removal of the components of the Old Covenant; but rather a new spiritual arrangement and understanding of these components. God didn't do away with priesthood, but replaced the order of Aaron with the order of Melchisedec (Heb 5-7). God didn't throw away his moral precepts, but wrote them on our hearts by the Holy Ghost. God stopped the continual blood sacrifices (AD 70); but accepted the blood sacrifice of His Son as the eternal replacement. The true tabernacle in heaven has replaced the copy on earth; and now we live with the blessings of the fulfilled types and shadows.

We can "rest" in the letter of the New Covenant scriptures to our own condemnation, just as they did in the Old. Paul had just stated:

2 Cor. 2:15 *"For we are unto God a sweet savour of Christ, in them that are saved, and in them that perish: 16 To the one we are the* **savour of death unto death***; and to the other the* **savour of life unto life***. And who is sufficient for these things?"*

The preaching of the gospel can also minister death if received by a hard and impenitent heart which rejects the spiritual understanding of the letter of the Gospel.

Clarke on 2 Cor. 3:6 "The apostle does not mean here, as some have imagined, that he states himself to be a minister of the New Covenant, in opposition to the Old; and that it is the Old Covenant that kills, and the New that gives life; but that the New Covenant gives the proper meaning of the Old; for the Old Covenant had its letter and its spirit, its literal and its spiritual meaning. The law was founded on the very supposition of the Gospel; and all its sacrifices, types, and ceremonies refer to the Gospel. The Jews rested in the letter, which not only afforded no means of life, but killed, by condemning every transgressor to death. They did not look at the spirit; did not endeavour to find out the spiritual meaning; and therefore they rejected Christ, who was the end of the law for justification; and so for redemption from death to every one that believes. The new covenant set all these spiritual things at once before their eyes, and showed them the end, object, and design of the law; and thus the apostles who preached it were ministers of that Spirit which gives life.

Every institution has its letter as well as its spirit, as every word must refer to something of which it is the sign or significator. The Gospel has both its letter and its spirit; and multitudes of professing Christians, by resting in the LETTER, receive not the life which it is calculated to impart. Water, in baptism, is the letter that points out the purification of the soul; they who rest in this letter are without this purification; and dying in that state they die eternally. Bread and wine in the sacrament of the Lord's Supper, are the letter; the atoning efficacy of the death of Jesus, and the grace communicated by this to the soul of a believer, are the spirit. Multitudes rest in this letter, simply receiving these symbols, without reference to the atonement, or to their guilt; and thus lose the benefit of the atonement and the salvation of their souls. The whole Christian life is comprehended by our Lord under the letter, Follow me. Does not any one see that a man, taking up this letter only, and following Christ through Judea, Galilee, Samaria, &c., to the city, temple, villages, seacoast, mountains, &c., fulfilled no part of the spirit; and might, with all this following, lose his soul? Whereas the SPIRIT, viz. receive my doctrine, believe my sayings, look by faith for the fulfillment of my promises, imitate my example, would necessarily lead him to life eternal. It may be safely asserted that the Jews, in no period of their history, ever rested more in the letter of their law than the vast majority of Christians are doing in the letter of the Gospel. Unto multitudes of Christians Christ may truly say: Ye will not come unto me that ye may have life."

The Letter simply sets forth order and obligation to worship in spirit and truth – to acknowledge this without performance is self condemning. Observing the Lord's Supper without the expected heart attitude is more condemning than not knowing to do it; because the person going through the motions is acknowledging their obligation and accountability for what it means. With baptism also, resting in the letter is self-condemning. To go through the motions without the heart and spirit of the matter is mockery and brings no life.

So, again we see that this Scripture is consistent with our position. The Jews in Acts 21, who after believing in Jesus were zealous of the Law, reveal to us that, after the heart turns to the Lord and the veil is removed, the Law becomes more glorious. The spiritual understanding of the Law makes it come alive; and the spiritual fulfillment of the Ceremonial Law is the very atonement of Christ that saves us. Originally the New Covenant included submission to Moses' Law and a proper appreciation for it in the light of Christ being the Messiah and the Lamb of God. The Old Covenant being ended doesn't mean all the components of the covenant are ended. The New Covenant is a new arrangement which includes much of the old components. The New Covenant is updated with Christ's fulfillment of the ceremonial laws; but we are still in a covenant with the **same God – He hasn't changed.** His manifestations of Himself, i.e. His opinions, judgments, moral standards, etc., have been consistent.

What about Romans 6:14?

Ro 6:14 For sin shall not have dominion over you: for ye are not under the law, but under grace. 15 What then? shall we sin, because we are not under the law, but under grace? God forbid.

Notice the word "sin". When we are under grace we still don't have license to sin. Sin is the transgression of God's Law; so we don't have license to transgress the law when we are not under the law, but under grace. How can this be? "Under the law" means facing the law alone in God's court without the grace of salvation through Christ's atonement. If we must deal with the law alone, we are all doomed and sin has dominion over us, i.e. we are conquered and destroyed by it. If we are under the grace of the gospel, then when we fail to keep God's Law, we are not hopelessly doomed, but have a chance to get back up, get cleansed and forgiven, and go on in the narrow way. In this arrangement, it is not necessary that sin have dominion over us; but victory is within our reach.

Some teach from passages like Romans 6:14 that: we are saved by grace; but the Old Covenant saints were saved by works. This is not the case, as every example given in the New Covenant of salvation by grace through faith was from an Old Covenant person – read Hebrews 11. Paul tells us in Galatians that the gospel was preached to Abraham; and in Hebrews 4 we are told it was preached to Israel. The Gospel is simply the good news that we are not hopelessly awaiting a court date in which God's law is going to condemn us to hell for our transgressions; but that God has devised means of atonement whereby we can be pardoned, and received back again into full citizenship and son-ship.

Nobody has ever been justified before God through Moses' Law alone (Rom. 3:20); because the blood of bulls and goats could never take away sin (Heb. 10:4). Everyone who has ever been justified has been justified by faith in God's redemption plan through Christ. This plan is offered over and over in the Old Covenant – and the spiritual ones understood. Those who offered the blood of bulls and goats with humble faith in God's grace were justified by their obedient faith in God's salvation program; but not by the blood of the sacrifices. Their sins were actually paid for in Jesus – so they were forgiven on credit you could say.

Ro 6:14 *For sin shall not have dominion over you: for ye are not under the law* **(Facing God's Law in court)***, but under grace* **(Facing God with Jesus as your Savior)***. 15 What then? shall we sin* **(trespass God's Law)***, because we are not under the* *law, but under grace? God forbid. 16 Know ye not, that to whom ye yield yourselves **servants to obey**, his servants ye are to whom ye obey; whether of sin **(transgression of God's Law)** unto death, or of obedience **(to God's Law)** unto righteousness? 17 But God be thanked, that ye were the **servants of sin**, but ye have **obeyed** from the heart that **form of doctrine** which was delivered you. 18 Being then made **free from sin,** ye became the **servants of righteousness.***

The Law of Moses, the schoolmaster, taught man that God had a plumb-line (Moral Law) which showed we were crooked; and so we had to run to the tabernacle where through offerings and sacrifices we could find grace when we failed. BUT, if we were not striving to live up to the plumb-line, we were not eligible for the offer of grace through sacrifices. The Law taught us this because this is the very arrangement now in Christ's kingdom. If you are not striving to walk in the light - obeying God's Word, you are not eligible for Christ's priesthood and salvation thereby (I John 1:7-9).

So, shall we trespass God's Law because we are not hopelessly facing a court date with God's plumb-line without a Savior? GOD FORBID! Know ye not that committing willful transgression of God's Law leaves you without the grace of Christ's sacrifice and priesthood? This is the message of the apostle, and is also stated in his other writings in different terms. Listen:

***Heb 10:26** For if we **sin wilfully after** that we have received the knowledge of the truth (Gospel), there **remaineth no more sacrifice for sins,** 27 But a certain fearful looking for of judgment and fiery indignation, which shall devour the adversaries. 28 He that despised Moses' law died without mercy under two or three witnesses:* **(Num 15)** *29 Of **how much sorer punishment**, suppose ye, shall he be thought worthy, who hath trodden under foot the Son of God, and hath counted the blood* *of the covenant, wherewith he was sanctified, an unholy thing, and hath done despite unto the Spirit of grace?* (see also Heb. 2:1-3; 12:25)

If we can still SIN while we are under Grace, and SIN is the transgression of the Law (I John 3:4); then we are still under obligation to God's Moral Law while under Grace. The blessing is that we don't have to have a forensic justification through a perfect record or self atonement (which is impossible). We must strive to fulfill the righteousness of the Law of God, but when we fail, we have an advocate in Christ Jesus, who through his sacrifice and priesthood allows us to get up, get clean, and get going again! This is what it means to be under GRACE and not simply under LAW.

1 Jn 2:1 *My little children, these things write I unto you, that ye* **sin** *not. And if any man* **sin***, we have an advocate with the Father, Jesus Christ the righteous:*

1 Jn 3:4 Whosoever committeth sin transgresseth also the law: for sin is the transgression of the law.

Gal 2:16 *Knowing that* **a man is not justified by the works of the law***, but by* **the faith of Jesus Christ***, even we have believed in Jesus Christ, that we might be justified by the faith of Christ, and not by the works of the law:* **for by the works of the law shall no flesh be justified...21** *I do not frustrate the grace of God:* **for if righteousness (Justification) come by the law, then Christ is dead in vain.**

Justification through the Law of Moses apart from Christ's atonement was a Jewish misconception – **it was never the truth.** We are justified through following "the faith of Christ" – not Christ's personal faith, but his teaching – "the faith once delivered to the saints".

Rom 10:3 *For they* **(the Jews)** *being ignorant of God's righteousness* **(justification),** *and going about to establish their* own righteousness **(justification)**, *have not submitted themselves unto the righteousness* **(Justification)** *of God. 4 For Christ is the end* **(goal and aim)** *of the law for righteousness* **(justification)** *to every one that believeth.*

Christ is the goal and aim of the Law's teaching about justification (having a righteous standing before God). The Law only atoned for sins in type, and God forgave on "credit" until Jesus could pay the debt; and thereby justify God's forgiveness and forbearance with man's sin in the Old Covenant.

Ro 3:24 *Being justified freely by his grace through the redemption that is in Christ Jesus: 25 Whom God hath set forth to be a propitiation through faith in his blood, to declare* **[God's justification]** *for the remission of sins that are past* **(Old Covenant),** *through the forbearance of God; 26 To declare, I say, at this time* **[God's justification]***: that he* **(God)** *might be* ***just,*** *and the **justifier** of him which believeth in Jesus.*

Jesus paid the debt, and justified God's pardoning us on credit. THUS, the gospel of salvation through Christ is seen every time pardon is offered or given in the Old Testament. THUS the gospel of salvation by grace is the only salvation offered in the OT. Here is one example

Isa 1:18 *Come now, and let us reason together, saith the LORD:* **though your sins be as scarlet, they shall be as white as snow; though they be red like crimson, they shall be as wool. 19 If ye be willing and obedient,** *ye shall eat the good of the land: 20 But* **if ye refuse and rebel, ye shall be devoured with the sword:** *for the mouth of the LORD hath spoken it.*

If this were salvation by works there would be no mention of forgiveness, cleansing, pardon, etc. Notice repentance and obedience are necessary to receive the grace of cleansing and pardon. God saves eternally with the same principles that He saves temporally as spoken of here.

What does Luke 16:16 mean?

Lu 16:16 _The law and the prophets were until John: since that time the kingdom of God is preached, and every man presseth into it._

Mt 11:12 _And from the days of John the Baptist until now the kingdom of heaven suffereth violence, and the violent take it by force. 13 For all the prophets and the law prophesied until John. 14 And if ye will receive it, this is Elias, which was for to come._

It is obvious to the student of Scripture that the law and the prophets were the sole teachers and pointed forward until John came in the role of Elijah as the forerunner of the Messiah. Look in the last book of the Old Covenant; and then go to the last chapter; and you'll see that the role of John the Baptist (Elijah) is what is spoken of as the next step in God's program.

Mal 4:5 _Behold, I will send you Elijah the prophet before the coming of the great and dreadful day of the LORD: 6 And he shall turn the heart of the fathers to the children, and the heart of the children to their fathers, lest I come and smite the earth with a curse._

Clarke: _The law and the prophets were until John]_ "The law and the prophets continued to be the sole teachers till John came, who first began to proclaim the glad tidings of the kingdom of God: and now, he who wishes to be made a partaker of the blessings of that kingdom must rush speedily into it; as there will be but a short time before an utter destruction shall fall upon this ungodly race. They who wish to be saved must imitate those who take a city by storm-rush into it, without delay, as the Romans are about to do into Jerusalem."

"They were the instructors concerning the Christ who was to come, till John came and showed that all the predictions of the one, and the types and ceremonies of the other were now about to be fully and finally accomplished; for Christ was now revealed."

People have greatly misunderstood the preaching of the Kingdom of God. **When Jesus was among them, the Kingdom of God was among them. When Jesus was with them, the Kingdom of God was with them.** Jesus was the king who would eventually sit on the throne of His father David, so to be one of His disciples was to come into the Kingdom of God as a faithful subject of the King; but Luke 19 is clear that His Kingdom on earth would be at His return. This concept has been confused partly due to a mistranslation and a lack of following the context and meaning of Jesus' words.

Lu 17:21 Neither shall they say, Lo here! or, lo there! for, behold, the kingdom of God is within you.

According to the context this verse should be translated "among you", and not "within you". Listen to the context.

*Lu 17:20 And when he was demanded of the Pharisees, when the **kingdom of God should come,** he answered them and said, The kingdom of God cometh not with observation: 21 Neither shall they say, Lo here! or, lo there! for, behold, the kingdom of God is [among] you. 22 And he said unto the disciples, **The days will come, when ye shall desire to see one of the days of the Son of man, and ye shall not see it.***

Jesus is the King, and when He is there, the Kingdom of God is there. So when John the Baptist began

303

preparing the way of the LORD – the KING, he was preaching the Kingdom of God. King Jesus had to first suffer, die, make atonement, be received to heaven, and then return before He actually would set up His Kingdom on earth (Luke 19). Those servants who were to "occupy" till the King returned "having obtained the kingdom" were under His Lordship and were His subjects; but not in the kingdom in the sense they would be later when He returned.

Jesus is making note that, since John's preaching concerning the kingdom of God, men are pressing into it, and must press vigorously or "violently" to enter the strait and narrow gate. Up until this time being a Jew was "going with the flow"; but now it would be "swimming upstream against the flow" to enter the kingdom of God as proclaimed by John, because the religious authorities were not acknowledging Christ as their King. This truth in no way changes the fact that God's Moral Law is eternal and always relevant; and when the circumstances are the same, the application will always be the same.

It is clear from the following passage that Christians were obligated to fulfill the moral laws of God, here called the "law of liberty", the "word", the "royal law", and the "Scriptures". The same God that commanded the Moral Law commanded the Gospel salvation for those who repent of trespassing His Law. They run together in perfect harmony. By following the Spirit, we fulfill the righteousness of the Law, which is obeying the Gospel. The Gospel is simply the good news that all who repent and reconcile with God by a humble return to His Law and Lordship have hope of pardon through the grace of Christ's atonement.

Jas 1:22 But be ye <u>doers of the word</u>, and not hearers only, deceiving your own selves. 23 For if any be a <u>hearer of the word</u>, and not a doer, he is like unto a man beholding his natural face in a glass: 24 For he beholdeth himself, and goeth his way, and straightway forgetteth what manner of man he was. 25 But whoso looketh into the <u>perfect law of liberty</u>, and continueth therein, he being not a forgetful hearer, but a doer of the work, this man shall be blessed in his deed....2:8 If ye <u>fulfil the royal law</u> according to the scripture, <u>Thou shalt love thy neighbour as thyself</u>, ye do well: 9 But if ye have respect to persons, <u>ye commit sin,</u> and are <u>convinced of the law as transgressors</u>. 10 For whosoever shall keep the <u>whole law</u>, and yet offend in one point, he is guilty of all. 11 For he that said, <u>Do not commit adultery, said also, Do not kill. Now if thou commit no adultery, yet if thou kill, thou art become a transgressor of the law.</u> 12 So speak ye, and so do, as they that shall be judged by the <u>law of liberty.</u>

Notice that being "doers of the Word" and "obeying the Law of God" are the same in James' mind. God's Law is the way to freedom, but sin brings debt. Jesus, in the "Lord's Prayer" said, "forgive us our **debts**, as we forgive our debtors". Jesus also said, "Whosoever committeth sin is the servant of sin". Jesus and James are speaking of sin as transgression of God's Moral Law. Obeying God is liberty from sin's snare; God's justification is liberty from the Law's condemnation; and these are not only New Testament concepts; but were understood in the Old Testament. Liberty is being delivered from the quick-sand of sin and condemnation, and walking on the firm path of God's commandments.

Ps 119:45 And I will walk at **liberty**: for **I seek thy precepts.**

2Co 3:17 Now the Lord is that Spirit: and **where the Spirit of the Lord is, there is liberty.**

The Spirit of God will only lead into fulfilling the righteousness of the Law of God through Moses. If you continue in St. James' line of thinking you come to another passage to consider:

*Jas 4:11 Speak not evil one of another, brethren. He that speaketh evil of his brother, and judgeth his brother, **speaketh evil of the law**, and **judgeth the law: but if thou judge the law, thou art not a doer of the law, but a judge.** 12 **There is one lawgiver**, who is able to save and to destroy: who art thou that judgest another?*

Those who set themselves up to judge Moses' Law are thus not being doers of that law, but judges of God's own inspired law. They need to remember that there is one lawgiver and judge, who is able to save and destroy, and they had better get down from their high and lofty position, and become humble doers of the Word!

What About John 1:17?

Joh 1:17 For the law was given by Moses, but grace and truth came by Jesus Christ.

Is John telling us that there was no grace or truth before Jesus came? Of course not; there is no way anyone could validate such a ridiculous interpretation. Noah found grace in the eyes of the Lord, and God's Word is truth from start to finish. If you look closer you will see that John had a particular thing in mind when using these words, which he had previously introduced.

*Joh 1:14 And the Word was made flesh, and dwelt among us, (and we beheld his glory, the glory as of the only begotten of the Father,) **full of grace and truth.** 15 John bare witness of him, and cried, saying, This was he of whom I spake, He that cometh after me is preferred before me: for he was before me. 16 **And of his fulness*** *have all we received, and grace for grace.* 17 *For the law was given by Moses,* **but grace and truth came by Jesus Christ.**

John doesn't see Jesus' work starting when He showed up on earth; but as he says in this chapter, "In the beginning was the Word..." John is simply comparing the two essential parts of the redemption plan: God's Law, by which is the knowledge of sin, was given to convict mankind and show us our need of redemption (Ro 3:20; Ga 3:19); and "grace and truth" which are John's words for "the Gospel", which brings justification, redemption, reconciliation, and a heavenly High Priest to facilitate our ultimate salvation. The Law was given through Moses with the types and shadows; but the "substance" which actually saves and redeems came through Jesus as the Lamb of God and High Priest in the heavens.

"Curiously this great word charis (grace), so common with Paul, does not occur in John's Gospel save in Joh 1:14,16,17, though alêtheia (truth) is one of the keywords in the Fourth Gospel and in 1John, occurring 25 times in the Gospel and 20 in the Johannine Epistles, 7 times in the Synoptics and not at all in Revelation (Bernard)." (Robertson's NT Word Pictures)

<u>John is not saying truth and grace showed up when Jesus arrived on earth; but that the truth of all the Old Testament types and shadows; and the grace thereby dispersed to mankind was through the sacrificial work of redemption that Jesus accomplished for us.</u> The Law did not belong to Moses, but was God's Law – the work of the WORD; and it was to bring us to an understanding of our desperate need of the LAMB OF GOD to be our sin offering. It all works harmoniously together; and is all a part of God's gracious truth for our salvation. John stops

using the word "grace"; but continues to employ the word "truth", in contradistinction to the Gnostic's errors, as his expression of the "faith once delivered to the saints". Anyone reading his epistles can see this at once.

Who Was Saved by Works?

We've already covered this to some degree, so I'll keep this section short. **No fallen man has ever been saved by their works.** Salvation by works means **"self-atonement"** or **"sinless perfection"**, which needs no atonement – a forensic justification. If you don't have a perfect record of righteousness before God through perfect obedience or self - atonement, then you have no hope of being saved by "works" according to the Bible definition. If keeping Moses Law atoned for sins, so Jesus didn't need to die, then you could be saved and counted righteous by the deeds of the Law (Gal. 2:21); but the Bible declares that all have sinned, and the blood of bulls and goats cannot take away sin; so the sacrifice of Jesus as a sin offering to make atonement for sin, was the only option that propitiated God.

*Ga 3:21 Is the law then against the promises of God? God forbid: for **if there had been a law given which could have given life, verily righteousness** (justification) *should have been by the law.*

Works of repentance and obedience to Christ are necessary to make one eligible to receive the benefits of the atonement of Christ; but this is not salvation by works. The term "works" is determined by the context, and is generally used differently by Paul in his epistles than by James in his. While James speaks of **obedience to Christ**, being "**doers of the word**", or "**exercising faith**" when using the word "**works**"; Paul is speaking of **self-**

atonement through the Ceremonial Law or being **sinless** when using the word "**works**". One of the "works" (James) is necessary for salvation, while the other "works" (Paul) is impossible and therefore cannot save us. That is why Paul says we are saved by faith and *not works*; while James says, "faith *without works* is dead".

James is speaking of faith in action, like us obeying the doctor and taking his medicine because we have faith in him. These works are necessary or our faith is dead as we have already spoken of. Paul is speaking about works of perfect performance or works to atone for our own sins, so that our righteous standing with God is a reward based on a debt God owes us, rather than grace to the undeserving (Ro 4). Paul in Ephesians and Romans is saying, "You cannot save yourself, and must put faith in God's gracious program"; while James is saying, "You'd better exercise your faith, not just sit on it". When Paul speaks of "works" or "deeds of the Law", he is speaking of men striving to save themselves with their own methods. When James speaks of "works", he is speaking of men actually following God's method, not just talking about it. They perfectly agreed with each other, but were dealing with different errors and teaching different principles.

Did Israelites all believe they were saved by works?

Though some fell into the error of assuming God was indebted to them simply because they were circumcised children of Abraham and practiced Moses' Law; the **spiritual** Israelites knew that their salvation was grace and not their due reward.

*Job 19:25 For I know that my **redeemer** liveth, and that he shall stand at the latter day upon the earth: 26 And though*

309

after my skin worms destroy this body, yet in my flesh shall I see God:

Job acknowledging the need for a redeemer to save him reveals that he well knew he could not save himself or atone for his own sins.

2Sa 14:14 *For we must needs die, and are as water spilt on the ground, which cannot be gathered up again; neither doth God respect any person:* **yet doth he devise means, that his banished be not expelled from him.**

This statement reveals these people knew that their reconciliation with God was due to means graciously devised by him whereby we could be pardoned and not expelled eternally. They obviously knew they could not remedy the situation by themselves.

Jon 8:56 *Your father Abraham rejoiced to see my day: and* **he saw it,** *and* **was glad.**

Ga 3:8 *And the scripture, foreseeing that God would justify the heathen through faith, preached before the* **gospel unto Abraham,** *saying, In thee shall all nations be blessed.*

He 4:1 *Let us therefore fear, lest, a promise being left us of entering into his rest, any of you should seem to come short of it. 2* **For unto us was the gospel preached, as well as unto them***: but the word preached did not profit them, not being mixed with faith in them that heard it.*

I could fill this book with quotes from the OT concerning salvation by grace through faith. Paul, when illustrating Salvation by Faith, uses Abel, Enoch, Noah, Abraham, Isaac, Moses,....all the way to us. When James speaks of justification by a "faith that works" he goes back to Abraham and Rahab. In Romans, when Paul wants to illustrate our faith being imputed to us for righteousness, he speaks of Abraham and David. Why? Because we are all saved by the same principle - Through Christ's sacrifice and priesthood God imputes righteousness to us by cleansing our record and pardoning us when we repent and begin exercising faith in Him.

He 11:4 By faith Abel offered unto God a more excellent sacrifice than Cain, **by which he obtained witness that he was righteous, God testifying of his gifts:** and by it he being dead yet speaketh. 5 By faith Enoch was translated that he should not see death; and was not found, because God had translated him: for before his translation he had this testimony, that he **pleased God.** 6 But without faith it is impossible to please him: for he that cometh to God must **believe that he is, and that he is a rewarder of them that diligently seek him.** 7 By faith Noah, being warned of God of things not seen as yet, **moved** with fear, **prepared** an ark to the saving of his house; by the which he condemned the world, and **became heir of the righteousness (Justification) which is by faith....**13 These **all died in faith,** not having received the promises, but having seen them afar off, and were persuaded of them, and embraced them, and confessed that they were strangers and pilgrims on the earth. 14 For they that say such things declare plainly that they seek a country. 15 And truly, if they had been mindful of that country from whence they came out, they might have had opportunity to have returned. 16 But now they desire a better country, that is, an heavenly: wherefore God is not ashamed to be called their God: for he hath prepared for them a city. 24 By faith Moses, when he was come to years, refused to be called the son of Pharaoh's daughter; 25 Choosing rather to suffer affliction with the people of God, than to enjoy the pleasures of sin for a season; 26 **Esteeming the reproach of Christ greater riches than the treasures in Egypt: for he had respect unto the recompence of the reward.** 27 By faith he forsook Egypt, not fearing the wrath of the king: for he endured, as seeing him who is invisible.

This is the same way you must be saved. You must strive to fulfill the righteousness of the Law through the

Spirit, and follow the conditions of the covenant you are in so the atonement is applied to you for sins committed. This is the only way you can have a relationship with the Father!

Ro 8:3 *For what the law could not do, in that it was weak through the flesh, God sending his own Son in the likeness of sinful flesh, and for sin, condemned sin in the flesh: 4 That the* righteousness of the law might be fulfilled in us, *who walk not after the flesh, but after the Spirit. 5 For they that are after the flesh do mind the things of the flesh; but they that are after the Spirit the things of the Spirit. 6 For to be carnally minded is death; but to be spiritually minded is life and peace. 7 Because the* carnal mind is enmity against God: for it is not subject to the law of God, *neither indeed can be. 8 So then they that are in the flesh cannot please God. 9* But ye are not in the flesh, but in the Spirit, *if so be that the Spirit of God dwell in you. Now if any man have not the Spirit of Christ, he is none of his.......13 For if ye* live after the flesh, ye shall die: *but if ye* through the Spirit do mortify the deeds of the body, ye shall live. *14 For as many as are* led by the Spirit of God, they are the sons of God.

2Co 6:17 *Wherefore come out from among them, and be ye separate, saith the Lord, and touch not the unclean thing;* and I will receive you, *18 And* will be a Father unto you, and ye shall be my sons and daughters, *saith the Lord Almighty. 7:1* Having therefore these promises, *dearly beloved,* let us cleanse ourselves from all filthiness of the flesh and spirit, perfecting holiness in the fear of God.

What is Legalism?

Legalism is a form of salvation by works. Legalism is the Judaizer's attempt to bring Gentile believers under the Ceremonial Law and circumcision - basically undoing what God and the Apostles established through Cornelius and the decision in Acts 15. Here are the Legalists:

Ac 15:1 *And certain men which came down from Judaea taught the brethren, and said,* **Except ye be circumcised after the manner of Moses, ye cannot be saved......**5 *But there rose up certain of the sect of the Pharisees which believed, saying,* **That it was needful to circumcise them, and to command them to keep the law of Moses**.

The Legalists are **not** those who say we must obey Jesus or the moral laws of God; but those who say that the atonement of Jesus and following the faith of Christ (the faith once delivered...) is not enough **by itself**. They would declare that circumcision and the Ceremonial Law is still necessary for justification to Gentile converts. What these legalists were demanding had been the proper mode of operation in the churches for the first twelve years after Pentecost, but God opened the doors to receive Gentiles without Judaism through Peter in the case of Cornelius (Acts 10); and thus changed the program. Some Jews did not want to accept this, and kept preaching Judaism to the Gentile Christians. They implied that the non-Jew converts were incomplete in their salvation unless they came under Judaism. Paul refuted this and declared that they were complete in following Christ Jesus.

Col 2:8 *Beware lest any man spoil you through philosophy and vain deceit, after the tradition of men, after the rudiments of the world, and not after Christ. 9 For in him dwelleth all the fulness of the Godhead bodily. 10 And* **ye are complete in him***, which is the head of all principality and power: 11 In whom also* **ye are circumcised with the circumcision made without hands***, in putting off the body of the sins of the flesh by the circumcision of Christ:*

It is very important to understand which epistles are refuting Judaizers/legalists, and which are refuting Gnostics. Paul was refuting Judaizers in most of his epistles. The Gnostics used Paul's epistles, which speak of salvation by grace without the Ceremonial Law, to say that our **performance** doesn't affect our **position** in Christ. How did they get this from Paul's epistles? Well, like many today, when Paul said "law" they assumed it meant all laws or rules of conduct. They failed to see that "law" is determined by context; and that Paul only declared the Gentiles to be free from the covenant obligations in the ceremonial laws, **not** from obedience to God's moral laws of holiness and righteousness – and **not** from obedience to Christ or His Apostles. The epistles of James and John countered these heretical misconceptions of the Gnostics to declare plainly that our performance/obedience **does** affect our position with God.

When Paul told Timothy to get the church in order by laying down certain rules, he was not being a legalist.

I Tim 2:9 *In like manner also, that women adorn themselves in modest apparel, with shamefacedness and sobriety; not with broided hair, or gold, or pearls, or costly array;*

For Timothy to enforce these principles by deliberate "do's and don'ts", church standards, and rules of conduct, was not legalism either. Our obedience to Christ and his Apostles **is** necessary for our salvation; because we will not be eligible for Christ's atonement if we are rebellious. However, thinking that asceticism, circumcision, ceremonies and rituals are **means of atoning for our own sins** or **helping Jesus atone for our sins** is a form of salvation by works or "legalism". Atoning for my sins or helping Jesus atone for my sins is **impossible** and **wrong thinking;** but repenting and obeying Jesus, so He will apply His atonement to me, and be my High Priest/Savior

is true and right thinking. Jesus is the "author of eternal salvation to **all them that obey Him**" (Heb. 5:9).   Where does that leave those who don't?

*He 5:9 And being made perfect, he (Jesus) became the author of eternal salvation **unto all them that obey him;***

Chapter Twenty Three
Let God Be True, But Every Man A Liar

Ro 3:4 *God forbid: yea,* **let God be true, but every man a liar;** *as it is written,* **That thou mightest be justified in thy sayings,** *and* **mightest overcome when thou art judged.**

The apostle was telling us that whenever it seems to our finite mind that God has done something inconsistent or unjust we must fall back on the reality that God is infinitely more knowledgeable in these areas than we are – thus we are to allow God's words, opinions, and judgments to stand as true, holy, and just; and all those who find fault to stand as liars. This is the only sensible approach when dealing with someone so much higher than we are.

Job 40:8 Wilt thou also disannul my judgment? wilt thou condemn me, that thou mayest be righteous?

Sadly, this is the sin of the Marcionite/Mennonites when they demean Moses' Law to exalt their interpretations of Jesus.

Nu 23:19 *God is not a man, that he should lie; neither the son of man, that he should repent: hath he said, and shall he not do it? or hath he spoken, and shall he not make it good?*

I Sa 15:29 *And also the Strength of Israel will not lie nor repent: for he is not a man, that he should repent.*

Ps 119:89 *For ever, O LORD, thy word is settled in heaven.*

Isa 40:8 *The grass withereth, the flower fadeth: but the word of our God shall stand for ever.*

Mal 3:6 *For I am the LORD,* **I change not;**

Jon 8:58 *Jesus said unto them, Verily, verily, I say unto you, Before Abraham was, I am.*

Ro 11:29 *For the gifts and calling of God are without repentance.*

Heb 1:12 *And as a vesture shalt thou fold them up, and* **they shall be changed:** *but* **thou art the same,** *and thy years shall not fail.*

Heb 13:8 *Jesus Christ the* **same** *yesterday, and to day, and for ever.*

Jas 1:17 *Every* **good gift** *and every* **perfect gift** *is from above, and cometh down from the Father of lights,* **with whom is no variableness, neither shadow of turning.**

1 Pe 1:25 *But the word of the Lord endureth for ever. And* **this is the word which by the gospel is preached unto you.** (Quoting Isaiah above)

The immutability of God and of Christ are so clearly stated in the Scriptures that it is unthinkable that any would challenge the concept; yet some blockheads insist on trying to make God a liar. Marcion thought he solved this fanciful dilemma by saying there was really *two gods;* but this also makes God a liar; for God said there was only ONE. God never repents in the sense of changing His purpose *because there is a better way or a higher course to follow.* His ways do not evolve or improve. Mennonite defenders like Ste. Marie argue that *O, yes, God is unchanging; but His moral judgments change from one covenant to another*; which only reaveals the shallowness of their thinking organ. The Bible clearly shows there to be ONE unchanging GOD; and God himself declares this in no uncertain terms. The reason Marcion and friends are bent on making God a liar in one case or the other is because they do not want their pet doctrines found to be error. If God and Christ are immutable in their moral consititution as the Bible teaches, then JESUS WAS NOT TEACHING ANYTHING CONTRARY TO THE OLD TESTAMENT LAW OF MOSES. Let's look at a couple places where they labor to make God a liar.

Lev 18

In Leviticus eighteen God gives commands forbidding many types of improper marriage practices, fornication, incest, and other lewd activity. In the list God says that one cannot marry a sister. At the end God says

Lev 18:24 Defile not ye yourselves in any of these things: for in all these the nations are defiled which I cast out before you: 25 And the land is defiled: therefore I do visit the iniquity thereof upon it, and the land itself vomiteth out her inhabitants. 26 Ye shall therefore keep my statutes and my judgments, and shall not commit any of these abominations; neither any of your own nation, nor any stranger that sojourneth among you: 27 (For all these abominations have the men of the land done, which were before you, and the land is defiled;) 28 That the land spue not you out also, when ye defile it, as it spued out the nations that were before you. 29 For whosoever shall commit any of these abominations, even the souls that commit them shall be cut off from among their people. 30 Therefore shall ye keep mine ordinance, that ye commit not any one of these abominable customs, which were committed before you, and that ye defile not yourselves therein: I am the LORD your God.

Upon first glance one may assume that God saw the marriage of a sister as a vile abomination. Now, in light of this it would seem that God changed His opinion on this matter; because when creating mankind He made it necessary for men to marry their sisters and said it was "very good". The Marcionites jump for glee when they find this; for it is just what they were looking for to prove that Jesus also taught contrary to God's previous moral judgments. There are, however, some fundamental flaws in this Marcionite exuberance.

How can we let God be true and every Marcionite a liar when the facts seem to testify against us? First, we follow the Apostle's admonition for interpretation of the Scriptures; we believe God's testimony of His own unchanging nature; and we look closer for an explanation that is true and consistent with God's way of doing things.

First, we need to understand that when something is said to be "good" *while it is also safe and productive*; but later said to be "bad" *when it becomes dangerous and unproductive*, this is **not** a change in the moral constitution of God; but a necessary change in judgment due to *a change in the nature of the situation*. God's law of love was not violated when men married their sisters and were fruitful and replenished the earth as God commanded; but 2500 years later when men's genetics had sufficiently broke down so that marrying sisters became a dangerous and unproductive enterprise, God forbad it. When it became dangerous, due to the possible corruption of the offspring, it would then indeed violate God's law of love. It is very unloving to deliberately produce a retarded or handicapped child by acting irresponsible. God knew about genetics and DNA even when others did not.

Now, what is the context for what God said in Leviticus eighteen? Do you understand that Moses' Law consisted of Genesis, Exodus, Leviticus, Deuteronomy, and Numbers? So any Israelite who read Leviticus **also**

had the history of Genesis in their mind as a **contextual backdrop**. They could see that Abraham married a sister and was the friend of God, while Sodom practiced other matters listed in Leviticus eighteen and were destroyed. They could clearly see that not everything in the Levitical list was equally obnoxious to God. Marrying sisters was not so much a moral issue, but a civil ordinance which prohibited that which was now dangerous and unproductive to society; but in and of itself, apart from the danger, was not abominable to God. This is common sense to anyone who is willing to believe God's Word. God never cast a shadow upon the morality of those early men who married sisters like He did upon Cain's murder, Reuben's immorality, Sodom's "exceeding" sinfulness, the ungodly marriages before the flood, or even the disrespect paid to Noah by Ham. Did God send the flood because they were marrying sisters? Did God overthrow Sodom for marrying sisters? No, but He did for the other matters in the list. Listen to how Leviticus eighteen begins:

*Lev 18:1 And the LORD spake unto Moses, saying, 2 Speak unto the children of Israel, and say unto them, I am the LORD your God. 3 **After the doings of the land of Egypt, wherein ye dwelt, shall ye not do: and after the doings of the land of Canaan, whither I bring you, shall ye not do:** neither shall ye walk in their ordinances. 4 Ye shall do my judgments, and keep mine ordinances, to walk therein: I am the LORD your God. 5 Ye shall therefore keep my statutes, and my judgments: which if a man do, he shall live in them: I am the LORD.*

Now, listen to the ending again:

*Lev 18:24 Defile not ye yourselves in any of these things: **for in all these the nations are defiled which I cast out before you: 25 And the land is defiled: therefore I do visit the iniquity thereof upon it, and the land itself vomiteth out her*** *inhabitants. 26 Ye shall therefore keep my statutes and my judgments, and shall not commit any of these abominations; neither any of your own nation, nor any stranger that sojourneth among you: 27 **(For all these abominations have the men of the land done, which were before you, and the land is defiled;) 28 That the land spue not you out also, when ye defile it, as it spued out the nations that were before you.***

Obviously God has in view some practices of the heathen nations which we don't even know all the particulars of; but was not saying that *"now He feels this way about Abel, Seth, and Abraham too"*. That is nonsense! God did not change His moral compass, but forbad something that had become dangerous along with other matters which were NEVER good, and could NEVER be good in **any** circumstance.

The reason Mennonites want to prove God changed His mind is because in the Law of Moses God allowed divorce and remarriage under certain circumstances as a remedial ordinance to keep peace and holiness in society; but they interpret Jesus as forbidding ALL remarriage and calling it adultery. They so love their pet doctrine that they wish to make God a liar over it. This is idolatry, not Christianity. Jesus and the Apostles are in perfect harmonious agreement with God's inspired directives in Deuteronomy concerning marriage, divorce, and remarriage – and to the Marcionite's dismay, my books prove it. *"Let God be true, but every [marcionite] a liar"*

What about Polygamy?

Some believe that God allowing polygamy in the OT, but not allowing it in the NT is a sure sign that Jesus spoke contrary to the Law; but they are building on false assumptions. Let's look at where the Law of God taught and commanded polygamy: _____.

322

That's right! He didn't. What does the **Law** teach us about polygamy?

First, it teaches us that God took only one rib and made only one woman for Adam. Then God made the declaration that they **two** should become **one** flesh. This should be all that needs to be said to show God's will. The Law also tells us where polygamy started.

Ge 4:19 *And Lamech took unto him two wives: the name of the one was Adah, and the name of the other Zillah.*

Polygamy came from the corrupt line of Cain. The first time we see this in the godly line is when Sarah initiated it between her maid, Hagar, and Abraham since she was childless. It was not in faith, but in unbelief; and has caused innumerable problems – It is the source of the conflict between the Jews and Arabs to this day. The next time is when Laban cheats Jacob and this ends with Jacob marrying two sisters – something the Law of Moses later forbade (Lev. 18:18). Notice how God allowed man to make mistakes and reap the consequences. God allowed Jacob to continue in this situation; but forbid future generations from following the unwise example.

These bad examples led to the practice, and when God brought the people out of Egypt, they had been affected by the pagan environment they were in. God chose wisely not to abruptly stop this situation, but to regulate it.   The Law gave regulations for those who chose this route; but it never commended it as God's will or choice for marriage. God patiently chose to allow it under the circumstances; but the Law in Genesis makes it clear that it was not the original intent of God.

Polygamy and divorce exist under similar principles:

1. Neither was in the garden or God's original intention.
2. Both were a result of man's sin and innovations.
3. 2500 years after these practices were established by men – God stepped in and gave instructions to keep people from being treated unjustly and to regulate the situation.
4. God's handling of the matter was to deal with what man had established in his carnality in the most loving manner possible.
5. It was allowed within a system of laws and accountability where injustice could be restrained.
6. We are now to suppress both; but when confronted with either, we must deal with it justly as God commanded. We are not to promote either one.

God knew that multiple wives would cause much unrest and trouble in the home, as well as hinder the husband from being led by God. God commanded kings not to multiply wives, lest they turn the man's heart from God; which multiply wives always seemed to do in one way or another. Men have a hard time following God without catering to the whims of the wife, and multiple wives multiply the problem. Consider the failures of men in this area, including Adam, Abraham, Jacob, Sampson, Gilead, David, Solomon, Ahab, etc. Consider the family strife caused by polygamy with these and other Old Testament examples.

God commanded for kings not to multiply wives and gold (Deut. 17:17); but then He patiently tolerated it while they learned the hard way that attention to detail in God's Law was the best route. God allowed them to walk in their carnal stupidity and reap the natural consequences in order to prove the wisdom of His instructions.

Pr 5:15 *Drink waters out of thine own cistern, and running waters out of thine own well. 16 Let thy fountains be dispersed abroad, and rivers of waters in the streets. 17 Let them be only thine own, and not strangers' with thee. 18 Let thy fountain be blessed: and rejoice with **the wife of thy youth.** 19 Let her be as the loving hind and pleasant roe; let her breasts satisfy thee at all times; and be thou ravished always with her love. 20 And why wilt thou, my son, be ravished with a strange woman, and embrace the bosom of a stranger? 21 For the ways of man are before the eyes of the LORD, and he pondereth all his goings.*

Why did God patiently tolerate it when He did not tolerate other things? God doesn't micromanage the affairs of men, but allows men to make their own choices; and then reap the consequences. God gave a written law when He came into covenant with Israel as a nation. This nation was already well into the practice; and God saw fit to allow it to continue under certain regulations. Only those rich enough to care for more than one wife had more; and as long as they were justly taken care of, they were possibly better off than if desolate. Ruth was happy to "find rest" in Boaz's household; and would have rather been the second wife than left desolate. These wives helped populate and build the nation of Israel, which cause was worthy of consideration while God's "church" was a nation. The heathen were multiplying quickly and God's people needed to keep up to some degree. Sometimes a man took two wives because his first was barren, and he wanted an heir to preserve his name in Israel – similar to Abraham. Sarah obviously wanted a child enough to even promote the idea. This same issue validated the Levirate marriage as well (Deut. 25:5); which was actually a command of God to preserve family inheritance in Israel. After man's fall came death, war, and hardship; and women were better off protected in marriage than not; multiple children were needed; and there was a race for survival with the ungodly nations. These dynamics made it expedient for God to allow the arrangement and regulate it.

Many of these issues ceased to be as important once the Messiah came and God's "church" ceased to be a nation and became assemblies of believers among all nations. The overall testimony of polygamous marriages in the Bible, with their complex dynamics, reveals that God's original plan was far superior for peace in the home. If God allowed it, that is His business, and we have no right to squawk. God didn't have to check in with us first. We can also know that God still feels the same way and Jesus agreed with God 100% and still does. Jesus was not embarrassed by what Moses allowed, because it was Jesus who commanded and inspired Moses. The Apostles did not separate polygamos marriages. Here are God's wise regulations.

Ex 21:10 If he take him another wife; her food, her raiment, and her duty of marriage, shall he not diminish. 11 And if he do not these three unto her, then shall she go out free without money.

The wife had recourse to the authorities and could divorce if the man took another wife and diminished her care. Jesus preached against the abuse of such a precept; but didn't change the precept.

De 21:15 If a man have two wives, one beloved, and another hated, and they have born him children, both the beloved and the hated; and if the firstborn son be hers that was hated: 16 Then it shall be, when he maketh his sons to inherit that which he hath, that he may not make the son of the

326

beloved firstborn before the son of the hated, which is indeed the firstborn: 17 But he shall acknowledge the son of the hated for the firstborn, by giving him a double portion of all that he hath: for he is the beginning of his strength; the right of the firstborn is his.

In the New Covenant God calls us back to HIS LAW; which always gave directives in the light of the original intent and not contrary to it. Jesus always referred back to God's Law when dealing with issues; but pointed out the difference between "original intent" and "remedial directives for particular needs among fallen people". **All God's Laws were to be interpreted in the light of God's original intentions**. Genesis revealed God's original plan before sin came upon the scene. We are now striving to live up to the holiness God originally designed; but still must use the remedial directives to help solve sin's problems. When a man came to Christ or the Apostles with two wives, he was accepted in to the church, not told to divorce. This man could not, however, be a church leader because they did not want polygamy to be set up as an **example** before the church.

1 Ti 3:2 *A bishop then must be blameless, the husband of* **one wife,** *vigilant, sober, of good behaviour, given to hospitality, apt to teach;*

1 Ti 3:12 *Let the deacons be the husbands of* **one wife***, ruling their children and their own houses well.*

Tit 1:6 *If any be blameless, the husband of* **one wife***, having faithful children not accused of riot or unruly.*

With these wise and patient steps, monogamy was restored and polygamy ceased in the faithful Christian churches. God expects more from Christians because they have been given more light. We are not responsible to build the nation of Israel and preserve our name or our

327

brother's name for an inheritance in the land.   God obviously NEVER saw polygamy in the same light as He sees immorality of many other sorts. Polygamy is never called adultery in the Bible, which proves that Jesus was not calling remarriage adultery; but was referring to the unjust divorce in the overall transaction. If the man had kept both wives, it would not have been called adultery.

God has not, however, changed His moral compass concerning polygamy. If we go to the mission field into a culture where polygamy is the common and accepted practice, we are not to demand divorce and monogamy; but are to follow the loving example of the Apostles in applying God's Law in its proper and original intent. When the same situations present themselves, God's Laws are always the wisest, most appropriate, and most loving thing to do; because they are GOD'S INFINITE WISDOM AND LOVE APPLIED TO THAT SCENARIO – and NO MAN can improve on that.

What about Musical Instruments?

Here is an issue where some would declare that God has changed his mind; but a careful study reveals that God has been very gracious in accepting man's show of affection.   To sing praises to God with musical instruments is still pleasing to God when it accompanies a sincere heart of reverence rather than a cloaked show off session and gratification of the flesh.

The spiritual climate and order where God chose to establish the church of Jesus Christ was one that did not employ the ancient instrumental worship of the Jews; but we are told that the synagogues just had prayer, reading, a sermon, and singing.   The worship with musical instruments seems to be confined to Temple worship or personal use, and was not a part of the synagogue service. The Psalms which recommend this type of worship are speaking of Temple worship.

Jesus and His Apostles set up the church after the pattern of the synagogue and the Temple was destroyed. This seems to indicate that since the Temple is gone, and we are following the pattern of the synagogue, we should continue the church's worship after the way the Apostles started it. The order of the synagogue was a God ordained arrangement which Jesus used and endorsed. When Christian Jews were kicked out of the Jewish synagogues they started Christian synagogues, which we call churches – both words refer to an *assembly.*

Jas 2:2 For if there come unto your **assembly** a man with a gold ring, in goodly apparel, and there come in also a poor man in vile raiment; {**assembly: Gr. synagogue**}

Just as all other parts of the Ceremonial Law that required the Temple are now done away, so it seems that the Temple worship with musical instruments was also done away; at least for public worship.

Did Jesus imply that worship would change?

Jn 4:20 Our fathers worshipped in this mountain; and ye say, that in Jerusalem is the place where men ought to worship. 21 Jesus saith unto her, Woman, believe me, the hour cometh, when ye shall neither in this mountain, nor yet at Jerusalem, worship the Father. 22 Ye worship ye know not what: we know what we worship: for salvation is of the Jews. 23 **But the hour cometh, and now is, when the true worshippers shall worship the Father in spirit and in truth: for the Father seeketh such to worship him.** 24 God is a Spirit: and they that worship him must worship him in spirit and in truth. 25 The woman saith unto him, I know that Messias cometh, which is called Christ: when he is *come, he will tell us all things. 26 Jesus saith unto her, I that speak unto thee am he.*

The woman of Samaria knew that when the Messiah came, He would explain hard issues and answer hard questions. In the matter of worship Jesus clearly says there is going to be a change from a more ceremonial worship in a certain place to a more spiritual worship without a specific location. This was facilitated in the synagogues spread all over the civilized world as God's fertile field intended for the rapid spread of the Gospel. Jesus preached in the synagogues and His churches were established after the order of the synagogue; so let's just keep the same basic pattern. Here are the positive commands in the New Covenant:

Heb 13:15 *By him therefore let us offer the **sacrifice of praise** to God continually, that is, the **fruit of our lips** giving thanks to his name.*

Eph 5:19 Speaking *to yourselves in psalms and hymns and spiritual songs, **singing** and making **melody in your heart** to the Lord;*

Col 3:16 *Let the word of Christ dwell in you richly in all wisdom; **teaching and admonishing** one another in psalms and hymns and spiritual songs, **singing** with grace in your hearts to the Lord.*

Jas 5:13 *Is any among you afflicted? let him pray. Is any merry? let him **sing** psalms.*

I have nothing personal against musical instruments; but simply believe the church is wiser to continue with the pattern Jesus set. There may be reasons for this pattern which we do not know. It is not a moral change in God, as nothing has been forbidden in this area which was previously commanded in the Law; and only those who really tune in and care will even catch what I am saying and follow it. God is gracious, but reveals His will to those who tune in and care.

There are some cautions concerning musical instruments and we can see how they have been and are being abused for the gratification of the flesh. Children who are taught to play instruments are in great danger of becoming "performers" rather than "worshippers". They practice and practice for the eyes and ears of men. Most people won't even bother with the hard work and time involved in learning an instrument if they cannot perform for someone. If I let my little girl labor and toil and learn to play the piano, then every time the grandparents or others visit there will be the temptation to say, "Show them what you've learned". Then the little girl's labor is rewarded by what? By performing and hearing the "O that is so nice" response of the audience. And how is it that you show your skill on an instrument? By playing slow and reverent? No, but usually by playing fast. I've seen the fruit of all this first hand, and believe that acapella worship is pleasing to God and attended with less danger.

The churches were patterned after the synagogues where they had no musical instruments; and the early Christian churches rejected musical instruments in group worship. I found an interesting article from Thy Word is Truth website, and felt it was worthy of posting here:

"Acapella means "as in the chapel." The music of the church was acapella for centuries. The first organ was introduced in worship by Pope Vitalian I some 670 years after Christ. When it threatened the division of the Catholic church it was removed. However some 130

331

years later it was again introduced, this time successfully though there was still some opposition. The Greek Catholic Church refused it and still refuses it. Martin Luther rejected the organ as an "ensign of Baal." John Calvin said of the organ in worship (things had not yet reached the orchestra stage), "It is no more suitable than the burning of incense, the lighting of tapers or revival of the other shadows of the law. The Roman Catholics borrowed it from the Jews." John Wesley, when asked about the use of the organ in worship, brusquely replied, "I have no objection to the organ in our chapels provided it is neither seen nor heard." Adam Clarke, a great Methodist commentator and a contemporary of John Wesley, said, "I am an old man and an old minister, and I here declare that I have never known instrumental music to be productive of any good in the worship of God, and have reason to believe that it has been productive of much evil. Music, as a science, I esteem and admire, but instruments of music in the house of God I abominate and abhor. This is the abuse of music, and I here register my protest against all such corruptions in the worship of that Infinite Spirit who requires His followers to worship Him in spirit and in truth." Charles Spurgeon was perhaps the greatest Baptist preacher who ever lived. He preached for twenty years in the Metropolitan Baptist Tabernacle of London, England to 10,000 people every Sunday. The mechanical instrument never entered the tabernacle of Spurgeon. When asked why he did not use the organ in worship, he cited 1 Cor. 14:15: "I will pray with the spirit, and I will pray with the understanding also: I will sing with the spirit and I will sing with the understanding also." He added, "I would as soon pray to God with machinery as to sing to God with machinery."

Bob Williams in a scholarly article, Origins of Christian Worship, shares the following:

"A significant difference is seen between the dramatic worship exhibited in the temple (both the first and the second) and the restrained and subdued gatherings in the synagogues. While the focus in the temple seemed to be mainly upon exuberant worship and praise through sacrifice and music (both vocal and instrumental), it seems that the main focus in the synagogues was not so much upon public worship, but rather upon instruction in the Law. The worship of the synagogues was apparently limited to recitation of prayer, chanting of the Psalms, and Bible reading and instruction... While it has been suggested by a few that the early Christians may have reintroduced a form of melodious singing similar to that found previously in the temple, the vast majority of scholars state that the music of Christian worship was limited to the same plain chant as had been used in synagogue worship, and that it would be several centuries before the introduction of choral melody and/or four-part harmony (or reintroduction, if indeed temple singing was similar to modern day church singing)...**It appears that the manner of worship seen in the early church was originally just a continuation of what the Jews had been doing for the previous 500 years (adding only the agape feast and Lord's Supper on the first day of the week).** This was followed by further gradual changes and variations, but the basic fundamental aspects of historical worship (singing, prayer, instruction, Lord's Supper) remained constant. Perhaps this is close to what Jesus had in mind when He stated that worship would not remain confined to specific places, but should always be done in spirit and in truth (John 4:21-24)."

In Heaven – God's Temple – we again see musical instruments in group worship being used. This may just be symbolic, as many other things in the book of Revelation are. It is worthy of note that only harps (very mild instruments) are seen in this heavenly worship. Harp music would certainly be more fitting for Heaven than what people usually play on other instruments. Contemporary Christian bands would really feel cramped if all they had were harps!

Re 5:8 And when he had taken the book, the four beasts and four and twenty elders fell down before the Lamb, having every one of them harps, and golden vials full of odours, which are the prayers of saints.

Re 14:2 And I heard a voice from heaven, as the voice of many waters, and as the voice of a great thunder: and I heard the voice of harpers harping with their harps:

Re 15:2 And I saw as it were a sea of glass mingled with fire: and them that had gotten the victory over the beast, and over his image, and over his mark, and over the number of his name, stand on the sea of glass, having the harps of God.

Maybe due to abuse, God stopped the instrumental worship providentially, but will allow it again when we are fully sanctified in Heaven.

What about Old Covenant Fancy Dress, Jewelry, and the Pursuit of Riches?

Due to the fact that many see some differences between what is commanded to NT believers and what was tolerated in the OT; it is important to explain why this is so. We know that God's promises and blessings took on first a natural earthly tone; but then the earthly types were shown to refer to spiritual blessings, not just earthly. This is why the "promised land" was first speaking of

Canaan, but now is heaven. God used earthly types, goals, blessings, and promises to teach about heavenly realities and lead us to understand the nature of the spiritual blessings. Israel was supposed to demonstrate God's blessings upon a nation that obeyed Him; but now we are sent into all nations to proclaim the promise of Christ's kingdom and a heavenly home. It is all still working for the same goal of man's salvation and reconciliation with God.

The greater the light and understanding one has been given, the more God expects of them. When God shines more light, He expects a greater spirituality in us; but this doesn't mean God has changed His view or moral constitution. This does not equal the charge that God commanded one thing in the OT and then said it was evil in the NT. God's patience in discipling and growing people cannot be construed as a change in His moral constitution and judgment – don't confuse the two. We don't expect new converts to have full understanding and mature living immediately; but that doesn't reflect a change in our church's moral teaching or standards.

God tolerated carnal practices among the Jews in matters of fancy dress, wearing jewelry, seeking riches, etc.; but these were not His ultimate goals for them; and spiritual Jews avoided such frivolities as they understood God's mind on it. He was dealing with a **nation** of people who were not all mature and Spirit filled. His promises to them were **earthly temporal types** of the **spiritual riches and possessions promised to us in the NT**. The Israelites were promised earthly inheritance and riches if they obeyed God's Law; and if any nation obeys God's Laws today it will cause them to prosper as well. God is not opposed to prosperity or riches; but is opposed to selfish and proud **usage** of such. The Spiritual Israelites understood this was only a type of something heavenly in the future; and confessed themselves strangers and pilgrims on the earth – **Read Hebrews 11.** Jesus will indeed reign on this earth; and when He does the earth will prosper as never before and all will be rich. God has no problem with riches; but doesn't want us to trust in them, be selfish with them, decorate ourselves with them, become proud through them, or be poor stewards of them. He knows our tendencies.

In the New Covenant, with Spirit filled saints composing the body of Christ/ the Church, God has commanded a more spiritual walk that seeks eternal riches, spiritual blessings, humble pursuits, and a counter culture of spirituality and holiness. We are still supposed to be diligent and prosper through obeying God's wise laws. We are to teach whatever nation we are in the principles of God's Laws so that nation can prosper; but in these last days, we are to be proclaiming a coming kingdom, not just building an earthly one, like Israel. We have much greater light and understanding, so more spirituality is expected of us. We have a commission to preach the Gospel around the world, and that is to be our focus in stewardship. Are we living up to the light we have received, or seeking to live on a lower level?

***1Ti 2:8** I will therefore that men pray every where, lifting up holy hands, without wrath and doubting. 9 In like manner also, that women adorn themselves in modest apparel, with shamefacedness and sobriety; not with broided hair, or gold, or pearls, or costly array;*

The Apostles clearly forbid Christians wearing that which exalts and focuses on the temporal, sensual, carnal, and prideful appetites of this world. This is also contrary to our focus of stewardship in spreading the Gospel – that money could be better used!

1Pe 3:1 Likewise, ye wives, be in subjection to your own husbands; that, if any obey not the word, they also may without the word be won by the conversation of the wives; 2 While they behold your chaste conversation coupled with fear. 3 Whose adorning <u>let it not be that outward adorning of plaiting the hair, and of wearing of gold, or of putting on of apparel;</u> 4 But let it be the hidden man of the heart, in that which is not corruptible, even the ornament of a meek and quiet spirit, which is in the sight of God of great price.

God does not want our "adorning" or "decorating" of ourselves to be with jewels, clothes, ribbons, bows, etc.; but he wants our "adorning" to be spiritual attitudes and actions. This was not made as clear in the OT; but is very clear in the NT. God expects more from those who have the Holy Spirit indwelling them along with the example and teachings of Christ, than those who didn't have that. But this is no change of God's moral constitution at all; and we are not taking something the Law taught and making it sin as Marcionites do. Paul and Peter who gave these exhortations did not see any conflict between this and the *righteousness of God's Law* being fulfilled in believers.

*1Ti 6:6 But godliness with contentment is great gain. 7 For we brought nothing into this world, and it is certain we can carry nothing out. 8 And having food and raiment let us be therewith content. 9 But they that **will be rich** fall into temptation and a snare, and into many foolish and hurtful lusts, which drown men in destruction and perdition. 10 For the **love of money is the root of all evil**: which while some coveted after, they have erred from the faith, and pierced themselves through with many sorrows. 11 But thou, **O man of God, flee these things; and follow after righteousness, godliness, faith, love,*** *patience, meekness. 12 Fight the good fight of faith, lay hold on eternal life,*

Jesus taught us to not lay up treasure upon earth, but to lay up treasure in Heaven. He said it was easier for a camel to go through the eye of a needle, than for a rich man to enter heaven. Some spiritual Jews understood this. Consider what Jonadab taught his children – Jer 35. Read Paul's commentary on the subject in Hebrews 11; and also consider the lives of the prophets like Elisha with his rebuke of Gehazi:

2Ki 5:26 And he said unto him, Went not mine heart with thee, when the man turned again from his chariot to meet thee? Is it a time to receive money, and to receive garments, and oliveyards, and vineyards, and sheep, and oxen, and menservants, and maidservants?

Spiritual Israelites understood that though God promised prosperity to the nation when they obeyed His laws, the prosperity in itself was dangerous to their spiritual life, and could cause them to trust in their riches rather than God. Trusting in riches or compromising righteousness for riches is condemned in all of God's Word. God still blesses nations and communities with prosperity when they obey His Word; but the emphasis in the NT is on our stewardship as messengers of the Gospel and ambassadors of Christ to the world.

When Jacob needed God's help and wanted his family to get right with God, he commanded them to get rid of their strange gods; and they also took off their ear rings and buried them all under a tree.

Ge 35:1 And God said unto Jacob, Arise, go up to Bethel, and dwell there: and make there an altar unto God, that appeared unto thee when thou fleddest from the face of Esau thy brother. 2 Then Jacob said unto his household, and to all that were with him, Put away the strange gods that are among you, and be clean, and change your garments: 3 And let us arise, and go up to Bethel; and I will make there an altar unto God, who answered me in the day of my distress, and was with me in the way which I went. 4 And they gave unto Jacob all the strange gods which were in their hand, and all their earrings which were in their ears; and Jacob hid them under the oak which was by Shechem.

When God was angry with Israel, He commanded them to put off their Jewelry and humble themselves while He decided what to do with them.

Ex 33:4 *And when the people heard these evil tidings, they mourned: and no man did put on him his ornaments. 5 For the LORD had said unto Moses, Say unto the children of Israel, Ye are a stiffnecked people: I will come up into the midst of thee in a moment, and consume thee: <u>therefore now put off thy ornaments from thee,</u> that I may know what to do unto thee. 6 And the children of Israel stripped themselves of their ornaments by the mount Horeb.*

It is clear from the "whole counsel of God" that He has tolerated many things; but those who love Him and seek to please Him can see that there is another way that He has always prefered. I want to walk this way. God's Law of love would always desire us to prosper; but then use that prosperity in a wise and charitable manner for the furtherance of the truth.

The New Covenant does not contradict the morality of God's Law, but clarifies it, shines more light on it, and gives more power to fulfill it. What God desired from man from the beginning should be more and more fulfilled as we grow in grace and walk in the same Spirit that inspired the Scriptures from Genesis to Revelation.

How is Divorce different from Polygamy, Jewelry, etc.?

Some will think we are not being consistent. They will say that God's dealing with divorce is the same as God's dealing with polygamy, jewelry and the other issues we've shown are somewhat different now from the OT allowances. **However there is a big difference.** Deut. 24:1-4 was God's own instructions for what to do when immoral conduct violated the marriage covenant. What God commanded as the best thing to do; and what God tolerated or allowed are two very different things. God's forbearance and God's instructions are fundamentally different: One is God's statement of what is appropriate in this situation; and the other is God's tolerance of man's innovations. One originates in God's mind and the other is due to man's fallen nature. One is God's remedy and the other is God's patience and forbearance with man. God never gave positive commandments where the solution to a problem was polygamy, wearing jewelry, fancy clothes, and pursuing riches. The only time polygamy was given as a solution was in the levirate marriage which only applied to Israel as a nation until Messiah came; and even this was not compulsory as we see in the book of Ruth and Deut 25:5-10.

God deals differently with a nation than with individuals. In Israel God worked through the nation; but also maintained a remnant who were truly spiritual seekers of truth. In the church, we ONLY have the remnant of regenerated seekers of truth; and so God expects the church to walk more spiritual than the nation.

Some things were tolerated with restrictions placed on them to keep them from becoming too harmful; but they were never positively commanded as a righteous way to solve a problem like Deut. 24:1-4. We can do without polygamy, jewelry, fancy clothes, etc; but when sin violates the marriage covenant, we still need to know what to do. The instructions given in the New Testament are consistent with the Law, not contrary to it, because they are based on the Law. Jesus was answering questions about the Law when He rebuked their abuse of God's Law. Paul based his instructions on the Law (Romans 7 and I Cor. 7).

Our book, "What The Bible Really Teaches About Divorce And Remarriage" deals more fully with the details. You can order your copy from booksellers online, or contact us.

Whatever issue arises where there seems to be a difference between the New Testament and the Old; we need to keep in mind that God never changes His morality, and Jesus is the "Word" of God from Genesis to Revelation. Jesus inspired the Scriptures from Genesis to Revelation; and He is the same yesterday, today and forever. Erroneous dispensationalism, easy believism, unconditional eternal security (once saved, always saved), and many other heretical teachings, would be cleared up if people could only understand God's consistent flow of light from Genesis to Revelation. Extreme teachings that pit the New Testament Scriptures against the Old; and pit the teachings of Jesus against Moses' Law are not only dangerous and sinful, but also misrepresent God's grace, justice, and wisdom.

2Ti 2:15 *Study to shew thyself approved unto God, a workman that needeth not to be ashamed, **rightly** **dividing the word of truth.***

Chapter Twenty Four
On The Proper Usage
Of "Early Church" Writings

*Php 3:17 Brethren, be followers together of me, and **mark them which walk so as ye have us for an ensample.** 18 (For many walk, of whom I have told you often, and now tell you even weeping, that they are the enemies of the cross of Christ: 19 Whose end is destruction, whose God is their belly, and whose glory is in their shame, who mind earthly things.)*

Even in St. Paul's day there were **many** *walking* as false teachers who caused confusion concerning the terms of reconciliation with God; which literally made them **enemies** of the cross of Christ. The purpose of Christ's sacrifice on the cross was to reconcile man with God; and all who hinder this sacred work are enemies of His cause. Paul warned of grievous wolves and false apostles who will masquerade as ministers of righteousness; but are actually ministers of Satan. All the Apostles warned numerous times about false prophets and false teachers, so is it any wonder that many of the prominent voices of the 2nd century and onward were teaching and practicing contrary to the Apostles of Christ? We must judge every writer and teacher by the **teaching** and **example** of the Apostles of Christ or we are **sure** to err. We can **never** use some "early church" writer as our basis to "understand" the Apostles.

I hope you understand that the **only** "early church" writings from the first century are the Scriptures themselves. The other "early church" writings are from men who were usually removed from Christ and the Apostles by over 100 years, and were not endorsed by any of the Apostles. Ignatius, Polycarp, and Clement of Rome, are the ones who probably knew the Apostles, and they didn't write much.

When I was a young pastor frustrated with the inconsistent and erroneous Baptist doctrine that I had been taught growing up and in college, I was excited to read the "Apostolic Fathers". Why? Because they are pretty consistent in one area – repentance and obedient faith as necessary for salvation. They did not believe in Calvinistic or Antinomian "Eternal Security"; and so they helped undergird my conclusions against those errors. However, over many years of study leading to greater familiarity with the Scriptures, history, and all the Patristic writings; I have come to realize these men are not safe guides, especially the later ones. Not because they don't agree with my conclusions; but because they are inconsistent with themselves, the Apostles, history, and the Hebrew roots of the gospel.

A prime indicator of pagan corruption and superstition in these early times can be seen in their baptism practices. This is one way we can know the Didache is not as early as some would like to imagine, as it requires fasting before baptism – something the apostles didn't practice or teach. Just as you can look at the "Youth Group" in churches today as a prime indicator of how worldly the congregation is, you can look at baptism practices in these early churches to know how corrupt they had become. Even as early as Tertullian (160-220AD)

344

you have much superstitious ceremonialism and shocking error added to the simple rite of baptism.

When we are going to enter the water, but a little before, in the presence of the congregation and under the hand of the president, we solemnly profess that we disown the devil, and his pomp, and his angels. Hereupon we are thrice immersed, making a somewhat ampler pledge than the Lord has appointed in the Gospel. Then when we are taken up (as new-born children), we taste first of all a mixture of milk and honey, and from that day we refrain from the daily bath for a whole week. We take also, in congregations before daybreak, and from the hand of none but the presidents, the sacrament of the Eucharist, which the Lord both commanded to be eaten at meal-times, and enjoined to be taken by all alike. As often as the anniversary comes round, we make offerings for the dead as birthday honours. We count fasting or kneeling in worship on the Lord's day to be unlawful. We rejoice in the same privilege also from Easter to Whitsunday. We feel pained should any wine or bread, even though our own, be cast upon the ground. At every forward step and movement, at every going in and out, when we put on our clothes and shoes, when we bathe, when we sit at table, when we light the lamps, on couch, on seat, in all the ordinary actions of daily life, we trace upon the forehead the sign. (De Corona Militis Chap 3)

W.A. Mackay, in his book, *Water Baptism - The Doctrine Of The Mode*, reveals the following sad decay in mainline churches under the leadership of these "Ante-Nicene Fathers." What is said below applied to Tertullian's baptisms as well.

"Even in the Apostle's days there was a disposition on the part of many to depart from the simplicity of the Gospel. And this was particularly the case with regard to the sacraments of the Church (See I Cor. ch. 11:19-34, and Ch. 1:14). But in the second and third centuries we find the state of things deplorable indeed. The disposition to ascribe peculiar virtue to external forms had gone on constantly increasing, until by-and-by, nude immersions, accompanied with excorcism

(magical powers), anointing, and every species of superstitions, fairly ran riot in unseemingly and scandalous practice. It was thought that there was a saving virtue in the very water of baptism. Just as it was believed that the bread and wine, after consecration, became the real body and blood of Christ, so it was believed that the water of baptism, after the invocation, possessed the real presence of the Spirit. The natural conclusion from this was that the more water the better, and that the water should be applied to the whole body so that the regeneration might be complete. We, therefore, now find trine or three-fold immersions in a nude state, accompanied with exorcism, unction, the giving of salt and milk to the candidate, clothing him in snow-white robes, and crowning him with evergreens"

The Ante-Nicene writers at this period were Gentiles who came from paganism and viewed the Scriptures from their world view rather than from the Jewish viewpoint of Christ and the Apostles. Their erroneous presuppositions led to Roman Catholicism steeped in pagan overtones. This is an undeniable historic fact; and those who quote the Patristic writers to defend their positions, rather than building solely on the Scripture, are strangely quiet about this or are ignorant of it. My use of the Patristic writers keeps these facts in view; but many who use them do not. All heresy comes from ripping the Scriptures from their proper historical Jewish context and original intent; and the Ante-nicene writers are notorious for this.

Patristic writers prove they are unworthy of trust and leadership in doctrine by the gross errors they endorsed and practiced in their day in their own congregations and lives. This fact sadly doesn't faze modern Mennonites who use the Patristic writings as long as they can find a quote or statement to defend their own Marcionite errors. I've shown numerous times, and in many instances, that the quote does, in fact, **not** defend their

346

point or that the one quoted was grossly in error and not worthy of joining hands with. This doesn't stop them from assuming that, just because a Patristic writer says something, it is therefore the "official church position" and worthy of trust. This assuming is a glaring revelation of stubborn ignorance as to the true nature of these men they quote.

I use Tertullian and Irenaeus to show that these men knew better than to interpret Jesus as correcting Moses and understood that Moses' Words were Jesus' Words. I also declare that even though they knew this, they still contradicted themselves and spoke things contrary to not only Moses, but the Apostles of Christ. They interpreted Scripture from their Gentile perspective and missed the context and Hebrew roots of the teachings of Jesus. NO modern Mennonite who uses these men to try and support their error would follow these men on most of their other interpretations, beliefs, and practices! They would not attend their churches! But why not? If these men indeed represent the "*official church position*", and thus reveal to us the *proper understanding* of Jesus' teachings and the Apostles' instructions, as Mennonites conveniently claim in the realms they agree with; then why not follow them on every aspect? Why? Because they don't agree with each other and they have blatant and obvious pagan overtones and errors -- That's why. So why put so much weight on their interpretations of Scripture in **any** area? The Mennonites use them when it is convenient; and at the same time conveniently overlook the gross errors and bad practices of the same men they hold up as authorities. My use of them is different and I will explain how.

I use Tertullian to prove that the Corinthians practiced women's head veil and understood Paul that way, as opposed to "long hair" being the veil; and also that they didn't cover their faces. This is **historic fact** gleaned from Tertullian arguing a completely different issue and referring to the Corinthian's own practice. That Tertullian lived during the time when Corinth was still a practicing Christian Congregation; and knew what their long standing practice and belief was on this topic is valuable historic information. I also use Tertullian's words to prove that the exception clause in Matt 19:9 was not "invented" by Erasmus as foolish people have asserted; because it was in Tertullian's Bible. Using these men to establish **historic data** of this sort **is appropriate**. What is **not appropriate** is when men twist the Scriptures so as to fit the beliefs found in some of the Patristic writers. What is **not appropriate** is to imply that the beliefs of the Ante-Nicene writers are the "official church position" from the Apostles on a subject; when in reality that is far from the truth in many areas. What is **not appropriate** is to build doctrine on what the Patristic writers said while ignoring the Hebrew context of the Scriptures.

When Tertullian writes his apology to the authorities he declares publicly to them that Christians filled their ranks including government and military – even reminding them of some historic facts *before their time* to demonstrate his point; but later gives his opinion that Christians really should not be in the military. Now, which is the "official church position"? Which one shows what Christians in general had believed and practiced even before Tertullian's time? Obviously whether or not Tertullian believed it was right, there were enough Christians in the government and military as to clear him from lying to the authorities. He couldn't have written

348

such a thing to the public leaders if the majority of Christians were pacifists and it was the "official church position" to be so. We can use his statement to the authorities because it was a *historic fact* reported in *public view* and not just a *personal opinion*; whereas his personal interpretation only shows what he personally believed on that subject on that day. The Patristic writers are full of opinions; but these are certainly not "official church positions" as any study of history and Scripture will reveal. Isolated cases of pacifism prove nothing more than cases of Marcionism, Gnosticism, false gospels, pagan influences or mistakes on historic facts like Irenaeus' error on the age of Jesus. What if the "popular" Christian writers of today all wrote their beliefs? Would people 1000 years later know what the true faithful Christians believed? Consider the state of the first century churches of Asia in Revelation chapters 2 and 3 if you think things were just rosy in the late second, third, and fourth centuries when these Ante-Nicene writers lived.

So, there is a correct usage of historic **uninspired** writings and there is an incorrect usage. The same usage is proper today with men's writings. If you look at the overall fruit and beliefs of an individual, you can tell whether to even read their interpretations or not; and some of those whom Mennonites seem to prefer are not worthy of following – like Hermas. We should only build doctrine on clear statements of Scripture in their historical Jewish usage and context; but we can gain historical insights through other writings including those of Jewish Rabbis and even pagan Gentiles. No Christian writings outside the Scriptures are inspired and worthy as foundations for doctrine. Christian writings ancient or modern are merely heretical doctrines of ignorant men unless they are properly representing the teachings of Scripture. How ironic and sad that the Apostles said, "*All scripture is given by inspiration of God, and is profitable for doctrine, for reproof, for correction, for instruction in righteousness";* but Marcion sympathizers prefer uninspired writers OVER the Old Testament!

Those who I have debated on these issues are continuously revealing an ignorance or bias concerning the true nature of the "early church" and the proper use of "early church writings". I hope this short article will help the sincere seeker of truth to understand the difference in their usage and my usage – as they are not the same.

Let me give you an example of how the Ante-Nicene writings are not even understood properly many times. In the Caneyville Letters and in Ste. Marie's attempted refutation you will hear them quoting from the Ante-Nicene writings thinking they are refuting my position. First, when I have annihilated their error from the Scriptures, I need not worry about some writer later on. Second, those who attempt to refute my stand don't even understand much of the "early church writings" which they quote. When they read the word "law", they obviously can't tell whether we are speaking of Moses' Law as "the Old Covenant", the "Ceremonial Law" or the "Moral Law". In the Scriptures the word "law" is used in all three of these ways; and you must understand the context to know what is being said – NOT ASSUME. Irenaeus used the term *Law* to refer to the *Old Covenant* as Paul does in Galatians, which was indeed replaced with something better; and wasn't referring to the Moral Law of God, which was not replaced, because there is nothing better.

If we can believe Irenaeus' own words, and **if** he is free from contradicting himself; then he can **never** support their case. If he actually does later on, then he is obviously confused, because the statement below leaves no room for the other side of the controversy. If Irenaeus believes the quote below, then he is on my side. He is probably the earliest writer to address these issues (130-202AD).

Irenaeus against Marcionism

"CHAP.XII.--IT CLEARLY APPEARS THAT THERE WAS BUT ONE AUTHOR OF BOTH THE OLD AND THE NEW LAW, FROM THE FACT THAT CHRIST CONDEMNED TRADITIONS AND CUSTOMS REPUGNANT TO THE FORMER, WHILE HE CONFIRMED ITS MOST IMPORTANT PRECEPTS, AND TAUGHT THAT HE WAS HIMSELF THE END (fulfillment) *OF THE MOSAIC LAW.*

"1. For the tradition of the elders themselves, which they pretended to observe from the law, was contrary to the law given by Moses. Wherefore also Esaias declares: "Thy dealers mix the wine with water,"(6) showing that the elders were in the habit of mingling a watered tradition with the simple command of God; that is, they set up a spurious law, and one contrary to the [true] law; as also the Lord made plain, when He said to them, "Why do ye transgress the commandment of God, for the sake of your tradition?"(7) For not only by actual transgression did they set the law of God at nought, mingling the wine with water; but they also set up their own law in opposition to it, which is termed, even to the present day, the pharisaical. In this [law] they suppress certain things, add others, and interpret others, again, as they think proper, which their teachers use, each one in particular; and desiring to uphold these traditions, they were unwilling to be subject to the law of God, which prepares them for the coming of Christ. But they did even blame the Lord for healing on the Sabbath-days, which, as I have already observed, the law did not prohibit. For they did themselves, in one sense, perform acts of healing upon the Sabbath-day, when they circumcised a man [on that day]; but they did not blame themselves for transgressing the command of God through tradition and the aforesaid pharisaical law, and for not keeping **the commandment of the law, which is the love of God."**

"2. But that this is the first and greatest commandment, and that the next [has respect to love] towards our neighbour, **the Lord has taught, when He says that the entire law and the prophets hang upon these two commandments**. Moreover, **He did not Himself bring down [from heaven] any other commandment greater than this one**, but renewed this very same one to His disciples, when He enjoined them to love God with all their heart, and others as themselves. **But if He had descended from another Father, He never would have made use of the first and greatest commandment of the law; but He would undoubtedly have endeavoured by all means to bring down a greater one than this from the perfect Father, so as not to make use of that which had been given by the God of the law. And Paul in like manner declares, "Love is the fulfilling of the law:"**(1) and [he declares] that when all other things have been destroyed, there shall remain "faith, hope, and love; **but the greatest of all is love;"**(2) and that apart from the love of God, neither knowledge avails anything,(3) nor the understanding of mysteries, nor faith, nor prophecy, but that without love all are hollow and vain; **moreover, that love makes man perfect; and that he who loves God is perfect, both in this world and in that which is to come.** For we do never cease from loving God; but in proportion as we continue to contemplate Him, so much the more do we love Him."

"3. **As in the law, therefore, and in the Gospel [likewise], the first and greatest commandment is, to love the Lord God with the whole heart, and then there follows a commandment like to it, to love one's neighbour as one's self; <u>the author of the law and the Gospel is shown to be one and the same.</u> For the precepts of an absolutely perfect life, <u>since they are the same in each Testament</u>, have pointed out [to us] the same God**, who certainly has promulgated particular laws adapted for each; but the more prominent and the greatest [commandments], without which salvation cannot [be attained], **He has exhorted [us to observe] <u>the same in both</u>."**

He says in Chapter II of this same document:

"3. But since the **writings (litera) of Moses are the words of Christ**, He does Himself declare to the Jews, as John has recorded in the Gospel: "If ye had believed Moses, ye would have believed Me: for he wrote of Me. But if ye believe not his writings, neither will ye believe My words."(3) **He thus indicates in the clearest manner that the writings of Moses are His words**. If, then, [this be the case with regard] to Moses, so also, beyond a doubt, the **words of the other prophets are His [words], as I have pointed out**. And again, the Lord Himself exhibits Abraham as having said to the rich man, with reference to all those who were still alive: "If they do not obey Moses and the prophets, neither, if any one were to rise from the dead and go to them, will they believe him."(4)"

Irenaeus could not believe that **love** fulfilled both covenants and then believe what modern Mennonites believe! If you can't understand this, then I cannot help you. It is principally impossible. *If* love allowed divorce and remarriage among Israelites when immorality marred that marriage; *but* Jesus said that to obey Moses' Law *now* is committing adultery; *then* **LOVE CANNOT FULFILL BOTH**; and Irenaeus' statement, "...**the precepts of an absolutely perfect life, since they are the same in each Testament**," simply cannot be true. *If* love taught men to defend the damsel in distress, the weak, and the innocent blood in the OT; *but* Jesus taught that we must be pacifists and allow the damsel to be raped while we pray; *then* how does LOVE fulfill both Jesus and the Law? *If* love taught men to swear by God in calling upon God to be witness of earthly transactions; *but* Jesus taught that this very precept "cometh of evil"; *then* how does love fulfill both the Law and Jesus?

353

Jesus did **not** teach a higher moral ethic; but taught the **same** ethic that JESUS also taught in the OT through Moses - As Ireneaus just stated: "...**the Lord has taught, when He says that the entire law and the prophets hang upon these two commandments**. Moreover, **He did not Himself bring down [from heaven] any other commandment greater than this one**, but renewed this very same one to His disciples, when He enjoined them to love God with all their heart, and others as themselves. **But if He had descended from another Father, He never would have made use of the first and greatest commandment of the law; but He would undoubtedly have endeavoured by all means to bring down a greater one than this from the perfect Father, so as not to make use of that which had been given by the God of the law."**

If there were deceivers propagating false doctrine within the very apostolic churches themselves even while the Apostles were alive; can you build doctrine on some uninspired opinion 100 plus years removed from the Apostles? Where did the early church end up? Which direction did these men lead those mainline churches? It ended up in Catholicism – eastern and western. If a doctrine is not clearly and consistently taught in the Scriptures, then quoting some uninspired man 100+ years removed from the Apostles certainly doesn't validate it! There is a proper and improper way to use historic writings. Look and see all that these men practiced and believed before building your doctrine on a singular opinion that you liked.

Acts 20:25 *And now, behold, I know that ye all, among whom I have gone preaching the kingdom of God, shall see my face no more. 26 Wherefore I take you to record this day, that I am pure from the blood of all men. 27 For I have not shunned to declare unto you all the counsel of God. 28 Take heed therefore unto yourselves, and to all the flock, over the which the Holy*

*Ghost hath made you overseers, to feed the church of God, which he hath purchased with his own blood. 29 For I know this, that **after my departing shall grievous wolves enter in among you, not sparing the flock. 30 Also of your own selves shall men arise, speaking perverse things, to draw away disciples after them.** 31 Therefore watch, and remember, that by the space of three years I ceased not to warn every one night and day with tears.*

If you wish to see a demonstration of the misuse and false assumptions when using the Ante-Nicene writers, then read the debates that I've had with these people where I expose the false conclusions they jump to with the Ante-Nicene writers.   Paste this address into your browser and read their letter with my response:

http://www.thefaithoncedelivered.info/web-living_faith_000087.htm

Chapter Twenty Five
The *Two Kingdom* Mis-Conception

Modern Mennonites are continually touting their "Two Kingdom Concept" which they think explains and justifies their false teaching. Their whole foundation is a misconception and false assumption based on reading their own presuppositions into the text of Scripture. They love to use the following verse, but usually only quote the first half and not the part I have emboldened. They somehow think this proves their pacifism.

Joh 18:36 *Jesus answered, My kingdom is not of this world: if my kingdom were of this world, then would my servants fight,* **that I should not be delivered to the Jews: but now is my kingdom not from hence**.

Jesus will reign immortal with heavenly authority and omnipotent control; but first He had to conquer Satan, taking away the keys of death and hell; redeem mankind from the sentence of death; and fulfill all the legal transactions to claim His position as the second Adam regaining what Adam lost to Satan at the fall. This whole process is certainly above and beyond this world's means and methods of obtaining a kingdom. Jesus wasn't an insurrectionist who desired to overthrow the earthly governments and reign as another one of them. He told Pilate that if this were the goal, then obviously His disciples would have fought off those who arrested Him. This is why Peter was rebuked for his inappropriate use of the sword. Jesus had told him to have and carry a sword in the context of self defense against criminal action; but not against the government.

The word *kingdom* simply means *realm, property, dominion,* or *rule.* There are many kingdoms spoken of in the Bible. Everywhere you had a king, you had a kingdom over which he ruled and had jurisdiction. When the Bible speaks of a kingdom in opposition to God's kingdom, it is speaking of the kingdom of Satan who sometimes uses earthly kingdoms by deceiving them. The kingdoms of men are ordained under God's kingdom, and He is the King of kings who spiritually rules over all kingdoms of human government. The earthly kingdoms can either serve God's interests or Satan's depending on the heart of the king.

Da 4:30 The king spake, and said, Is not this great Babylon, that I have built for the house of the kingdom by the might of my power, and for the honour of my majesty? 31 While the word was in the king's mouth, there fell a voice from heaven, saying, O king Nebuchadnezzar, to thee it is spoken; The kingdom is departed from thee. 32 And they shall drive thee from men, and thy dwelling shall be with the beasts of the field: they shall make thee to eat grass as oxen, and seven times shall pass over thee, **until thou know that the most High ruleth in the kingdom of men, and giveth it to whomsoever he will....** *4:34 And at the end of the days I Nebuchadnezzar lifted up mine eyes unto heaven, and mine understanding returned unto me, and I blessed the most High, and I praised and honoured him that liveth for ever,* **whose dominion is an everlasting dominion, and his kingdom is from generation to generation:**

1Ch 6:15 And Jehozadak went into captivity, when the LORD carried away Judah and Jerusalem by the hand of Nebuchadnezzar.

2Ch 36:22 Now in the first year of Cyrus king of Persia, that the word of the LORD spoken by the mouth of Jeremiah might be accomplished, the LORD stirred up the spirit of Cyrus king of Persia, that he made a proclamation throughout all his kingdom, and put it also in writing, saying, 23 Thus saith Cyrus king of Persia, All the kingdoms of the earth hath the LORD God of heaven given me; and he hath charged me to build him an house in Jerusalem, which is in Judah. Who is there among you of all his people? The LORD his God be with him, and let him go up.

God is the ultimate ruler of this world; but He has not obligated Himself to micro-manage the world. He is rightly allowing men to "sleep in the bed they made" so they can experience the results of their rebellion to Him and see that their way was not so smart. God is allowing men to make choices and reap the consequences as God's Spirit continues to convict men's hearts and also sift the hearts of men for the final judgment. The Almighty has ordained human government as an extension of His own government; but when the men in office do not honor this fact and thus do their own business, they receive God's judgment. Human government is delegated by God to men; but they often rebel against this reality.

Ro 13:1 Let every soul be subject unto the higher powers. For there is no power but of God: **the powers that be are ordained of God**. 2 **Whosoever therefore resisteth the power, resisteth the ordinance of God:** and they that resist shall receive to themselves damnation. 3 For rulers are not a terror to good works, but to the evil. Wilt thou then not be afraid of the power? do that which is good, and thou shalt have praise of the same: 4 **For he is the minister of God to thee for good**. But if thou do that which is evil, be afraid; for he beareth not the sword in vain: **for he is the minister of God, a revenger to execute wrath upon him that doeth evil**. 5 Wherefore ye must needs be subject, not only for wrath, but also for conscience *sake. 6 For for this cause pay ye tribute also: **for they are God's ministers**, attending continually upon this very thing. 7 Render **therefore** to all their dues: tribute to whom tribute is due; custom to whom custom; fear to whom fear; honour to whom honour.*

We are to view all earthly authority as an extension of God's kingdom and government even if they don't realize or recognize the fact. We are to honor and respect them in that manner.

1Ti 2:1 *I exhort therefore, that, first of all, supplications, prayers, intercessions, and giving of thanks, be made for all men; 2 **For kings, and for all that are in authority; that we may lead a quiet and peaceable life in all godliness and honesty. 3 For this is good and acceptable in the sight of God our Saviour;** 4 Who will have all men to be saved, and to come unto the knowledge of the truth.*

Tit 3:1 *Put them in mind to be subject to principalities and powers, to obey magistrates, to be ready to every good work,*

1Pe 2:13 *Submit yourselves to every ordinance of man for the Lord's sake: whether it be to the king, as supreme; 14 Or unto governors, as unto them that are sent by him for the punishment of evildoers, and for the praise of them that do well. 15 For so is the will of God,*

If they are ignorant of this reality and tell us to transgress God's Law, then we appeal to the higher power and respectfully disobey the lower power. The same is true with **all** authority: Husband and wife, parent and child, school teacher and student, bishop and congregation, etc. All of those under authority must ultimately obey God over their earthly authority; but still see the earthly authority as an extension of God's government to be obeyed when it is in line with God's Law. If the local police officer commands me to violate the law of the state, then I appeal to the higher authority; but the police are still part of the state government and not an opposing kingdom.

The TWO OPPOSING KINGDOMS that will ultimately clash in the final battles that end all battles are the Kingdom of God and the Kingdom of Satan. We are in one kingdom or the other by **what we believe and practice**; not where we live, what language we speak, or what office we fill. Every career, office, or lawful activity can serve one or the other. This is the only *two kingdom concept*; and it runs through the entire Bible.

Gen 3:15 *And I will put enmity between thee and the woman, and between **thy seed and her seed**; **it shall bruise thy head, and thou shalt bruise his heel.***

Ac 26:18 *To open their eyes, and to turn them **from darkness to light**, and from the **power of Satan unto God**, that they may receive forgiveness of sins, and inheritance among them which are sanctified by faith that is in me.*

He 2:14 *Forasmuch then as the children are partakers of flesh and blood, [Christ] also himself likewise took part of the same; **that through death he might destroy him that had the power of death, that is, the devil;***

2Th 2:8 *And then shall that Wicked be revealed, **whom the Lord shall consume with the spirit of his mouth, and shall destroy with the brightness of his coming:** 9 Even him, whose coming is after the **working of Satan** with all power and signs and lying wonders,*

1 Jo 3:8 *He that committeth sin is of the devil; for the devil sinneth from the beginning. **For this purpose the Son of God was manifested, that he might destroy the works of the devil.***

Re 12:7 *And there was war in heaven: Michael and his angels fought against the dragon; and the dragon fought and* *his angels, 8 And prevailed not; **neither was their place found any more in heaven**. 9 And the great dragon was cast out, that old serpent, called the Devil, and Satan, **which deceiveth the whole world**: he was cast out into the earth, and his angels were cast out with him.*

* **Re 20:1 And I saw an angel come down from heaven**, having the key of the bottomless pit and a great chain in his hand. 2 And he laid hold on the dragon, **that old serpent, which is the Devil, and Satan, and bound him a thousand years**,...10 And the **devil that deceived them** was cast into the lake of fire and brimstone, where the beast and the false prophet are, and shall be tormented day and night for ever and ever.*

Mennonites/Amish, due to their Marcionite thinking, believe the church is Christ's present Kingdom and the peace spoken of in Christ's Kingdom is due to Christians being pacifists. They teach that the world's governments are one kingdom, and Christ's Church is an opposing kingdom – hence their "two kingdom concept". They say if you participate in the government as a soldier, magistrate, police officer, governor, etc. then you are opposing and betraying Christ and His Kingdom. Therefore they conclude that Christians must be pacifists who cannot participate in the government at all. They wish to believe that all the glories of Christ's prophesied kingdom are now happening in THEIR PACIFIST CHURCH. Wow, that's a stretch.

Can you believe they get this from reading the Bible? Well, actually they don't. They get it by reading their own ideas into the Bible as they rip it out of its historical Hebrew context. They terribly confuse the separation of church *government* and state *government* with the separation of *Christians* and government *offices.* Christians can and should fill any God ordained office where they can serve Christ's ends and be salt and light –

362

like Daniel and Mordecai. The Apostles all believed and taught this. They baptized public officials and received them into communion while they were still holding office; and never said one word even close to the doctrine of these pacifists.

The local sheriff, police, mayor, judge, governor, soldier or even the president can all serve either Satan's kingdom or Christ's Kingdom from their position as a public servant. They can serve either kingdom just the same as the local mechanic, grocer, merchant, electrician, carpenter, or farmer. Actually those in public office are called the *ministers of God*; but the others are never given this title for farming, building, or dealing in merchandise. As John the Baptist was proclaiming the coming Messiah and preparing men for the kingdom of God he baptized soldiers and told them to be content with their wages. Jesus said the centurion who had great faith would be the type that would make it to heaven; the Apostles all baptized public officials, soldiers, jailers, governors, etc. and never taught that they were serving in some kingdom opposed to Jesus Christ. Our book "Resist Not Evil?" deals with all this more in depth.

Jesus was telling Pilate the *nature* of His kingdom, not that it was an opposing kingdom to the earthly governments or would never be on earth. Jesus will someday come to claim His rightful place on David's throne and reign over all the earth as the prophets have foretold. This has not happened yet.

What did Jesus plainly say about His Kingdom?

Lu 19:11 And as they heard these things, he added and spake a parable, because he was nigh to Jerusalem, and because they thought that the kingdom of God should immediately appear. 12 He said therefore, A certain nobleman *went into a **far country to receive for himself a kingdom, and to return.** 13 And he called his ten servants, and delivered them ten pounds, and said unto them, **Occupy till I come**. 14 But his citizens hated him, and sent a message after him, saying, We will not have this man to reign over us. 15 And it came to pass, that **when he was returned, having received the kingdom,** then he commanded these servants to be called unto him, to whom he had given the money, that he might know how much every man had gained by trading. 16 Then came the first, saying, Lord, thy pound hath gained ten pounds. 17 And he said unto him, **Well, thou good servant: because thou hast been faithful in a very little, have thou authority over ten cities**. 18 And the second came, saying, Lord, thy pound hath gained five pounds. 19 And he said likewise to him, **Be thou also over five cities**...27 **But those mine enemies, which would not that I should reign over them, bring hither, and slay them before me.***

I try not to be too dogmatic on my interpretations or conclusions concerning "end-time" prophecies; but it seems that many Scriptures cannot be fulfilled without Jesus reigning with His saints on planet earth over mortal unregenerate nations (Rev 20, Zech 14). How will we who are saved reign with Christ (Rev 5:10)? Over whom will we reign? Why would Jesus rule the nations with a rod of iron, if they were all converted people (Ps 2:9; Re 2:27; Re 12:5; Re 19:15)? In Revelation 2:27 it says those who overcome in this life will also reign with a rod of iron over the nations and consequently "as the vessels of a potter shall they be broken to shivers:" – the meaning is all too clear, is it not?

We don't know how this Kingdom will occur exactly; but we do know a few things about it. Just looking at this parable we can see that the Kingdom of God **was not to immediately appear**; that **Jesus would be gone for a long time** (Mt 25:19) to **receive for himself a kingdom and return**; that **his servants were to be occupied doing his**

business while he was gone; and that **when he returned, having received the kingdom, he would both reward his faithful servants with positions of authority and judge those who opposed him or were unfaithful.**

We, the Christian Church, are in the category of **"occupying" till he comes**. He is coming to reign; and his faithful servants will reign with Him over "cities" of people. Who exactly will they be? Will it be on this earth? Will believers be immortal, while those over whom they reign are still mortal? We can be confident on some points; but cannot be dogmatic on all the details. Below are some observations about Christ's Kingdom that are quite certain:

#1 It is not here now in the sense that we are to expect it in the future. Were those servants who were commanded to "occupy" already in the kingdom? Yes and No. They were already under their king and serving him; but not yet in the kingdom that was coming. The disciples were with Jesus when he told the Pharisees, "The Kingdom of God is [among] you" and they knew what that meant; but they still asked Jesus in Acts 1:6, "Wilt thou at this time restore again the kingdom to Israel?" We are now to be waiting for a coming kingdom, striving to be worthy to inherit it, and being tested to see if we are faithful in little so we can then be trusted with much (five or ten cities, etc.). Notice in the following Scriptures the difference between *NOW* and *LATER* when Jesus returns. I will insert and N for NOW, and a L for LATER.

Mt 5:5 Blessed are the meek (N): for they shall inherit the earth. (L)

Mt 5:10 Blessed are they which are persecuted for righteousness' sake (N): for theirs is the kingdom of heaven. (L)

Mt 5:19 *Whosoever therefore shall break one of these least commandments, and shall teach men so (N), he shall be called the least in the kingdom of heaven (L): but whosoever shall do and teach them (N), the same shall be called great in the kingdom of heaven. (L)*

Mt 5:20 *For I say unto you, That except your righteousness shall exceed the righteousness of the scribes and Pharisees (N), ye shall in no case enter into the kingdom of heaven.(L)*

Mt 6:10 *Thy kingdom come. Thy will be done in earth, as it is in heaven.*

Mt 7:21 *Not every one that saith unto me, Lord, Lord, (N) shall enter into the kingdom of heaven (L); but he that doeth the will of my Father which is in heaven. (N)*

Mt 25:34 *Then shall the King say unto them on his right hand, Come, ye blessed of my Father, inherit the kingdom prepared for you from the foundation of the world:*

Ac 1:6 *When they therefore were come together, they asked of him, saying, Lord, wilt thou at this time restore again the kingdom to Israel?*

Ac 3:21 *Whom the heaven must receive until the times of restitution of all things, which God hath spoken by the mouth of all his holy prophets since the world began.*

This time of restitution relates to "the regeneration" spoken of in Mt 19:27 below in #2

Ac 14:22 *Confirming the souls of the disciples, and exhorting them to continue in the faith, and that we must through much tribulation (N) enter into the kingdom of God. (L)*

1Co 6:9 *Know ye not that the unrighteous (N) shall not inherit the kingdom of God? (L)*

2Th 1:5 *Which is a manifest token of the righteous judgment of God, that ye may be counted worthy of the kingdom of God (L), for which ye also suffer (N)*

2Ti 4:1 *I charge thee therefore before God, and the Lord Jesus Christ, who shall judge the quick and the dead at his appearing and his kingdom;*

2Ti 4:18 *And the Lord shall deliver me from every evil work, and will preserve me unto his heavenly kingdom: to whom be glory for ever and ever. Amen.*

He 12:28 *Wherefore we receiving a kingdom which cannot be moved,(L) let us have grace, whereby we may serve God acceptably with reverence and godly fear: (N)*

Jas 2:5 *Hearken, my beloved brethren, Hath not God chosen the poor of this world rich in faith, and heirs of the kingdom which he hath promised to them that love him?*

2Pe 1:11 *For so an entrance shall be ministered unto you abundantly into the everlasting kingdom of our Lord and Saviour Jesus Christ.*

#2 We who have suffered with Christ here and faithfully finished our course will reign with Him over other people. Zechariah 14 seems to say it will be those left after Christ conquers the world.

Zech 14:16 *And it shall come to pass, that every one that is left of all the nations which came against Jerusalem shall even go up from year to year to worship the King, the LORD of hosts, and to keep the feast of tabernacles. 17 And it shall be, that whoso will not come up of all the families of the earth unto Jerusalem to worship the King, the LORD of hosts, even upon them shall be no rain.*

Mt 19:27 *Then answered Peter and said unto him, Behold, we have forsaken all, and followed thee; what shall we have therefore? 28 And Jesus said unto them, Verily I say unto you,*

That ye which have followed me, in the regeneration when the Son of man shall sit in the throne of his glory, ye also shall sit upon twelve thrones, judging the twelve tribes of Israel.

Lu 22:28 *Ye are they which have continued with me in my temptations. 29 And I appoint unto you a kingdom, as my Father hath appointed unto me; 30 That ye may eat and drink at my table in my kingdom, and sit on thrones judging the twelve tribes of Israel.*

1Co 6:2 *Do ye not know that the saints shall judge the world? and if the world shall be judged by you, are ye unworthy to judge the smallest matters?*

2 Tim 2:11 *It is a faithful saying: For if we be dead with him, we shall also live with him: 12 If we suffer, we shall also reign with him: if we deny him, he also will deny us:*

Re 2:26 *And he that overcometh, and keepeth my works unto the end, to him will I give power over the nations: 27 And he shall rule them with a rod of iron; as the vessels of a potter shall they be broken to shivers: even as I received of my Father.*

Re 5:10 *And hast made us unto our God kings and priests: and we shall reign on the earth.* (compare Zech 14:16)

#3 Christ's Throne is called the Throne of his father David. Christ is called the "Son of David". This Kingdom is future.

Mt 25:31 *When the Son of man shall come in his glory, and all the holy angels with him, then shall he sit upon the throne of his glory:*

Lu 1:32 *He shall be great, and shall be called the Son of the Highest: and the Lord God shall give unto him the throne of his father David:*

Ac 2:30 *Therefore being a prophet, and knowing that God had sworn with an oath to him, that of the fruit of his loins,* *according to the flesh, he would raise up Christ to sit on his throne;*

#4 We are now to spread the glad tidings of this coming kingdom and call men to the hope and preparation for it. We are now in the highways and hedges compelling people to come to the wedding.

Mt 22:9 Go ye therefore into the highways, and as many as ye shall find, bid to the marriage.

Lu 8:1 And it came to pass afterward, that he went throughout every city and village, preaching and shewing the glad tidings of the kingdom of God: and the twelve were with him,

Ac 8:12 But when they believed Philip preaching the things concerning the kingdom of God, and the name of Jesus Christ, they were baptized, both men and women.

Ac 14:22 Confirming the souls of the disciples, and exhorting them to continue in the faith, and that we must through much tribulation enter into the kingdom of God.

Ac 19:8 And he went into the synagogue, and spake boldly for the space of three months, disputing and persuading the things concerning the kingdom of God.

Ac 20:25 And now, behold, I know that ye all, among whom I have gone preaching the kingdom of God, shall see my face no more.

Ac 28:23 And when they had appointed him a day, there came many to him into his lodging; to whom he expounded and testified the kingdom of God, persuading them concerning Jesus, both out of the law of Moses, and out of the prophets, from morning till evening.

Ac 28:31 Preaching the kingdom of God, and teaching those things which concern the Lord Jesus Christ, with all confidence, no man forbidding him.

Now, with these definite principles in mind, let us consider a few things. If there is coming a kingdom where the "Just One" will reign with a Rod of Iron; will enforce righteousness on the earth; will reign on the throne of his father David; will have His saints reigning with him; etc....And, If we are now to be proclaiming the glories and hopes of this King and Kingdom, so men will repent and prepare their hearts for the coming King....And, If we are seen now as ambassadors for this coming kingdom of righteousness....where does pacifism come in??? It simply doesn't fit; and the church of Jesus Christ on earth now is not THE kingdom; but is waiting and preparing for and preaching the **coming kingdom**. The church is betrothed as the King's Bride; but the marriage has not taken place. We are therefore in some degree in His realm or "kingdom"; but not in the fullest sense. IF what we have now is a taste and foreshadowing of the coming kingdom, THEN THERE SHOULD BE NO MATERIAL DIFFERENCE IN THE FOUNDATIONAL PRINCIPLES, DOCTRINES, OR ETHICS.

Those who continually tout their "two kingdom concept" are teaching that this world and its governments are one kingdom and the church is Christ's Kingdom; but this is a stretch and abuse of the Scriptures, especially with how they apply it in pacifism, non-participation in government, etc. The Bible presents the Kingdom of Satan in war with the Kingdom of God; but not the *Two Kingdom Concept* fabricated by pacifists.

We will not be pacifists in Christ's Kingdom - that is sure. The peace that comes on the earth will not be due to pacifism, but a rod of iron (Ps 2:9; Re 2:27; Re 12:5; Re 19:15). It is prophesied that the peace Jesus brings on the earth with His sword and rod will cause the nations to cease fearing the threat of danger, so they will beat their swords into plowshares and their spears into pruning hooks, and will learn war no more – **but not because they are pacifists, but because they are SAFE under Christ's reign.**

Isa 2:4 *And he shall judge among the nations, and shall rebuke many people: and they shall beat their swords into plowshares, and their spears into pruninghooks: <u>nation</u> shall not lift up sword against <u>nation,</u> neither shall they learn war any more.*

Isa 9:6 *For unto us a child is born, unto us a son is given: and the government shall be upon his shoulder: and his name shall be called Wonderful, Counsellor, The mighty God, The everlasting Father, The Prince of Peace. 7 Of the increase of his government and peace there shall be no end, upon the throne of David, and upon his kingdom, <u>to order it, and to establish it with judgment and with justice</u> from henceforth even for ever. The zeal of the LORD of hosts will perform this.*

Mic 4:1 *But in the last days it shall come to pass, that the mountain of the house of the LORD shall be established in the top of the mountains, and it shall be exalted above the hills; and people shall flow unto it. 2 And many nations shall come, and say, Come, and let us go up to the mountain of the LORD, and to the house of the God of Jacob; and he will teach us of his ways, and we will walk in his paths: for the law shall go forth of Zion, and the word of the LORD from Jerusalem. 3 And he shall judge among many people, and rebuke strong <u>nations</u> afar off; and they shall beat their swords into plowshares, and their spears into pruninghooks: <u>nation</u> shall not lift up a sword against <u>nation,</u> neither shall they learn war any more. 4 But they shall sit every man under his vine and under his fig tree; and <u>none shall make them afraid:</u> for the mouth of the LORD of hosts hath spoken it.*

We know this is not speaking of the church age – *while we are are occupying till He comes*, **because Jesus**

371

said the following concerning the church age, which we are presently experiencing:

Mt. 24:4 And Jesus answered and said unto them, Take heed that no man deceive you. 5 For many shall come in my name, saying, I am Christ; and shall deceive many. 6 And ye shall hear of wars and rumours of wars: see that ye be not troubled: for all these things must come to pass, but the end is not yet. 7 For nation shall rise against nation, and kingdom against kingdom: and there shall be famines, and pestilences, and earthquakes, in divers places. 8 All these are the beginning of sorrows. 9 Then shall they deliver you up to be afflicted, and shall kill you: and ye shall be hated of all nations for my name's sake. 10 And then shall many be offended, and shall betray one another, and shall hate one another. 11 And many false prophets shall rise, and shall deceive many. 12 And because iniquity shall abound, the love of many shall wax cold. 13 But he that shall endure unto the end, the same shall be saved. 14 And this gospel of the kingdom shall be preached in all the world for a witness unto all nations; and then shall the end come.

We are in this age of turmoil waiting for the **coming** Kingdom of Christ. We are to be preaching the glad tidings of this Kingdom, not some present pacifist kingdom of our imagination. We are ambassadors for the *coming* Kingdom of Christ.

In Revelation we see this scenario laid out for us:

The "Israel of God" brings forth the Messiah, who is caught up to heaven: (Acts 3:21)

Re 12:5 And she brought forth a man child, who was to rule all nations with a rod of iron: and her child was caught up unto God, and to his throne.

The "Church" flees to the wilderness and Christians are persecuted by Satan who knows he has a short time left.

Re 12:11 And they overcame him by the blood of the Lamb, and by the word of their testimony; and they loved not their lives unto the death. 12 Therefore rejoice, ye heavens, and ye that dwell in them. Woe to the inhabiters of the earth and of the sea! for the devil is come down unto you, having great wrath, because he knoweth that he hath but a *short time.*

The gospel is preached around the world:

Re 14:6 And I saw another angel fly in the midst of heaven, having the everlasting gospel to preach unto them that dwell on the earth, and to every nation, and kindred, and tongue, and people,

Jesus (the child brought forth by the woman) returns to judge, conquer, and reign with the rod of iron (see also Zech 14)

Re 19:11 And I saw heaven opened, and behold a white horse; and he that sat upon him was called Faithful and True, and in righteousness he doth judge and make war. 12 His eyes were as a flame of fire, and on his head were many crowns; and he had a name written, that no man knew, but he himself. 13 And he was clothed with a vesture dipped in blood: and his name is called The Word of God.

Jesus is called the *Word of God* – Would that be the Word of God through Moses or the Word of God through Jesus? If Marcionites are correct, then we have a real problem; but if Jesus is not correcting Moses, then the *problems* vanish.

Believers who have died or were caught up come with Him to judge and reign (Jude 14,15; 1Th 4:17)

Re 19:14 And the armies which were in heaven followed him upon white horses, clothed in fine linen, white and clean. 15 And out of his mouth goeth a sharp sword, that with it he should smite the nations: and he shall rule them with a rod of iron: and he treadeth the winepress of the fierceness and wrath

373

of Almighty God. 16 And he hath on his vesture and on his thigh a name written, KING OF KINGS, AND LORD OF LORDS.

In Revelation 20 we see Satan bound for 1000 years while Jesus and His saints reign on the earth over mortals. We see that these people are mortals who can still be deceived and rebel against Christ when Satan is loosed.

Re 20:1 And I saw an angel come down from heaven, having the key of the bottomless pit and a great chain in his hand. 2 And he laid hold on the dragon, that old serpent, which is the Devil, and Satan, and bound him a thousand years, 3 And cast him into the bottomless pit, and shut him up, and set a seal upon him, that he should deceive the nations no more, till the thousand years should be fulfilled: and after that he must be loosed a little season. 4 And I saw thrones, and they sat upon them, and judgment was given unto them: and I saw the souls of them that were beheaded for the witness of Jesus, and for the word of God, and which had not worshipped the beast, neither his image, neither had received his mark upon their foreheads, or in their hands; and they lived and reigned with Christ a thousand years. 5 But the rest of the dead lived not again until the thousand years were finished. This is the first resurrection. 6 Blessed and holy is he that hath part in the first resurrection: on such the second death hath no power, but they shall be priests of God and of Christ, and shall reign with him a thousand years. 7 And when the thousand years are expired, Satan shall be loosed out of his prison, 8 And shall go out to deceive the nations which are in the four quarters of the earth, Gog and Magog, to gather them together to battle: the number of whom is as the sand of the sea. 9 And they went up on the breadth of the earth, and compassed the camp of the saints about, and the beloved city: and fire came down from God out of heaven, and devoured them. 10 And the devil that deceived them was cast into the lake of fire and brimstone, where the beast and the false prophet are, and shall be tormented day and night for ever and ever.

What Laws will Jesus enforce while reigning over unregenerate mortals on the throne of David? Well, listen to Jesus, the King:

*Mt 5:17 Think not that I am come to destroy the law, or the prophets: I am not come to destroy, but to fulfil. 18 For verily I say unto you, **Till heaven and earth pass**, one jot or one tittle shall in no wise pass from the law, till all be fulfilled. 19 Whosoever therefore shall break one of these least commandments, and shall teach men so, he shall be called the **least in the kingdom of heaven**: but whosoever shall do and teach them, the same shall be called **great in the kingdom of heaven.***

Will Jesus enforce the "golden rule" in His Kingdom? What is that? O, yea, it is the Law and the prophets, remember? Will the two greatest commandments be the rule of Christs' Kingdom – what is that? O, yea, it is what the Law and the prophets all *hung from* i.e. were teaching and communicating. Is there any question then?

After the 1000 year reign we see the final judgment:

Re 20:11 And I saw a great white throne, and him that sat on it, from whose face the earth and the heaven fled away; and there was found no place for them. 12 And I saw the dead, small and great, stand before God; and the books were opened: and another book was opened, which is the book of life: and the dead were judged out of those things which were written in the books, according to their works. 13 And the sea gave up the dead which were in it; and death and hell delivered up the dead which were in them: and they were judged every man according to their works. 14 And death and hell were cast into the lake of fire. This is the second death. 15 And whosoever was not found written in the book of life was cast into the lake of fire.

So, we are supposed to be representing this coming King and Kingdom by proclaiming the glories and virtues of both. We are to proclaim the justice and righteousness of this coming kingdom as a standard and pattern for present men and governments. We are to represent to men the rightness of our King's ways (God's Law of Love), and His claim upon men and the earth. We are to call men to **now** repent and **accept** Christ as their coming King, or face His wrath for their rebellion. This applies to the common civilian, the soldiers, the magistrates...Cornelius, Sergius Paulus, Felix, Agrippa, Festus, Lysias, the Ethiopian Eunuch, the Phillipian Jailor, and Caesar. This opportunity to repent and reconcile is the Gospel message we are to preach along with the glad tidings of the coming Kingdom of righteousness. All men in whatever office they hold should profess Jesus as the coming King and strive to serve Him with whatever authority they hold. We should all want God's Kingdom to come on earth as it is in heaven and try to uphold this in our jurisdiction with whatever influence we have – Just like all the godly leaders presented in the Bible record.

HOW CAN MEN DO THIS AND PREACH PACIFISM? They cannot! Pacifism is not the answer, and is not used or promoted to set up or maintain Christ's Kingdom. We need to now preach what the Bible says about righteousness in all of life including government, so men know what Jesus' reign will be like. This is what Paul preached to those in government:

Ac 24:24 And after certain days, when Felix came with his wife Drusilla, which was a Jewess, he sent for Paul, and heard him concerning the faith in Christ. 25 And as he reasoned of righteousness, temperance, and judgment to come, Felix trembled, and answered, Go thy way for this time; when I have a convenient season, I will call for thee.

We need to preach all the realms of holiness that will be active and operating in Christ's future kingdom while we pray, "Thy kingdom come, thy will be done on earth as it is in heaven". Would pacifism be appropriate to teach if we were now reigning on the earth with Christ in a millennial type reign that the Bible seems to predict? Would pacifism fit anywhere? No, we would have to then teach the type of non-resistance that we present in our books, which is consistent with righteous government action, and not some pacifism that Jesus never intended, and will not be promoting in His future kingdom.

Do pacifists pray for God's Kingdom to come and God's will to be done in earth as it is in heaven?   Are God's servants pacifists in Heaven?

Re 12:7 *And there was war in heaven: Michael and his angels fought against the dragon; and the dragon fought and his angels,*

In order for God's will to be done **in earth as it is in heaven** there must be war to subdue Satan and all who side with him. His is the opposing Kingdom! This is what Jesus will do when He returns and we must be doing this where we have jurisdiction now.

Would a pacifist speak in the manner Jesus does in the parables about himself or His Father coming back to slay those who refuse to submit to him? We've already seen what He said in Luke 19 about Himself when He returns.   In Mt 21 after Jesus cleanses the temple, the next day he is confronted by the religious leaders asking Him by what authority He is claiming to act as He is. Jesus gives a parable about a husbandman seeking to receive the fruit of his vineyard. He sends servants (prophets) to these people (Jewish leaders); but they kill and mistreat them; but then he sends his son (Christ).

Mt 21:37 But last of all he sent unto them his son, saying, They will reverence my son. 38 But when the husbandmen saw the son, they said among themselves, This is the heir; come, let us kill him, and let us seize on his inheritance. 39 And they caught him, and cast him out of the vineyard, and slew him. 40 When the lord therefore of the vineyard cometh, what will he do unto those husbandmen? 41 They say unto him, He will miserably destroy those wicked men, and will let out his vineyard unto other husbandmen, which shall render him the fruits in their seasons. 42 Jesus saith unto them, Did ye never read in the scriptures, The stone which the builders rejected, the same is become the head of the corner: this is the Lord's doing, and it is marvellous in our eyes? 43 Therefore say I unto you, The kingdom of God shall be taken from you, and given to a nation bringing forth the fruits thereof. 44 And whosoever shall fall on this stone shall be broken: but on whomsoever it shall fall, it will grind him to powder. 45 And when the chief priests and Pharisees had heard his parables, they perceived that he spake of them. 46 But when they sought to lay hands on him, they feared the multitude, because they took him for a prophet.

Is Jesus teaching pacifism? The definition of pacifism is: "The belief that **any** violence, including war, is **unjustifiable under any circumstances**, and that **all** disputes should be settled by peaceful means." One pacifist who has corresponded much with us said, *"Nonresistant people never find themselves involved in violence at any level."* So, is Jesus teaching pacifism? The prophets Jesus speaks of were martyrs, but they were not pacifists. Why would Jesus line Himself up with these other non-pacifist martyrs as though they all were of the same stripe?

Jas 5:10 Take, my brethren, the prophets, who have spoken in the name of the Lord, for an example of suffering affliction, and of patience.

Should we do this? Should we suffer as they did? They were not pacifists. So, we are to follow their example of suffering affliction – there must not be a conflict of principle.

Here is another example of His teaching.

Mt 22:2 *The kingdom of heaven is like unto a certain king, which made a marriage for his son, 3 And sent forth his servants to call them that were bidden to the wedding: and they would not come. 4 Again, he sent forth other servants, saying, Tell them which are bidden, Behold, I have prepared my dinner: my oxen and my fatlings are killed, and all things are ready: come unto the marriage. 5 But they made light of it, and went their ways, one to his farm, another to his merchandise: 6 And the remnant took his servants, and entreated them spitefully, and slew them. 7 But when the king heard thereof, he was wroth: and he sent forth his armies, and destroyed those murderers, and burned up their city.*

His servants were slain (martyrs); but does that mean they were non-resistant? They were the servants of a king who was certainly not. We know the Old Testament prophets were not pacifist. Jesus is telling what is going to happen to Jerusalem because they rejected Him. Is He teaching pacifism? If He meant to, He needed to convince His Father.

The Pilgrims who founded Plymouth seem to have had a decent handle on this principle. They honored and obeyed their authorities in England and Holland to the best of their ability without denying the faith. Some of their persuasion were burned at the stake and died as noble martyrs. They didn't take up arms against their rightful lords; but they did believe in defending themselves against criminals. When they set up Plymouth, they established government with military to protect the colony; but at the same time they made friends with all the neighboring Indians. They didn't make friends by being pacifists or they would have been killed. There was mutual respect developed because the Pilgrims could defend themselves and would. They were not war-mongers; but peace-lovers. They knew, however, that peace comes from proper government and putting down evil, not from being pacifists. As much as possible, they lived peaceably with all men in England, Holland, and America; but they didn't do this to the point of not protecting those under their care.

How can we preach pacifism and at the same time preach the glories of the coming kingdom of Christ? They are not the same! They are built on completely different principles. We would actually be making Christ act the hypocrite by presenting Him as sending ambassadors to proclaim that saints cannot partake in government; that all use of force is unholy and unchristian; that self-defense and protecting the weak is not righteous; and that pacifism is Christ's way – WHEN THESE ARE NOT PRINCIPLES OF HIS OWN KINGDOM! That would be hypocritical of Christ's kingdom, would it not?

You say, "Well, we are not supposed to participate in *earthly* kingdoms, but only Christ's". Do you even know what this means? So, you believe it is OK for Jesus to be violent, but not man? Is this because He has authority and Jurisdiction? And what if Jesus delegates that authority to earthly government ("ministers of God" Rom. 13)? And how is this any different than when we reign with Jesus? Why then is it wrong for Christians to serve in government now? Do you not know that God has ordained earthly positions of government and labels earthly governors as His ministers and commands us to obey, honor, and pay them to do their work? Earthly governments are not enemies of Christ's Kingdom unless they are misusing their God ordained authority. The only reason Jesus will have to conquer when He returns is because men have used the God ordained positions unlawfully – the same will be true in apostate churches. Godly men will be placed in these very positions when Jesus reigns on the earth. We are supposed to honor and relate to earthly governments in righteousness as a testimony to them of what they *ought* to be. This is what Paul did when confronting those in authority.

If an earthly governor is also a Christian, can he not then serve Christ's Kingdom from that position by doing basically the same things he will do when he reigns with Christ? Of Course! Is this not Christ's will for earthly governments? Would it not be better if all government officials were Christians? Paul thought so; and Menno Simons thought so.

Pacifists are not just against "earthly governments", but are against "violence", which they define, not as the abuse of power, but as the **use of force in any way**. If the use of force to uphold law and order is wrong, then Jesus will be doing wrong. If the use of force to subdue the wicked and protect the innocent is bad, then Jesus and His saints will be bad. What is the primary purpose of God ordained earthly government as revealed in Romans 13? *"...for he is the minister of God, a revenger to execute wrath upon him that doeth evil."* Does it not say we are to pay taxes to them for **this very purpose?**

Should we not, as ambassadors for Christ's Kingdom, be preaching the very righteous and holy principles that actually operate in Christ's Kingdom, and will be the law when His Kingdom comes, and His Will is done in earth as it is in Heaven?? How can we claim to "seek first the kingdom of God and his righteousness" if we preach a different righteousness based on an effeminate aversion to "violence"; even when it is necessary to put down evil and protect the weak and innocent? The one schooled in pacifism must alter his thinking to see that holiness does not consist in an effeminate aversion to wrath, judgment, and the use of force; but rather God's holiness includes the appropriate masculine use of wrath, judgment and force to establish righteousness and put down evil. Pacifism is false piety, not LOVE.

Any time God is showing wrath or judgment He is simultaneously showing love and mercy. Wrath on evil men is simultaneously mercy on the victims and the innocent. This reality cannot be changed or altered; but is just the way it is. God is love in all He does, even when pouring out wrath on those who deserve it. Jesus was showing love for God and truth while whipping the men out of the temple. God's holiness includes the appropriate use of wrath and force with the simultaneous exercise of love and mercy. You cannot rightly love anyone unless you are also proportionately angry towards injustice against them.

The two kingdoms that are opposing each other on the grand battlefield of time are the Kingdom of Christ – **the seed**; and the Kingdom of Satan – **the serpent**. In the beginning God said the serpent would bruise the Seed's heel and the Seed would bruise the serpent's head. This will be the final victory.

God has not ordained any necessary office that can only be filled by lost men and cannot rather be filled much better by converted men. We are a part of this colossal battle as we stand up for righteousness and proclaim the truth of God's Word against Satan's deceptions in **all walks of life**. The church is to be a witness for the truth; but pacifism is no part of that truth. The Christians are to be salt in any position or opportunity where they can be; and serve to establish truth in every area of life. God's principles of righteousness are consistent from Genesis to Revelation – nay, rather from eternity to eternity!

Chapter Twenty Six
"The Son of David, The Son of Abraham"

Where do those words occur in the Bible? They are part of the first sentence in the New Testament Scriptures. It is a vital truth that the Messiah would be the Son of David and the Son of Abraham. The Bible declares that the Messiah would be the promised "seed" of Abraham (Ga 3:16); and would also be of the lineage of David as rightful heir to the Throne of David. God chose two special men and made promises to them that through their family line the Savior would come into the World to redeem mankind and reign victorious over the earth. The Jewish people knew of God's promises; were looking for such a Messiah; and many people called out to Jesus, "thou Son of David..." while He was ministering on earth. Everyone expected the Messiah to reign from Jerusalem on the throne of David, which is why Herod tried to kill the child. Gabriel confirmed this truth to Mary.

*Lu 1:31 And, behold, thou shalt conceive in thy womb, and bring forth a son, and shalt call his name JESUS. 32 He shall be great, and shall be called the Son of the Highest: and the **Lord God shall give unto him the throne of his father David: 33 And he shall reign over the house of Jacob for ever; and of his kingdom there shall be no end**.*

Zacharias prophesied so at the birth of John the Baptist:

*Lu 1:67 And his father Zacharias was **filled with the Holy Ghost**, and **prophesied**, saying,68 Blessed be the Lord God of Israel; for he hath visited and redeemed his people, 69 And hath raised up an horn of salvation for us in the **house of his servant David**; 70 **As he spake by the mouth of his holy prophets, which have been since the world began: 71 That we should be saved from our enemies, and from the hand of all that hate us;** 72 To perform the mercy promised to our fathers, and to remember his holy covenant; 73 The **oath which he sware to our father Abraham,** 74 That he would grant unto us, that we being **delivered out of the hand of our enemies might serve him without fear, 75 In holiness and righteousness before him, all the days of our life.***

All this will indeed happen. The godly Jews understood correctly what the prophets had told them about the Messiah, but they missed the part about His suffering; rising from the dead; and being received up to heaven until the appropriate time to reign. This was the point the Apostles continually argued from the Scriptures in order to convince the Jews that Jesus was indeed the Messiah; and was still coming to reign.

*Ac 17:2 And Paul, as his manner was, went in unto them, and three sabbath days reasoned with them out of the scriptures, 3 Opening and alleging, that Christ **must needs have suffered, and risen again from the dead;** and that this Jesus, whom I preach unto you, is Christ.*

*Ac 3:20 And he shall send Jesus Christ, which before was preached unto you: 21 **Whom the heaven must receive until the times of restitution of all things**, which God hath spoken by the mouth of all his holy prophets since the world began.*

Jesus was indeed the Messiah promised to Israel; and this is why the Disciples expected Him to set up His

Kingdom immediately. Jesus had spoken with them many days between the resurrection and the ascension specifically about the Kingdom; and they knew what it was going to be. They did not, however, understand there would be a long span of time between the ascension and the second coming until after the Holy Ghost came upon them at Pentecost and taught them these things.

*Ac 1:1 The former treatise have I made, O Theophilus, of all that Jesus began both to do and teach, 2 Until the day in which he was taken up, **after that he through the Holy Ghost had given commandments unto the apostles whom he had chosen**: 3 To whom also he shewed himself alive after his passion by many infallible proofs, **being seen of them forty days, and speaking of the things pertaining to the kingdom of God:** 4 And, being assembled together with them, commanded them that they should not depart from Jerusalem, but wait for the promise of the Father, which, saith he, ye have heard of me. 5 For John truly baptized with water; but ye shall be baptized with the Holy Ghost not many days hence. 6 When they therefore were come together, they asked of him, saying, **Lord, wilt thou at this time restore again the kingdom to Israel?** 7 And he said unto them, **It is not for you to know the times or the seasons**, which the Father hath put in his own power. 8 **But ye shall receive power, after that the Holy Ghost is come upon you: and ye shall be witnesses unto me both in Jerusalem, and in all Judaea, and in Samaria, and unto the uttermost part of the earth.***

Now, the point I wish to add to what we have already established is that the Jewish expectations of the Messiah coming to conquer and reign on the throne of David were **correct**; and are still valid. Jesus was, is, and will be what godly Jews expected Him to be: a righteous deliverer, conqueror, and King reigning on the throne of

David - **not** a pacifist changing Moses' Laws. Consider the following

Jesus filled three very important roles that the schoolmaster of the Old Testament foreshadowed: He was the "**SEED" of God's promise to Abraham** (Ga 3:16); He was a **Priest after the order of Melchisedec** (Heb 7); and He was the **Son of David who would reign forever on David's throne** (Lu 1:32,33).

These three offices are the manifestation of God's gracious will and design concerning Jesus the Messiah of Israel and Savior of the World. Now, there is a character; and there are values and principles attached to these people that cannot be ignored. David was the Heroic Warrior of Israel who delivered them from their enemies and gave them peace to serve God. He killed the ungodly giant and saved Israel from their enemies. This was a God ordained type of Jesus; and He will indeed fulfill it. He was called the *Son of David* numerous times during His ministry, and He never distanced himself from or rejected that title, though that title would definitely not fit a pacifist, and would greatly conflict with His teaching if He was teaching pacifism or changing Moses' Laws.

Next, He was the *seed of Abraham* and the *priest after the order of Melchisedec*. Consider the character and values of these men; as well as the circumstances in which God introduces them and manifests them.

Heb 6:13 For **when God made promise to Abraham**, *because he could **swear by no greater, he sware by himself**, 14 Saying, Surely blessing I will bless thee, and multiplying I will multiply thee. 15 And so, after he had patiently endured, he obtained the promise. 16 For men verily swear by the greater:* and an **oath for confirmation is to them an end of all strife.** *17 Wherein God, willing more abundantly to shew unto the heirs of* *promise* **the immutability of his counsel, confirmed it by an oath:** *18 That by two immutable things, in which it was impossible for God to lie, we might have a strong consolation, who have fled for refuge to lay hold upon the hope set before us: 19 Which hope we have as an anchor of the soul, both sure and stedfast, and which entereth into that within the veil; 20 Whither the forerunner is for us entered, even* **Jesus, made an high priest for ever after the order of Melchisedec.**

Heb 7:1 For this Melchisedec, *king of Salem,* **priest of the most high God,** *who* **met Abraham** <u>**returning from the slaughter of the kings,**</u> **and** <u>**blessed him**</u>*; 2 To whom also* **Abraham gave a tenth part of all**; *first being by interpretation* **King of righteousness**, *and after that also King of Salem, which is,* <u>**King of peace;**</u> *3 Without father, without mother, without descent, having neither beginning of days, nor end of life;* **but** <u>**made like unto the Son of God**</u>**;** *abideth a priest continually. 4 Now consider* **how great this man was,** *unto whom even the patriarch Abraham* <u>gave the</u> **tenth of the spoils.**

Now, don't miss this glaring truth about the character and values of God's Messiah. Imagine...the Apostle states all this without even a cautionary explanation due to these *supposed "opposite ethics"*. Abraham, the *father of the faithful*, had made at least 319 weapons and had them on hand for self defense and for standing with the locals in warfare when a just cause arose. He not only had a store of 319 weapons, but had taken the time and effort to train himself and his 318 servants to efficiently use them. The story is in Genesis fourteen.

Ge 14:14 And when Abram heard that his brother was taken captive, he **armed** *his* **trained** *servants, born in his own house, three hundred and eighteen, and pursued them unto Dan. 15 And he divided himself against them, he and his servants, by night, and smote them, and pursued them unto Hobah, which is on the left hand of Damascus. 16 And he* *brought back all the goods, and also brought again his brother Lot, and his goods, and the women also, and the people.*

Was Abraham wrong to believe in "just cause" as a validation of war and killing? Was he *"not trusting God"* in having weapons and in training his servants to use them? He had developed a very efficient fighting force as we can see from the story! He did indeed trust God; and God gave him the victory; but God never does for us what we can and should do for ourselves. This was indeed a "just cause"; and... guess what? The only time we meet with Melchisedec in the Scriptures is to bless Abraham for this **slaughter of the Kings**; and to even **receive tithes of the spoils!!** HA! Abraham got to pay God tithes on all those wicked kings' riches, including the kings of Sodom and Gomorrah.

So, Jesus is a priest **after the order** of this man? Paul presents this mysterious figure of the Old Testament in such a way that we wonder if he was not an actual appearance of the pre-incarnate Christ to Abraham! **NOTE:** His name is the **king of righteousness** and the **king of PEACE. Yes, Abraham did indeed restore the peace with the help of God**. This is the SAME way Jesus will bring PEACE to the earth. So, this is the Friend of God meeting on this occasion with the most vivid type of Christ in the Old Testament – what was God saying to us?

Ex 15:3 The LORD is a man of war: the LORD is his name.

Isa 42:13 The LORD shall go forth as a mighty man, he shall stir up jealousy like a man of war: he shall cry, yea, roar; he shall prevail against his enemies.

Re 19:11 And I saw heaven opened, and behold a white horse; and he that sat upon him was called Faithful and True, and in righteousness he doth judge and make war.

"But didn't Abraham love his enemies?"   He loved them as God loves His enemies. He would have aided them and helped them also in a righteous cause; but when they became unrighteous, and captured one whom he loved more; then his love for Lot's family superceded his love for them. God loved the people before the flood as well as the people of Sodom; but when they persisted in wickedness, God's Love of righteousness and His own faithful people necessitated the destruction of the wicked. Jesus loved and died for mankind; but He also brought about the destruction of the Jewish nation in AD 70, and He will return to destroy all opposition when He brings PEACE to the earth. Hell is far worse than death itself; yet Jesus will send His enemies to hell for their unrepentant and persistent rebellion against righteousness. The love of enemies doesn't trump every other concept in the Bible the way pacifists tend to imply. I should indeed try to help and convert my enemies; but protecting my family and standing for truth is priority. God's love means that we act appropriately, not that we act like effeminate pansies.

Notice also another interesting fact from our OT schoolmaster which is meant to lead us to Christ, and not away from Him.   The priests under the law (Mosaic Covenant) were not made with an oath; **but Jesus was**; and by *SO MUCH (the very oath of God)* He was declared to be a priest **forever** after the order of Melchisedec. He will never change this **priestly order – forever**. He is the priest of the New Covenant with His own blood sacrifice; but He is also the King of Peace and Righteousness; and He will reign over the earth to bring peace just like Abraham brought peace when he was blessed by this King of Peace.

*Heb 7:20 And inasmuch as **not without an oath** he was made priest: 21 (For those priests **were made without an oath; but this with an oath** by him that said unto him, The Lord sware and will not repent, Thou art a priest for ever after the order of Melchisedec:) 22 By **so much** was Jesus made a surety of a better testament. ...28 For the law maketh men high priests which have infirmity; but the word of the oath, **which was since the law**, maketh the Son, who is consecrated for evermore.*

Even though the priests under Moses' Law were appointed without an oath of confirmation; God chose to confirm Jesus as the Priest of the New Covenant after the order of Melchisedec **with an oath – the very oath of God.** The Apostle brings this forth without even a blush of Mennonite embarrassment. Of course, Paul knew that Jesus wasn't condemning righteous and lawful oaths as commanded in Moses' Law, for Paul himself used them NINE times in his Holy Spirit inspired epistles. Jesus knew that His very office was filling the role of *THE SON OF DAVID*, *THE SEED OF ABRAHAM*, and *THE PRIEST AFTER THE ORDER OF MELCHISEDEC*; and He knew that unlike the priests in the OT, His appointment was by the **oath** of God. Do you really imagine that Jesus taught contrary to all this?? Never.

If the Jesus presented to you in your denomination is different from the characteristics of the Biblical Jewish Messiah presented to you in this study, then you have **another** Jesus.

*2Co 11:3 But I fear, lest by any means, as the serpent beguiled Eve through his subtilty, so your minds should be corrupted from the simplicity that is in Christ. 4 For if he that cometh preacheth **another Jesus, whom we have not preached**, or if ye receive another spirit, which ye have not* *received, or another gospel, which ye have not accepted, **ye might well bear with him.***

This is what has happened to most of Christendom, including all those who teach the Marcionite concept that Jesus corrected Moses' Law and preached a different ethic from God's Word in the Old Testament. Will you follow it? Will you *bear with them*?

Chapter Twenty Seven
REVIEW: Bringing It All Together

IF you have understood the points which have been duly documented and proved from Scripture, then you realize we have totally annihilated the Marcionite/Mennonite position. There is no crack or crevice left for them to hide in. You will also realize that Satan's masterpiece deception has been revealed. The old Serpent has led a zealous group of people to embrace "another Jesus" and all the while believe they are "contending for the faith" of Jesus Christ. This is a serious situation that deserves all the attention we can give it while praying that we can cause a great awakening among those who have been so long deceived.

IF God says He is immutable, then He cannot change His moral compass, opinion, outlook, judgment, or purpose.

IF Jesus is the same yesterday, today, and forever, then He can never change His morality or moral judgment.

IF Jesus is the WORD who inspired the Scriptures, then He cannot correct the morality of the Scirptures without having changed His own morality.

IF God is LOVE, and all His Law and prophets express His Love, as Jesus said they did; then nothing Jesus could teach would be a higher ethic; for God's love does not evolve or improve; and there is no higher ethic than divine love.

IF Jesus taught a higher ethic, He would be wrong to also teach the lower ethic at the same time; but Jesus said the love He taught was the same that fulfilled the Law, and which the law and prophets expressed.

IF the New Covenant was God's Law written on men's hearts in a new and living way through the indwelling Holy Ghost, then everything Jesus and the Apostles taught was for this purpose.

IF the Law was our schoolmaster to bring us to Christ, then there could be no opposite ethic in the teachings of Jesus, for that would just testify that He was not the Messiah; and the law would lead us elsewhere.

IF Jesus taught a different ethic from God's Law, He would then be a false prophet; and the Jews were righteous for killing Him.

IF Jesus came changing and correcting Moses' Law, then John the Baptist, in the role of Elijah, was actually preparing people to reject Jesus, because John called them back to God's Ways as recorded in the Old Testament.

IF those who knew Moses' Law intimately, and so longed to have evidence to destroy Jesus, could not accuse Him at His trial of teaching contrary to Moses'

Law, then you can be sure that He never did! They couldn't accuse Him of breaking Moses' Law or teaching contrary to it; but you know they would have loved to do so, if it had been the case.

IF the righteousness of God's Law must be fulfilled in all believers to justify God's justification; then the moral law of God is eternal and obligatory upon all mankind; which is why the worldwide conviction of God's Spirit on man is called the "work of the Law" in Romans 2.

IF Jesus told His disciples to obey them that sit in Moses' seat, then He could not be teaching an opposite ethic. In Mt 23 Jesus clearly upholds the religious leader's right and responsibility to make application of God's Laws in the form of observances; and tells everyone listening to obey them.

IF ALL the Apostles and Jewish believers were still fully practicing Moses' Law; and only baptizing those who came under Judaism for the first twelve years after Pentecost; and Paul never taught Jews to forsake Moses (Ac 21); then most modern theology needs to go in the trash can, including Mennonite Marcionism.

IF there is but one Gospel for all time; and the true Grace of God commands us to live soberly, righteously, and godly; then most modern gospel preaching is also trash; and, again, God's morals have never and can never change.

IF we are to, *Be perfect even as Jesus' Father is perfect,* and, *Be holy even as God is holy*, then we can define Christ's teaching and terms by the example of the God of the Old Testament.

IF we are to follow the Apostles of Christ in order to properly understand and follow Christ, then we are to define Christ's teachings and terms by the Apostles example and teaching.

IF the Apostle John in AD 95 still believed that sin was the transgression of God's Law, then the moral law was still the standard to determine what was and was not sin.

IF Jesus was the pure Lamb of God, then He never transgressed or spoke contrary to God's Law; but had to keep it and teach it perfectly to be sinless.

IF Jesus died to pay for our transgressions of God's Law and make reconciliation between man and God on this basis; then He 100% agreed with God's Law; and could not be presenting any different ethic or morality.

IF Jesus was the SON OF DAVID, the SEED OF ABRAHAM, and the PRIEST AFTER THE ORDER OF MELCHISEDEC, then He could not fill the role that Marcionites/Mennonites try to put Him in teaching contrary to His calling. Every one of these connections would be contrary to His very purpose and message! He could not be condemning all oaths, when He was confirmed as Priest of the New Covenant with an oath – unlike the Old Testament priests.

IF Jesus came to reconcile man to God and serve as our High Priest to intercede to God on our behalf; and our transgressions of God's Law was the problem; Then Jesus, again, fully agreed with God and His Law. Reconciliation with God is not a compromise where we meet in the middle. Mankind MUST repent, submit again to God's Law, and strive to live out the righteousness of God's Law, or Jesus will not act as their High Priest applying His own blood or interceding on their behalf.

IF A = B; and C = A; then C = B! **IF LOVE** fulfills the Law *AND* the Law hangs from LOVE, which Jesus and the Apostles clearly taught; then Jesus and the Apostles preached the same ethic as Moses *OR* Jesus and the Apostles *DIDN'T PREACH LOVE*. IF Jesus taught God's Love *AND* said that ALL the Law of Moses taught LOVE, then *THEY TAUGHT THE SAME ETHIC*. If God's Love is what Jesus taught *AND* it fulfills the Law, then Jesus taught the same ethic as the LAW.

IF Malachi specifically said that the Messiah would preach against FALSE SWEARERS and ADULTERERS **as defined** and **consistent with** Moses' Law; then **GOD HIMSELF has told us plainly that Jesus was preaching consistent with Moses' Law and not contrary to it**; so there need be no more question about it; and the debate is OVER! Just stop squirming and accept God's beautiful Word, or you will prove yourself a God hating rebel who just serves his own end and agenda. Every rock solid point that we have made in this book would have to be false in order for Mennonite Marcionism to be true.

Don't rest on the fact that a large group of people would now be shown to be in error for this book to be accepted as truth. This excuse has been proven to be a *foundation of sand* too many times in history. If it is alright for a large group of people to preach much truth and do much good, but to also mix in heresy and error; then what is wrong with the JW's, Mormons, and Romanists after all? If it is OK for people to be doctrinally close; but reject the apostle's teaching on an important issue like this, then what was wrong with Diotrephes after all?

People have argued these sandy foundations against Jesus being the Messiah *("Have any of the rulers or of the Pharisees believed on him?"),* against the Apostle's doctrine, against those who have left Judaism, Catholicism, Mormanism, Islam, etc.; and it has also been used against most major scientific discoveries. On the text of Mt 13:57, where Jesus is rejected by his own countrymen because He was just the "carpenter's son"; Albert Barnes shares the following: *"Columbus, a native of Genoa, had, by patient study, conceived the idea that there was a vast continent which might be reached by sailing to the west. Of this his countrymen had no belief. Learned men had long studied the science of geography, and they had never imagined that such a continent could exist; and they were indignant that he, an obscure man, should suppose that he 'possessed wisdom superior to all the rest of mankind united.' It is accordingly a fact, that outside his own country he was obliged to seek for patrons of his undertaking; that there he received his first honours; and that to other kingdoms the discoveries of the obscure Genoese gave their chief wealth and highest splendour."* **Truth is truth is truth**;

and it is just like God to use a "nobody" to teach the truth and correct error, so as to *resist the proud and give grace to the humble.*

Now...What are you going to do with what you know? Can you humbly receive the truth? It will not go away! You can throw the book away; but the issue has been put in your lap; and God will hold you accountable for what you have read. **Now that you have heard the truth your salvation depends upon you walking in this light also. You cannot run and hide or play ignorant; for your very soul is at stake. If you don't speak God's truth and strive to live it — regardless of the consequences — you will not be saved.**

Don't stop short of victory! I encourage you to read our other studies for a full, in-depth treatment of these important issues. There is much more of the same clear Bible teaching waiting for the sincere lover of TRUTH. You may obtain a copy of these books free by contacting our ministry at the address below.

■ RESIST NOT EVIL? This book deals with the non-resistance and non-participation in government issues in more depth.

■ **What the Bible *Really* Teaches About Divorce And Remarriage** -- This book is an in-depth study of this topic specifically.

We invite sincere questions and will strive to answer them directly from the Word of God.

Living Faith Christian Fellowship
27216 Ingel Rd. Brookfield, MO 64628

Pastor Mark Bullen

To view correspondence with Anabaptist periodicals and individuals who wished to debate on these topics view these links on our Home Page.

www.thefaithoncedelivered.info

www.TheRightJesus.com

Also by Mark Q. Bullen

What the Bible Really Teaches About Divorce and Remarriage
ISBN: 978-0615627250

Do you realize Malachi foretold that Jesus would come and preach against adulterers and in the same prophecy commanded the people to keep obeying Moses' Law? (Malachi 3:1-5 and 4:4)

Do you realize that everything taught in the New Testament concerning marriage, divorce, and remarriage is consistent with God's moral law? (Romans 7:1; 1 Cor. 7:39)

Do you realize there is no evidence in church history or the Bible that the apostles or early Christians ever denied baptism and membership to converted couples due to divorce and remarriage in their past?

Do you realize the pilgrim church and Anabaptist believers did not deny baptism and church membership to couples with divorce and remarriage in their past?

Do you wish to know what the Bible REALLY teaches about divorce and remarriage?

...then carefully read this book with an open and honest heart seeking only for truth!

The Alien Exposed
ISBN: 978-0615954059

It is a foregone conclusion that certain groups of Christians, known collectively as Anabaptists, were identified by their piety and unrelenting love of the Truth. As a result of their devotion persecutions ensued, yet they held to the faith as they knew it, convinced of the necessity to walk in humble obedience to the Scriptures.

Books have been filled with the stories of men who sacrificed the comforts and even the necessities of life in order to obey the Word of God. Families were split apart; livelihoods were lost; homes and farms were left; and almost every comfort of life was traded for cruel persecution, infamy, poverty, and death. Why? Because they were like Moses, "Choosing rather to suffer affliction with the people of God, than to enjoy the pleasures of sin for a season; Esteeming the reproach of Christ greater riches than the treasures in Egypt: for he had respect unto the recompence of the reward. By faith he forsook Egypt, not fearing the wrath of the king: for he endured, as seeing him who is invisible." Heb. 11:25-27

It is love of Truth which compels men toward a great willingness to be conformed to the Scriptures. What they were raised with and taught to believe with all the fringe benefits of their "camp" were happily sacrificed for the joy of knowing they were right with God and obedient to His Word.

Do such men of self-abandoning devotion to truth still exist? Many claim the name or heritage of these Anabaptist people; but does the same love of truth still live on in them? We sincerely hope so; and this hope alone has provoked the prayerful writing of these pages.

Resist Not Evil???
ISBN: 978-0692367315

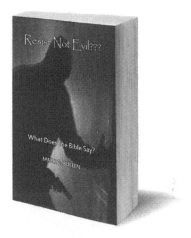

It seems people have the idea that God's ways must go completely contrary to man's reason in order to be divine and wonderful. Is it possible that God made man in His own image so we could understand and admire His wisdom and ways? God's ways are indeed contrary to selfishness, but not to true concepts of justice, mercy, and righteousness. In order to find God's truth on any subject, we must first flush all our personal feelings and prejudice on the subject. Next, we must decide to go wherever truth will take us, without first checking to see if we approve of the destination. If we must know where truth will take us before we get on for the ride, then we really don't want truth, but only our own security, ideas, and our "ism". If we want God's truth above all else, then we will let God's Word say what it says and love it, no matter where it takes us or what the cost.

Salvation Strait & Narrow
ISBN: 978-0692394311

A definitive look at Biblical Salvation.

The ways of God are infinitely wise, yet man willingly confuses and makes ambiguous plain teachings of Scripture to suit his own destructive predilections. This is nowhere more evident than in the doctrine of Salvation. In this book, God's Ways are proven to align with common sense. The subject is explained simply, understandably, and sensibly through elucidation of God's Word.

Available from Apprehending Truth Publishers
and your online book source.

For these and other titles offered by Apprehending Truth please visit us at:

www.ATPublishers.com
Buy the Truth and sell it not. ~ Proverbs xxiii, 23

Made in the USA
Lexington, KY
13 April 2017